Foundations in American History

From Discovery to Reconstruction

Howard J. Schwach

Additional Material
Evelyn M. Early

GLOBE BOOK COMPANY, INC.
Englewood Cliffs, New Jersey

Howard J. Schwach is a graduate of C. W. Post College, with a B.A. in history and social studies. He taught for several years in the New York City public school system. Mr. Schwach has written books, plays, newspaper and magazine articles for the student with reading handicaps, and has received three Educational Press Association awards. He is a contributor to the *University Home Independence Study Program*. His books include *Wild Tales, Plays About Sports, The Great Depression, Juveniles and the Law, Youth Crime and Punishment,* and *The Flight of Lucky Lindy.*

Cover Design: Arnie Cooper
Text Illustrations: Joe Pearson and Janet Wilson

ISBN: 0-87065-602-3

Printed in the United States of America
9 8 7 6 5 4 3

Table of Contents

PART   2
ROAD TO DISUNITY

Unit 1
The First Settlers Come To North America

Chapter 1
Introduction To History

1. Why do we study the past?

2. Many people have said that we need to understand the past and the mistakes that were made in the past. Then we will not make the same kinds of mistakes in the future.

3. Others say that we must study the past so that we will know who we are and where we came from. We will know about our "roots".

4. Many people feel that well-educated people should know about the past.

5. For all these reasons, and maybe for others, we study the past. We study events, reasons for those events, and the people who took part in those events. We call that study the study of history.

6. History is knowledge or information about the past. This book and the others that will follow will give you information. You need this information to understand how the problems of the past are related to today's problems, and perhaps to problems of the future.

7. The books will also help you to know more about yourself, those who came before you and the "roots" your family grew from.

8. It will also help you to know more about the country you live in.

How does a historian use these tools to study the past?

Historians

9. People who study history are called historians. Like people who do any kind of work, historians use certain tools in their work.

10. The main tools of historians are words. Historians study words like bankers study money. The words the historians study help them to understand the past.

11. Some of these words come in the form of things written by people who were there when the events were happening. They have left diaries or papers, or have written books about their experiences. These tell historians what happened and why. Historians call these **primary** or **first** sources because they come from the people who were in the "thick of the action."

12. Other words come from people who wrote about events they never saw happen. They may have written about the events years, even hundreds of years, after they happened. These are called **secondary** sources because the writer was not part of the action.

13. For example, a book about the writing of the Declaration of Independence by Thomas Jefferson, who was there, is a primary source. A book written today by a person who studied Jefferson's book would be a secondary source. The writer was not there when the event took place.

14. Most historians study as many primary sources as they can before writing their own books on a historical event. Often, this makes their book more useful because they get many viewpoints on what happened. Each person has a different viewpoint, or idea, about what happens.

Teaching History

15. Both primary and secondary sources are important to historians who want to teach history to others. These sources can be written or they can be such things as maps and pictures. If the maps and pictures were drawn when the event happened, they are primary sources. Pictures and maps drawn later are secondary sources.

16. Historians also use graphs and cartoons to tell their story. You will find all these tools of the historian in this book.

17. You will also find one other tool used many times in this book. This tool is called a **time line**. The time lines will help you see when, and in what order, the events of history happened.

18. Time lines are important, easy and fun to use. They make it easier to "see" what was happening in different places at any time during the history you will be studying. It's a little like using a road map to keep you moving in the right direction of your study of history.

Using Time Lines

In this book you will be studying events that took place at many different times in history. In most of the chapters of this book there will be a time line. These will show you what events are taking place in the chapters. The time lines below show you which part of history you will study in the first part of this book "Building a Nation". It also shows you how far apart the events are in time. Below the time lines you can see the numbers of the chapters. This shows you when you will be studying the different events in history.

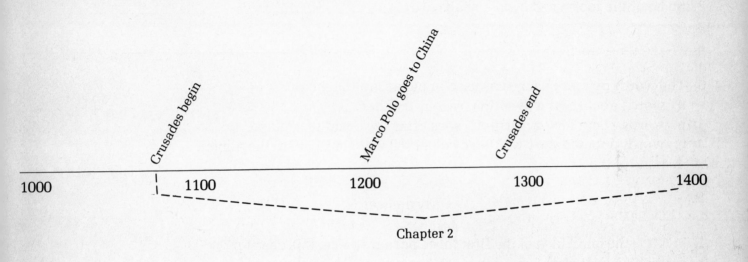

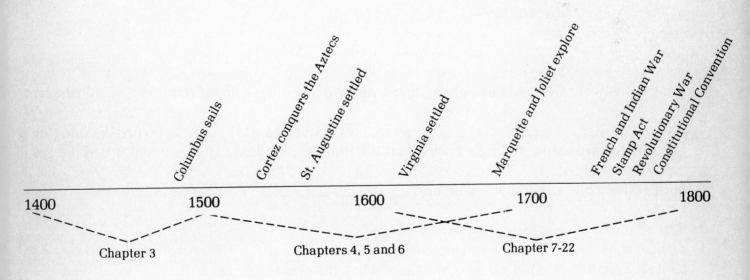

Understanding What You Read

1. Which of the following is **not** a reason for studying history?
   a. to find out about our roots
   b. to learn more about the past
   c. to be able to become a banker
   d. to be able to keep from making the mistakes of the past

   My answer is _____ . (2-3)

2. Some of the tools used by historians are _____ , _____ ,

   _____ , _____ , and _____ . (15-16)

3. The words **primary source** as used in paragraph 11 mean:
   a. words about history written by your teacher.
   b. words about history written years after the event took place.
   c. words about history written by a person who took part in the action.
   d. none of the above.

   My answer is _____ . (11)

4. What is the main idea of the first three paragraphs in this chapter?
   a. to tell why it is important to study history
   b. to tell why the author wrote this book
   c. to teach you how to read
   d. to tell you about your "roots"

   My answer is _____ . (1-3)

5. If my name were George Washington, and I was writing a book about the time I was President,

   it would be a _____ source for historians. (11) Suppose I were Washington's
   great, great-grandson writing a book about the time Washington was President. I had not been

   born at that time, so my book would be a _____ source. (12)

6. Secondary sources may be important because:
   a. they show many different viewpoints about the same event.
   b. it was written by a person who was there when the event took place.
   c. both of the above
   d. none of the above

   My answer is _____ . (12)

4

7. Make a time line for the important events of your life. First, look at the time line below which has been filled in. When you are finished, your time line might look like this one.

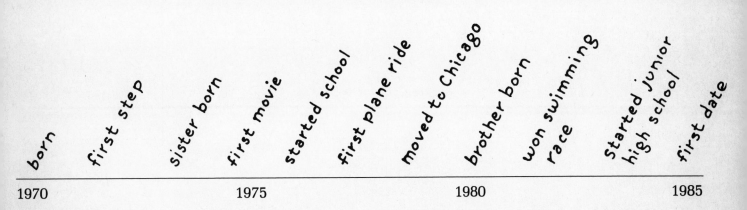

Begin by placing the year you were born over the line at the left of your time line below. Place the present year over the line at the right. How many years are there between the two lines? _____ What year should the line in the middle stand for? _____ Now draw along the time line all the events you think are important in your life. You might want to put in such things as when you started school or when younger brothers and sisters were born. How about when you broke your leg playing football. What other events do you think are important?

Chapter 2
Columbus And Before

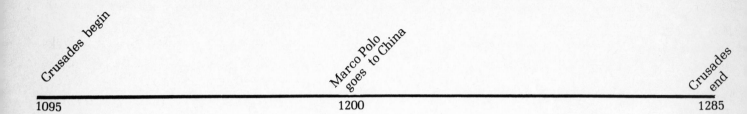

Crusades begin

Marco Polo goes to China

Crusades end

1095   1200   1285

1. The story of how America became a nation starts long before the explorers came to North America. In the time around 1000 much was known about Europe, Northern Africa, and the Middle East. Some things were known about other areas of the world. But nothing was known about the land across the sea — North and South America.

2. At that time many mapmakers showed the Earth as square. Ships that went beyond the horizon would fall off and never be seen again, it was thought. It took a war to change their minds.

3. Let's go back to the 11th century (1000 to 1099) when a group of people called **Turks** captured the small land of Palestine.

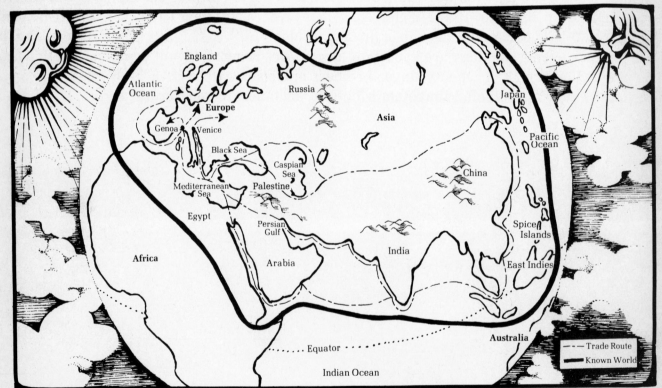

The Routes Followed By The Early Trade Ships

6

A Crusader goes forth to meet the Turks.

Palestine, at the eastern end of the Mediterranean Sea, was important to three religions of that day.

4. The Turks, who were Moslem and followed the teachings of Mohammed, believed that Palestine was a holy land. The Christians and Jews both believed that their religions were born in that area. For all three religions, the area was called the **Holy Land.**

5. The Turks, however, did not like outsiders coming to their land. They closed the Holy Land to all who did not believe in Mohammed and his teachings.

6. This made the European Christians very angry. In 1095, the Pope, the leader of the Christians, called on all his people to fight the Turks and to take back the Holy Land.

7. Thousands of Christian soldiers took up the call and went to Palestine to fight the Turks. This war, called the **Crusades**, lasted for 200 years. It ended in 1285.

8. The Christians never did drive the Turks out of Palestine. But the Crusades helped make history in another important way.

9. Most of the Crusaders came from Europe. They thought of Europe and the land around the Mediterranean Sea as the center of the world. They didn't know anything about the Far East — India and China — and of the goods made there.

10. The Middle East, the area around Palestine, was an exciting place for the Crusaders. They met people from the East there. The Crusaders saw things there they had never seen before, brought from India, China, and the islands near Southeast Asia. They found spices and silks, jewels and perfumes.

11. The Crusaders found that the world was larger than they thought. They wanted to find ways to get the new things they had seen to their homes in Europe.

Trade Routes Open

12. As more people in Europe found out about the goods brought back by the Crusaders from the Middle East, **trade routes** opened up.

13. Silks, jewels, perfumes and spices, such as pepper and cinnamon, were brought from India, China, and the Islands near Southeast Asia to Palestine. They were brought either by an overland route or by sea. (See map on page 6.)

14. From there they were picked up by Spanish, French, Portuguese or Italian ships, and carried to Europe.

15. Both routes were very long, hard, dangerous and expensive.

16. When the land route was used the goods had to be carried over deserts and mountains on the backs of camels. This took a long time and many dangers, such as storms and bands of robbers, faced the camel caravans.

17. The sea route brought the ships to the Red Sea. From there the goods were carried overland to the Mediterranean Sea. From the Mediterranean they were shipped to Europe. This trip was also long and dangerous.

18. Traders in many European nations began to look for other routes. They wanted to get the goods from India and China, called the **Indies**, to Europe in a safer and less expensive way.

19. The traders began to look at their maps. One way seemed to be to sail from Europe around the tip of Africa to the Indies.

20. In 1497 a Portuguese explorer named **Vasco Da Gama** did sail around Africa and then to India. Da Gama brought back lots of trade goods from the Indies.

21. Da Gama's route was longer than those traveled before, but it was safer and all by sea. Sea travel was cheaper than land travel and there was no worry about bandits stealing the goods.

22. Other Portuguese sailors followed Da Gama's route. The Portuguese soon became the masters of the Europe-to-Indies trade.

23. The Portuguese were not, however, the only people looking for a quicker, less expensive route to the Indies.

24. Some of these people did not believe that the world was flat. They believed that it was round like a ball.

25. If that were true, they reasoned, a sailor could reach the Indies not only by sailing east, but by sailing west as well.

26. **Christopher Columbus** was one of those people. He was sure that the world was round, and that by sailing westward he could reach the Indies.

27. On August 3, 1492 Columbus and his three ships set sail from Spain. They headed west to find a new route to the Indies.

28. What they found was the Americas.

Spotlight On What Columbus Knew About The World

29. Before Columbus began his sail westward in 1492, much was already known about the world even though many people believed that it was flat.

The Turk, with his scimitar held high, is ready to meet the Crusader.

8

30. The Crusaders brought back a lot of information about the Middle East. They also brought back stories of a nation called **Cathay** (China) further east.

31. Some brave men had traveled to that far-away nation. Among the best-known of these travelers was **Marco Polo**. In the thirteenth century (1200's) Polo and his two uncles visited Cathay. They lived at the court of the Emperor.

32. When they went back to Italy, Polo wrote of his experiences in the far-away land. He told of seeing an ocean east of Cathay and India.

33. About 1450 the first printing press, with movable type, was invented. Many books could then be printed quickly. Among the first books was one by Marco Polo. It told of his trip to Cathay and the sea to the east of Cathay and India.

34. After reading Marco Polo's book, many people believed that the sea to the east of China and India was the same sea that was west of Europe. They thought the world was round, and land in the east could be reached by sailing west.

35. More Europeans began to believe that this was true. One mapmaker named Paolo Toscanelli drew a map showing Europe with the Indies to the west rather than east.

36. Also around 1450, came the discovery of two instruments that would make a long trip by sea possible. These were the **compass** and the **astrolabe**.

37. Before the discovery of these two instruments most sailors kept their boats close to land. To get out of sight of land could mean falling off the edge of the square Earth, they thought.

38. But with a compass a sailor could tell the direction in which he were going. More important, it could show the direction of the land he had just left behind.

39. The astrolabe, like the later sextant, showed a sailor just where his ship was at any time. Ships could now go out of the sight of land with some hope of returning once again.

40. Columbus knew all of this before he set sail.

Understanding What You Read

1. Place the following historical events in the order in which they really happened. The event which took place first would be **1)**, and so forth.
   a. The Pope calls for the Crusades. (6)
   b. The Turks take Palestine. (3)
   c. Vasco Da Gama sails around the tip of Africa. (20)
   d. Columbus sails westward. (29)
   e. The Crusaders fight the Turks in Palestine. (7)

   My answers are 1) _____ , 2) _____ , 3) _____ , 4) _____ , and 5) _____ .

2. What is the main idea of this chapter?
   a. The Turks discovered America.
   b. Many people wanted to find a cheaper and quicker way to the Indies. Some of them believed that sailing west rather than east was the answer.
   c. People like silks and spices.
   d. The three major religions claimed Palestine as their Holy Land.

   My answer is _____ .

3. The Crusades were important because:
   a. the Turks were forced out of the Holy Land.
   b. many Christians fought there.
   c. Columbus was a general in one of the wars.
   d. many Crusaders learned a lot about the Indies and brought back products from there.

   My answer is _____ . (10-12)

4. **True or False:** Decide if the following statements are true or false. If a statement is false, change the **underlined** word to make it true. If it is true, mark a T in the spaces beside the letters.

   _____ a. Columbus believed that he could reach the Indies by sailing <u>East</u>. (26)

   _____ b. Columbus had read books about the Indies by such writers as <u>Marco Polo</u>. (31)

   _____ c. Columbus believed that the world was <u>flat</u>. (26)

5. Traders in Europe wanted to find a new route to the Indies because the old routes were

   _____ and _____ . (17)

6. A new invention that helped Columbus learn about the Indies was the _____ _____ .

   (33) Two other new inventions, the _____ and the _____
   helped him to sail out of the sight of land. (36)

7. **Map Study:** Look at the map on pg. 6 and then answer the following questions:

   a. The trade ships went through these bodies of water: _____ _____ , _____

   _____ , _____ _____ , _____ _____ , _____

   _____ and _____ _____ .

   b. Japan and the Spice Islands are in the _____ Ocean.

   c. _____ and _____ are cities in Europe.

   d. Part of the continent of _____ is below the Equator.

   e. The _____ _____ is between Africa and Europe.

Chapter 3
Columbus Sails To The New World

Printing press, compass, and astrolabe invented

Columbus sails

Vasco da Gama sails

1450   1492   1497

1. Christopher Columbus was born in Italy. He grew up dreaming of becoming a sailor. At the age of 14 his dream came true. He began sailing on Italian ships.

2. Not too much is known of Columbus' early life. It is known that he read books by such travelers as Marco Polo and also studied many map books.

3. Columbus was sure that he could reach the Indies by traveling west. But he could not get anyone to give him ships for the journey. He tried in Italy and Portugal, but they would not give him any money or ships.

4. Then he went to the king and queen of Spain. Spain was not getting goods from the Indies as quickly as the other European countries. They hoped that Columbus would find a way to get there by going west and make them rich. They gave Columbus three ships, a crew and the money he needed to make the trip.

5. Columbus and his three ships, the **Nina**, the **Pinta**, and the **Santa Maria**, set sail westward.

6. The following journal of the trip is like one which might have been written by a sailor on one of those ships. The map below will help you to trace the route of the voyage.

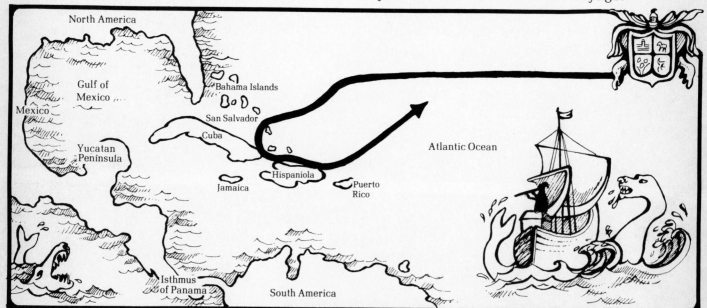

Explorations of Columbus in 1492

7. **August 3, 1492:** *We leave this day for the Indies. Our captain, Christopher Columbus, is about thirty years old. He seems like a good man and a good sailor. But many of us who sail with him on this journey think he is a little mad. He believes that the world is round and that, by sailing west, we can go east and reach the Indies. Does he not know that the waters of the sea boil past where we can no longer see land? Does he not know we will fall off the edge of the earth if we go any further than that point? Not even the sea monsters that wait for ships out there seem to bother him. We will have to wait and see. Perhaps he is right.*

8. **August 28, 1492:** *We have been at sea for many days. We in the crew now know that the captain was right about one thing. We have not yet fallen off the edge of the earth or seen even one sea monster hiding in the depths. Yet we see no land. It has been a hard journey. Each day we grow more afraid that we will never see our homes and families again.*

9. **October 12, 1492:** *Land! After thirty-three days at sea we have reached the Indies Sea. We have discovered many islands with many people. We have called them* **Indians** *after the place in which they live. We took all of these islands in the name of Spain.*

10. *One island — we call it Juana — is beautiful, with tall green trees, many mountains and rivers. The Indians there are very friendly, and they give us gold without asking much in return. They think that we have come from some sort of heaven.*

11. Columbus had not found the Indies. He really was in the Atlantic Ocean, not the Indian Ocean. The islands he discovered were off the coast of North America — first San Salvador and then Cuba, which he called Juana. And the people he called Indians were really Native Americans — the first Americans.

12. Columbus went back to Spain where he showed everyone the gold and other goods he brought back. He did not bring back silk or spices. He had not found a new route to the Indies. He sailed back to the New World three more times without ever finding what he was looking for.

13. Columbus died a poor man. He never dreamed of how important his discoveries were.

14. Many other explorers followed Columbus to the New World. They wrote letters and sent maps of what they had found to friends in Europe.

15. About the same time Columbus was making his third voyage to the New World, another explorer was also sailing for North America. His name was **Americus Vespucius.**

Columbus claims the New World for Spain.

16. Some of his reports and maps found their way to a German schoolteacher who was writing a new geography book. The schoolteacher drew a map of the New World. It really only showed a small part of the east coast and the islands Columbus had discovered. He called the New World **America** in honor of Vespucius and his voyage.

Did Columbus Really Discover America?

17. One question on which people who study history cannot agree is, "Was Columbus really the first non-Indian to step foot on the Americas?" We know the **Native Americans** were first. But who came next?

18. Here are some of the **theories** (unproven ideas) about who else might have discovered America:

19. Some say the **Norsemen** (Vikings) were the first to visit the Americas. This theory states that in the 9th and 10th centuries these strong sailors from **Scandinavia** (Sweden, Norway, Denmark) crossed the Atlantic looking for land and gold. They first settled in Iceland.

20. Many people say they went even farther west until they came to the northern part of North America.

Perhaps Phoenicians in a ship like this came to the New World before Columbus.

21. In 1965 a map dated from around 1440 was found. That **Viking Map** showed parts of northeastern Canada. That map seems to show that the Norsemen did come to North America before Columbus.

Viking flag of Leif Ericson

22. Some say the **Phoenicians** were the first to visit. In 1872 a slave in Brazil, South America, found a stone with strange carving on it. The stone was turned over to the National Museum.

23. Experts there found that the carving on the stone was Phoenician writing. The Phoenicians were a seagoing people who lived in what is now Israel and Lebanon around 2,000 years ago. Many people now believe that a Phoenician ship was blown off course and landed in South America.

24. The stories go on and on. Some believe that the Chinese came first. Others say an Irish priest came long before Columbus or anyone else.

25. Whoever is right, whoever came first, many followed in their footsteps. The New World soon became a place for French, English, Spanish, Portuguese and many others to look for fame and fortune.

Spotlight On Indians

26. Some 20,000 years ago there was an ice age on earth. Most of what is today North America was covered with ice.

27. There was a **land bridge** between Asia (now Russian Siberia) and North America (now Alaska).

28. That bridge, over 1,000 miles wide, brought North America its first immigrants — the Indians or Native Americans. These wandering fur-dressed people moved south to find warmth and food. They covered the American continent, bringing their own speech, customs and way of life.

29. By 1492, when Columbus ''discovered'' America, there were probably between one million and one and one-half million Indians in the Americas.

30. The Indians lived very far apart from each other, and there were few ties between the different tribes.

31. The Plains Indians in the west had to have animals for their food, housing and clothing. They moved all the time, following wherever the herds took them.

32. The Woodland Indians in the northeast were hunters. They had homes made of wood. They moved only when the hunting grew bad in their area.

33. The Desert Indians in the southwest were farmers. They stayed with their land, moving very little. They lived in mud or adobe houses.

34. All in all, there were about 2,200 tribes of Indians in North and South America.

35. We will study many of these tribes in greater depth in later chapters. The Indians, The First Americans, helped to shape later American history. Many fought against the coming of the ''White Man'' to their land. Many died while protecting their land.

Understanding What You Read

1. From what you read in paragraphs 6-10, what do you know about some of the men who sailed with Columbus?
   a. They believed they could find a new way to the Indies by sailing to the west.
   b. They were afraid of what might happen to them on the voyage.
   c. They often traveled to the New World.
   d. They never believed the stories about falling off the edge of the Earth or meeting sea monsters.

My answer is _____ . (6-10)

2. Columbus had three ships. They were the _____ , the _____ , and the _____ . (5)

3. Columbus named the inhabitants of the place he discovered Indians because he thought he had found _____ . (11)

4. The Island Columbus called **Juana** is today called _____ . (11)

5. The name **America** was given to the New World by a_____ _____in honor of the voyage of _____ _____ . (16)

6. Many people do not believe that Columbus was the first non-Indian to step foot on the Americas. Some theories say that the _____ , the _____ , the _____ and an _____ came before Columbus. (18-23)

7. The first immigrants to North America were the _____ who came across a _____ that connected the continents of _____ and _____ . (26-27)

8. **Map Study:** Look at the map on pg. 12 and then answer the following questions:

   a. Columbus first sailed to the islands of _____ , _____ and _____ .

b. These islands are surrounded by two bodies of water. They are the _____

and the _____ .

c. On his voyage in 1492 Columbus did not visit the islands of _____ ,

_____ , and _____ .

d. The islands Columbus discovered are closest to the coast of _____ .

9. **Find The Hidden Words:** All of the words below are hidden in the puzzle. They may be forward, backward, vertical, or upside-down. Find the words and circle them. The first one is done for you.

COLUMBUS   INDIES

PALESTINE   SILKS

TURKS   SPICES

MOHAMMED   CAMELS

CRUSADE   SPAIN

```
S  I  L  K  S  A  B  C
M  O  H  A  M  M  E  D
D  N  E  C  S  I  F  G
H  I  P  O  E  N  I  J
K  A  A  L  C  D  L  M
N  P  L  U  I  I  C  O
S  S  E  M  P  E  R  P
L  Q  S  B  S  S  U  R
E  S  T  U  R  K  S  T
M  U  I  S  V  W  A  X
A  Y  N  Z  A  B  D  C
C  D  E  E  F  G  E  H
```

Chapter 4
The Spaniards Come To The New World

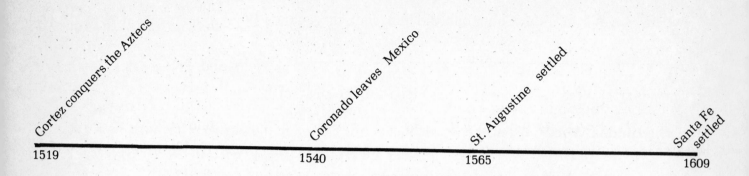

Cortez conquers the Aztecs — 1519

Coronado leaves Mexico — 1540

St. Augustine settled — 1565

Santa Fe settled — 1609

1. The return of Columbus with gold and other riches from the New World brought other explorers to Mexico and South America.

2. **Hernando Cortez** was a young Spaniard who went to Cuba to find his fortune. While in Cuba he heard stories of the gold to be found in Mexico and South America.

3. In 1519 he took some men and left Cuba to find the gold of the **Aztecs**, an Indian tribe living in those areas. (See map on page 19.)

4. Cortez had only 600 men, yet he was able to conquer one of the most powerful Indian tribes in the Americas.

5. There were many reasons why Cortez took the riches of the Aztecs so easily.

6. First of all, the Spaniards had horses. The Indians had never seen horses before. To their eyes the horse and rider were one large monster.

7. Secondly, the Spaniards had guns which made loud noises and frightened the Aztecs. The Spaniards also wore metal armor that kept the Aztec arrows from cutting through their skin. The Aztecs believed the Spaniards to be gods who had come to their land.

8. The Spaniards killed the Aztec king and took over the land and people. They made the Aztecs work in the mines, digging up gold and silver. The gold and silver was shipped back to Spain. In this way, Spain became one of the richest nations in the world.

9. But the Spaniards were still not happy. They wanted more money, more gold and silver. The Spanish Governor of Mexico had heard stories of cities made of gold to the north. He wanted that gold.

10. In 1540 a large group of men, led by **Francisco Coronado**, set out to find the cities of gold. Coronado's soldiers rode through northern Mexico and into what would later become Arizona, New Mexico, and Texas.

11. They found no gold. They found only the sand and mud houses of the Pueblo Indians who lived in those areas.

12. Coronado was angry that he had not found the cities of gold. He sent men off in different directions with orders to find them. They all returned without finding the cities. Some of

Spanish flag around 1500

them did find a deep canyon later named the Grand Canyon.

13. Coronado made up his mind not to give up without finding the cities of gold. He heard from an Indian that the cities were really to the east. His army marched again.

14. They found buffalo and grassy plains that extended as far as the eye could see. They found another kind of Indian, one who hunted with bow and arrow. But they found no golden cities.

15. Very sad, Coronado and his men returned to Mexico. But before they did, they claimed all the land over which they had traveled in the name of Spain. That land included much of Arizona, New Mexico, Texas and Oklahoma.

16. At the same time, other Spanish explorers such as **De Soto** and **Ponce De Leon** were exploring parts of Florida and the lower Mississippi River. One Spanish sailor, Cabrillo, sailed around South America and discovered part of what today is California.

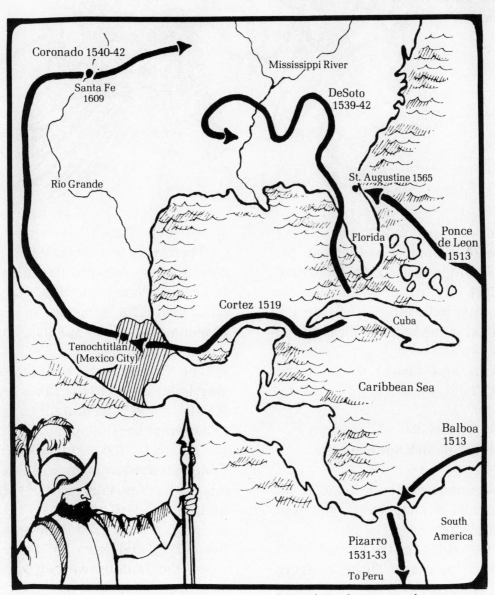

Spanish Exploration in the Americas

A Spanish Conquistador storms down on the Aztecs.

17. In 1565, the first Spanish settlement, **St. Augustine**, was built in Florida. St. Augustine is now the oldest city in North America. In 1609 the Spaniards built a city at Santa Fe, New Mexico. That is the second oldest city in North America.

18. The Spaniards now owned much of the Americas.

Spotlight On Spanish Settlements

19. By 1542 the Spaniards had founded an empire in the Americas that was larger than the United States is today.

20. The empire was ruled for the king of Spain by two men called **Viceroys**. These Viceroys each controlled one area.

21. There was one Viceroy for the Kingdom of New Spain — Mexico, the islands of the West Indies and North America. The other Viceroy controlled The Kingdom of Peru — Peru, Panama and the Spanish land in South America.

22. The Viceroy made sure that the king's law was followed and that taxes were collected. He also made sure that all the gold and silver mined went back to Spain.

23. Helping the Viceroys were the **Conquistadores**. They were soldier leaders who helped to take over the land from the Indians.

24. Indians were used to farm the land, watch the cattle, and work in the mines. In most cases the Indians were treated like slaves. They were made to work very hard for no pay.

20

They were not allowed to go where they pleased, to work for whomever they wanted, or to own any land.

25. One group of people complained about the treatment of the Indians. They were the **missionaries**, Catholic priests, who had followed the soldiers into the new territories. They came to bring religion to the Indians.

26. Wherever the missionaries went, they built missions. The missions can be found in all the countries in North, Central and South America. Missions were not only churches, but also places where people lived and worked.

27. The missions were often built like forts because many Indians did not want the missionaries to be there. They attacked the missions.

28. Those Indians who lived in the missions were taught religion as well as how to farm and tend sheep. They also learned to weave and make clothing.

29. Most Indians did not live in the missions. Many lived as slaves on large farms owned by the Spanish. These large farms were called **haciendas**.

30. The Spanish and the Indians did help each other in one way, however. The Spanish brought new crops such as sugar cane, coffee and cereal grains to the New World. They taught the Indians to grow these crops using new tools such as the iron hoe and the plow.

31. The Spanish also learned from the Indians. They learned to grow tobacco, potatoes, and squash. The Spanish also learned to grow Indian corn and make chocolate from cacao beans.

Missions like this were built by Spanish missionaries with the help of the Indians.

Understanding What You Read

1. Which of the following is **not** a reason why the Spaniards had such an easy time defeating the Aztecs.
   a. The Spaniards had horses.
   b. The Spaniards were better, stronger fighters than the Aztecs.
   c. The Spaniards had guns and armor.
   d. The Aztecs thought that the Spaniards were gods.

   My answer is _____ . (6-7)

2. Put the following historical events in the order in which they happened. The event which took place first would be **1)**, and so forth.
   a. The settlement of St. Augustine (17)
   b. The settlement of Santa Fe (17)
   c. Cortez defeats the Aztecs. (3)
   d. Coronado moves into America to look for the cities of gold. (10)
   e. Coronado's men find the Grand Canyon. (12)

   My answer is 1) _____ , 2) _____ , 3) _____ , 4) _____ , and 5) _____ .

3. In the space below, match the letters in **Column B** with the names in **Column A.**

   Column A

   1. Cortez (2-4)

   2. Aztecs (3)

   3. Coronado (10)

   4. Pueblos (11)

   5. St. Augustine (17)

   Column B

   a. first Spanish settlement

   b. defeated the Aztecs

   c. Indians in the Southwest United States

   d. Mexican Indians

   e. explored America

4. The land Coronado took for Spain included much of what today are the states of

   _____ , _____ , _____ ,

   and _____ . (15)

22

5. Most of the Indians who worked for the Spaniards were treated like _____ . (24)

6. The Catholic priests who followed the Spanish soldiers built _____ which were more like _____ than churches. (27)

7. The Spaniards taught the Indians how to grow such crops as _____ , _____ , and _____ , using such tools as the _____ , and _____ . In return, the Indians taught the Spanish how to grow _____ , _____ , and _____ . (30-31)

8. **Map Study:** Look at the map on pg. 19 and then answer the following questions:

   a. The Spanish explorer who went the farthest north was _____ .

   b. The two Spanish explorers who touched Florida were _____ and _____ .

   c. The two Spanish explorers who left from Cuba were _____ and _____ .

   d. The Spanish explorer who discovered the Mississippi River was _____ .

   e. The Spanish explorer who stayed in Mexico and never went to what is now the United States was _____ .

Chapter 5
The French Come To The New World

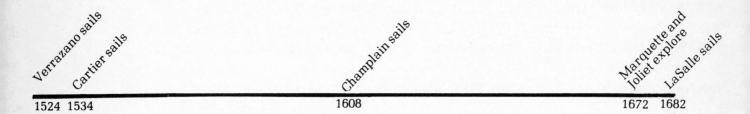

Verrazano sails

Cartier sails

Champlain sails

Marquette and Joliet explore

LaSalle sails

1524 1534   1608   1672 1682

1. The French looked at the riches coming to Spain from the New World and were unhappy. They too wanted some of the gold and other riches from that far-away land.

2. In 1524 the French king sent an Italian sailor named **Verrazano** to the New World. He was to find a new route to the Indies.

3. Verrazano sailed up and down the East Coast of America looking for a passage that would take him further west. He did not find it and returned to France.

4. A French sailor, **Jacques Cartier**, was sent next (See map on page 26.) In 1534 he left France looking for the **Westward Passage**, a river that would take ships west from the Atlantic to the Pacific Ocean. No such river existed, but explorers of that time did not know that.

5. But Cartier had somewhat more luck than Verrazano. He found the mouth of the St. Lawrence River in Canada. He began to follow the cold river westward, hoping it would take him to the Pacific Ocean and then to the Indies.

6. His trip ended much sooner than he thought it would. The river ended at a place with a high hill. He called it Mont Real, or **King's Mountain** in honor of the king of France. Mont Real later became Montreal, the capital of French-speaking Canada.

7. Cartier named the area **New France**, and claimed it in the name of the King of France. Cartier returned home to France. It would be more than 70 years before another Frenchman came to the mouth of the St. Lawrence.

8. In 1608 an explorer and fur trader by the name of **Samuel de Champlain** brought a group of settlers to the area. They built a fort and a settlement. Champlain sent out traders to buy furs from the Indians of the north and west of New France.

9. Champlain and his traders made friends with the Hurons, an Indian tribe that hunted and trapped in the northern woods. He brought missionaries to live with the Indians. He even lived with them himself for a time.

French flag of Samuel de Champlain

10. The missionaries were to bring Christianity to the Indians. They spread out in the heavy woods. They built small churches wherever they could find a group of Indians to live with.

11. Champlain also tried to find a Westward Passage. He explored the Great Lakes and discovered Lake Champlain. But he too could not find the passage to the Indies that so many had looked for without success.

More People Come To New France

12. The French continued to spread out. More and more traders and missionaries came to New France. They went into the woods to tend their traps and trade and live with the Indians. They built forts and trading posts along the rivers.

13. These forts were needed to protect the traders from the Indians. Although Champlain was friendly with the Hurons and other tribes, he helped them to attack their enemies, the Iroquois. The Iroquois did not like that and attacked fur traders and missionaries as often as they could.

14. Later the Iroquois helped the British in their fight against the French and the American colonies.

15. The governor of New France heard a story about a mighty river. In 1672 he called for **Father Marquette**, one of the missionaries who had been living among the Indians, and a fur trader named **Louis Joliet**. He sent them to find the river and see if it went to the Pacific Ocean.

16. The two set off on their trip in two canoes with five other men. As they went along, the weather got warmer and warmer. They were sure that they were heading south towards the Gulf of Mexico, not west towards the Pacific.

17. They were right. They were on the mighty **Mississippi River**. They were heading for the Gulf of Mexico. The two men got as far as the Arkansas River. Then they returned north.

18. In 1682 a young Frenchman named **Robert LaSalle** finished the trip by sailing all the way to the mouth of the river. He then claimed the entire Mississippi River in the name of France.

19. LaSalle wanted to build a chain of trading posts along the river. For that he needed money and the permission of the French king. He got both.

Many French fur traders were friendly with the Indians.

20. LaSalle and a large number of Frenchmen left New France and traveled down the Mississippi River. Their aim was to build a trading post at the mouth of the Mississippi — at what is now New Orleans.

21. They got lost and built their post on a small branch of the Mississippi farther west than they had planned. The French built more trading posts all the way from the Gulf of Mexico, up the Mississippi River to the Great Lakes and Canada.

22. France now owned much of the St. Lawrence and Mississippi River valleys and the land around them. The riches from this area came, not from gold and silver, but from fur and land. This gave France a valuable foothold in the New World.

23. The French did little to settle the land they ruled. The only real settlements in the New World were in Canada and along the St. Lawrence River.

24. Most of the other French outposts had only a few houses, and maybe a church. There

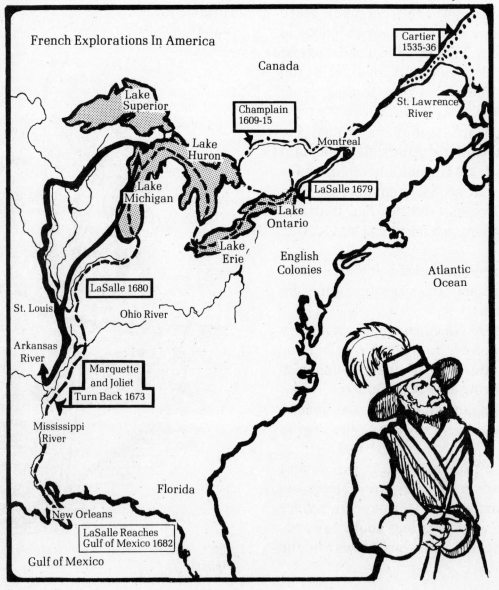

French Explorations In America

Cartier 1535-36

Canada

Lake Superior

Champlain 1609-15

St. Lawrence River

Lake Huron

Montreal

Lake Michigan

LaSalle 1679

Lake Ontario

Lake Erie

English Colonies

Atlantic Ocean

LaSalle 1680

St. Louis

Ohio River

Arkansas River

Marquette and Joliet Turn Back 1673

Mississippi River

Florida

New Orleans

LaSalle Reaches Gulf of Mexico 1682

Gulf of Mexico

Far to the North, the French built trading posts along rivers.

were just enough Frenchmen there to keep up the fur trade.

25. There were many reasons for this. First of all, the French were more interested in building an empire in Europe. They didn't want to build one in the American wilderness.

26. Secondly, because most French outposts were in the cold north woods, the government had a hard time finding colonists who wanted to come to the New World.

27. At one time the French king sent over a group of soldiers. He then fired them from the army. With no way back to France, they were forced to become fur traders along the Mississippi River.

28. The French colonies grew very slowly. By 1750, 100 years after the first Frenchmen came to the New World, only about 75,000 French settlers were living on the large amount of land that France had claimed.

Spotlight On The French Settlements

29. The French trading settlements along the St. Lawrence and Mississippi Rivers were rough, hard places to live and work.

30. Most of the people living in these outposts were men. They spent much of their time going up and down the river in canoes. They would either tend their own traps or trade with the Indians for furs the Indians had trapped.

31. Beaver was the main trade fur. Some men got rich on the beaver fur trade. These were the traders who bought the furs from the French trappers. They would then send the

furs to France. Little of that money went to the men who trapped the beaver.

32. During the summer the men lived in the woods alone or in pairs.

33. During the winter, the trappers and traders would live with an Indian tribe. They usually lived with either Algonquins or Hurons, both friendly tribes.

34. The strongest tribe in the area was the Iroquois. Many believe that the Iroquois was the strongest tribe east of the Mississippi River. The Iroquois were the enemies of both the Algonquins and the Hurons.

35. Because the French helped these two tribes, the Iroquois also became the enemy of the French traders and missionaries. Many French settlers were killed by the Iroquois.

36. The French king controlled his empire in America much like the Spanish king controlled his.

37. The French in America had no say over what they could do. The king ruled through a **Royal Governor**. Under him were men called **seigneurs**, who controlled large pieces of land. The lowest group of people were called the **habitants**. They were the workers.

38. The habitants were not as bad off as the Indians who worked for the Spanish. The habitants were not slaves, and they were free to go and work where they wished.

39. It was the law that all the furs, lumber and fish from the French colonies could be traded only with France or other French colonies. In this way France took much wealth from its New World holdings.

Understanding What You Read

1. The main idea of this chapter is:
   a. the French took lots of gold and silver from North America.
   b. the French settled parts of the St. Lawrence River valley and the Mississippi River valley from Canada all the way to the Gulf of Mexico.
   c. the French were very bad to the Indians, using them as slaves to catch beaver and other animals.
   d. most of the Frenchmen who came to the New World were missionaries who built fort-like missions to protect themselves.

   My answer is _____ .

2. **True Or False:** Decide if the following statements are true or false. If the statement is true, place a T in the space beside the letter. If the answer is false, change the **underlined** word to make it true.

   _____ a. The French first came to America because they wanted to find <u>furs</u>. (1)

   _____ b. <u>Cartier</u> sailed up and down the east coast of America looking for the Westward Passage before returning to France. (3)

   _____ c. <u>Verrazano</u> called the newly discovered area around Mont Real, New France. (5-6)

   _____ d. The <u>French</u> claimed most of the St. Lawrence and Mississippi River valleys for themselves. (22)

   _____ e. Louis Joliet was a French <u>missionary</u>. (15)

   _____ f. The French were friendly with an Indian tribe called the <u>Iroquois</u>. (9)

   _____ g. <u>LaSalle</u> was the first Frenchman to reach the Gulf of Mexico. (18)

3. **Map Study:** Look at the map on pg. 26 and then answer the following questions.

   a. According to the map, the first Frenchman to explore the New World was

   _____ , who came in the years _____ .

   b. Cartier came down the _____ River to where the city of

   _____ is today.

c. Champlain went farther _____ from the city of _____

to the Great Lakes during the years _____ .

d. Marquette and Joliet turned back when they reached the _____ River.

e. LaSalle, Marquette and Joliet all traveled south on the _____ River.

f. The first Frenchman to reach the Gulf of Mexico was _____ who reached

it in the year _____ .

g. The Frenchman to go farthest south was _____ .

4. **Word Search:** Find the hidden words listed in the puzzle below and circle them.

KING   INDIES

CHAMPLAIN   VERRAZANO

CARTIER   FRANCE

WEST   PACIFIC

FURS   RICHES

```
V A R I C H E S K V
E C H A M P L A I N
K A K K L Q P R N W
Y R L W Z E A S G I
P T V E R K C D K N
Q I W S Q I I F L D
S E R T Z X F U M I
F R A N C E I R N E
X U T X P M C S O S
V E R R A Z A N O T
```

Chapter 6
The British Come To North America

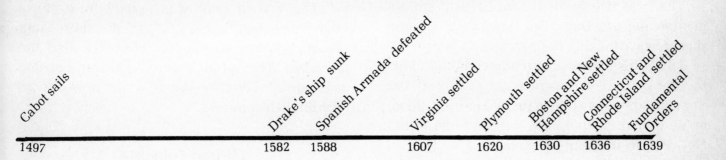

Cabot sails	Drake's ship sunk	Spanish Armada defeated	Virginia settled	Plymouth settled	Boston and New Hampshire settled	Connecticut and Rhode Island settled	Fundamental Orders
1497	1582	1588	1607	1620	1630	1636	1639

1. The French were exploring and settling the St. Lawrence and Mississippi River valleys. At the same time, other European nations were exploring and settling the east coast.

2. The first Englishman to come to the New World was a man from Bristol, England, named **John Cabot**. Cabot made his voyage in 1497, while Columbus was still making his voyages to the New World.

3. Like many others at that time, Cabot was looking for a way to get to the Indies by sailing westward.

4. Cabot and his men explored the shores of Nova Scotia, Newfoundland and Labrador. When he could not find the passage he was looking for, he returned to England. Before leaving, he claimed most of the east coast of North America for England.

English flag of John Cabot

5. Most people in England cared little about the New World. However, some traders found that trade with the Spanish colonies in Florida and on the Gulf of Mexico brought them much money.

6. The English traders also got slaves in Africa and brought them to the Spanish ports in America.

Trouble Between Spain And England

7. The Spanish government did not like the English trading with their colonies. They wanted the Spanish colonies to trade only with Spain. They ordered that all foreign (non-Spanish) ships entering ports at Spanish colonies be sunk.

8. **Sir Francis Drake** was a British ship's captain who traded with the Spanish. One day in 1582 his ship sailed into a port in Spanish America. His ship was sunk and most of his men were killed.

9. Drake got away and returned to England. He got a new, more powerful ship and sailed it to Spanish America. He sailed along the coast, taking riches from Spanish treasure ships. He also attacked Spanish settlements along the coast and took what he needed for supplies.

10. Other British sailors joined Drake. Soon the Spanish were losing more gold and silver than they were taking back to Spain.

11. The Spanish called the British sailors pirates and **Sea Dogs**. But they could not stop them from attacking their ships and land.

12. The British government allowed their ships to break the law because they wanted the Spanish to be less powerful in America. Also, many British people now wanted to go to the New World to set up colonies. But, as long as the powerful Spanish controlled the seas, they could not safely go.

13. Spain was angry at the British government for not stopping the Sea Dogs. The Spanish government got together a large fleet of ships.

Sir Francis Drake, called a Sea Dog by the Spanish, helped the English come to America.

They planned an attack on England. The fleet, called the **Spanish Armada**, sailed for England in 1588.

14. The British fleet was helped by a storm that destroyed many Spanish ships and pushed others off course. They defeated the Armada. The Spanish were no longer a strong sea power. The New World would now be safe for English colonists.

British Colonists

15. People came to America from England for many different reasons.

16. Many religious people came to America. They saw a chance to be free to practice their chosen religion.

17. Other religious people saw the chance to bring Christ to the "savages", the Native Americans they found there.

18. Many who came to America did not choose to come. They were sent by British judges who saw the New World as a good place to send "idle women and sturdy beggars". These were the people they wanted to get rid of.

19. Business people came to America. They could buy raw materials such as tobacco and furs from the colonists. They also saw the colonies as a large market for British goods.

20. Many small farmers who had worked for landlords in England saw the trip as a chance to have their own land.

21. With the threat of the Spanish out of the way, people belonging to each of these groups began to make their way to America.

22. The very first British colony in the New World was the **Jamestown Colony** in Virginia. Led by John Smith, settlers came to that colony in 1607. Jamestown was set up to trade New World goods with England.

Religious Freedom

23. Let's take a closer look at one reason people came to the New World. Many different groups came looking for one thing — religious freedom. By 1682, seven colonies had been founded in the New World by people looking for the freedom to worship as they wanted.

24. Why did they have to come to the New World for that?

25. Henry VIII, the king of England, started a **state church**. That was a religion that everyone who lived in England had to belong to and give time and money to. He called it the **Church of England**. It is also known as the Anglican Church.

26. A few groups would not join the Church of England.

27. One such group was called the **Pilgrims**. They wanted to break away from the Anglican Church. The Pilgrims were jailed and fined in England for starting their own church.

28. The Pilgrims then got permission to go to America. They were given a piece of land in

The Pilgrims aboard the *Mayflower* signing the Mayflower Compact. They came to America in search of religious freedom.

what is today New York State. But their ship, the **Mayflower**, was blown off course. It landed near Cape Cod, in Massachusetts.

29. They founded the Massachusetts Bay Colony with a settlement at Plymouth in 1620. Their leader was William Bradford.

30. The **Puritans** were another group of English people who wanted religious freedom. They were called Puritans because they wanted to "purify", or make clean, the Church of England.

31. They did not want to do away with the Church. They just wanted to change some of its ways. The Puritans were also treated badly in England because of their beliefs.

32. They came to the New World and settled at Boston in **Massachusetts Bay Colony** in 1630.

33. The Puritans came to America for religious freedom, but they gave none to their followers in the New World. They did not let non-puritans vote or make laws. Only one religion could be practiced in the colony.

34. Some Puritans thought that their leaders were acting as badly as the king.

35. Two such men decided to leave the Massachusetts Bay Colony and begin colonies of their own.

36. One was Roger Williams, a young Puritan minister. He believed that the leaders of the church should not also be the leaders of the colony. He also thought that the Indians should be paid for the land the colony took from them.

37. The Puritan leaders wanted to send Williams back to England, but he escaped in 1636. He was joined by others who believed as he did. They founded the **Rhode Island Colony** by settling a town called Providence.

38. The same year another minister, Thomas Hooker, left the Massachusetts Bay Colony with a group of people. He had many of the same reasons as Williams. Hooker and his people formed the **Connecticut Colony**.

39. Some left the Massachusetts Bay Colony for other reasons. In 1630 John Mason took a group of people to a more fertile farming area. They wanted to get away from the rocky soil of Massachusetts. Mason and his people settled in Portsmouth and founded the **New Hampshire Colony**.

40. By 1636 the four **New England** colonies had been formed and had colonists living in settlements there.

41. Each settlement was formed for special reasons, mostly religious ones. But they sometimes banded together for protection from the Indians and to help each other survive in the cold, snowy Northeast winters.

Spotlight On The British Colonies

42. The British colonies were different from the Spanish or French colonies. The people in the British colonies had the right to govern themselves. There was no Viceroy or Royal Governor to tell them what laws they must follow or which religion they were to believe in. From the beginning, the British colonists had their own ideas about how they wanted to live.

43. For example, in 1639 people in Connecticut were living under a **constitution**. A constitution puts into writing the laws governing a group of people. It also states the rights those people have. The constitution which the towns of Hartford, Windsor and Weathersfield in Connecticut wrote is called the **Fundamental Orders of Connecticut**. This is thought to be the first constitution of our time which would really work.

44. Three very different regions or areas in the British colonies soon began to develop. **New

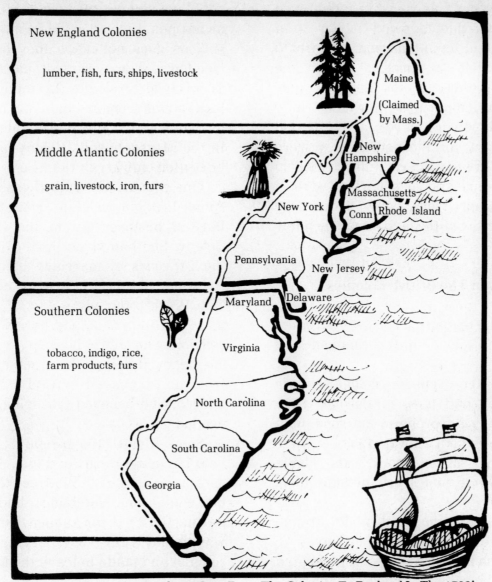

New England Colonies

lumber, fish, furs, ships, livestock

Middle Atlantic Colonies

grain, livestock, iron, furs

Southern Colonies

tobacco, indigo, rice,
farm products, furs

Maine
(Claimed by Mass.)

New Hampshire

Massachusetts

New York   Conn   Rhode Island

Pennsylvania

New Jersey

Delaware

Maryland

Virginia

North Carolina

South Carolina

Georgia

Products Sent From The Colonies To England In The 1700's

England, which you have read about in this chapter, was one. You will read about the **middle colonies** in Chapter 7. The last group were the **southern colonies**, which you will also read about in that chapter. The three regions were very different because each had a different climate and different kinds of land.

45. In each of the colonies there was a wealthy upper-class of people. Some of these people had been wealthy in England. Many had become wealthy only since coming to America. They were business people, shipowners and owners of large pieces of land.

46. About nine out of ten people in the British colonies made a living by farming. The others were traders, kept shops or gave other services needed by the colonists. Many of them were poor. Others were middle class, living a fairly good life.

47. Many of the newcomers were **indentured servants**. These people owed money to a person in England or in America who would pay for their trip to America. When the indentured servants got to America, they would work long enough to pay for their trip.

48. In a way, they were slaves for the period they had to work for the person they were indentured to. But most earned their freedom in a few years' time and got some land of their own. Some went from being indentured servants to being wealthy landowners in a few years.

Women In The British Colonies

49. Women in the British colonies were treated differently than those in the Spanish and French colonies.

50. Women in the Spanish colonies were treated as they had been in Europe. They were thought of as property or something their husbands owned. They had to obey their husbands, stay home, cook, and have children. They did not work outside their homes.

51. The few women who lived in the French trading posts were treated the same way.

52. Women in the British colonies were treated a little better than they had been in England. The main reason for this is that they were given more of a role outside of the home and more freedom.

53. Many were full partners with their farmer husbands. They had to be. Few farms could get along without the women working as hard as the men. Women gained a new respect.

54. This does not mean they had much real freedom. They were not usually educated. They could be beaten by their husbands. In England, a woman could be beaten by her husband with "any reasonable instrument". In the Massachusetts Colony a woman could be beaten only in self-defense.

55. One woman who gained great respect was Anne Hutchinson. She was married to a Puritan businessman in the Massachusetts Colony. She had given birth to 14 children in the 22 years of marriage before coming to America. She had two more children in the New World.

56. Mrs. Hutchinson had her own ideas about religion. She told whoever would listen that she believed that each person could know the truth and be saved by God without going to church. She believed that ministers were not needed.

57. Soon, almost 100 people were coming to hear her speak each Sunday.

58. The leaders of the Puritan Church did not like what Anne Hutchinson had to say. They put her on trial for saying those things. She was found guilty of speaking against her religion and made to leave the Massachusetts Colony.

59. She would not give up her beliefs. She went to Rhode Island and later to New York with some of her children. She was killed in New York during an Indian attack. To the end she would not give up what she believed.

Understanding What You Read

1. Look at the chart below and then answer the following questions:

Settlement Of The First British Colonies

Colony	Settlement	Leader	Date	Reason
Virginia	Jamestown	John Smith	1607	Trade
Massachusetts Bay	Plymouth	William Bradford	1620	Religious freedom
	Boston	John Winthrop	1630	Religious freedom
New Hampshire	Portsmouth	John Mason	1630	Religious freedom and better land
Connecticut	Hartford	Thomas Hooker	1636	Religious freedom
Rhode Island	Providence	Roger Williams	1636	Religious freedom

a. The settlement used as a trading center was _____ .

b. The colonies set up for religious purposes were _____ ,

_____ , _____ , and _____ .

c. The first British settlement in the New World was _____ in the colony

of _____ , settled in the year _____ .

d. In the spaces to the right of each colony place the name of the settlement and its leader:

	Settlement	Leader
Rhode Island	_____	_____
Connecticut	_____	_____
Massachusetts Bay	_____	_____

Virginia   _____   _____

New Hampshire   _____   _____

2. Place the following historical events in the order in which they happened. The first event would be **1)**, and so forth.
   a. Cabot's voyage to America (2)
   b. British colonists come to the New World in large numbers. (23)
   c. The defeat by the British of the Spanish Armada (13-14)
   d. Drake and the other Sea Dogs raid the Spanish treasure ships off the coast of America. (8-9)

   My answers are 1) _____ , 2) _____ , 3) _____ , and 4) _____

3. Some of the following statements are **facts**. That is, they really happened. Some of the statements are **opinions**. That is, they tell how someone thought or felt about something that happened. For example, **h** is an opinion. Place a **F** in the correct space if the statement is a fact, **O** if it is an opinion.
   a. Cabot explored the coast of Nova Scotia, Newfoundland and Labrador.
   b. The Spanish government was right in keeping British ships from trading at ports in Spanish America.
   c. Drake was leader of the Sea Dogs.
   d. The Sea Dogs had every right to raid and sink Spanish treasure ships because the Spanish had sunk Drake's ship.
   e. England won a battle with the Spanish Armada.
   f. Many people came to the New World so that they could practice the religion of their own choice.
   g. The Pilgrims were treated badly in their own country because they did not want to follow the Church of England.
   h. The Mayflower and its passengers would have been better off if they had reached New York, because it is warmer there.
   i. Roger Williams and Thomas Hooker were right to leave Massachusetts and form their own colonies.

   My answers are: a. _____ , b. _____ , c. _____ , d. _____ , e. _____ ,

   f. _____ , g. _____ , h. __**O**__ , i. _____ .

5. The first constitution in North America was written by three towns in _____ .

   It was called the _____ of _____ . (43)

Chapter 7
Europeans Come To The Middle And Southern Colonies

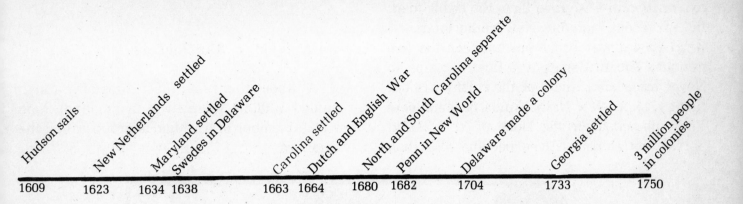

Hudson sails	New Netherlands settled	Maryland settled	Swedes in Delaware	Carolina settled	Dutch and English War	North and South Carolina separate	Penn in New World	Delaware made a colony	Georgia settled	3 million people in colonies
1609	1623	1634	1638	1663	1664	1680	1682	1704	1733	1750

1. In the 1600's some nations had colonies in the New World. Other European nations wanted to find a westward passage, a way to to reach the Indies by sailing west.

2. The Dutch kept trying for many years. They began in 1609, two years after the settlement of the Jamestown, Virginia colony. A Dutch ship called the **Half Moon** sailed along the east coast of the New World looking for the Westward Passage (See map on page 40.). Its Captain, **Henry Hudson**, was an Englishman, but he sailed for the Dutch.

3. Instead of finding a shorter way to the Indies, Hudson found a river that ran westward for a short time, and then north. He had found the New York river that now bears his name, the Hudson.

4. He also found that the Indians along the shores of the river were friendly. They were willing to trade for furs with the sailors on the ship.

5. When Hudson reported this news to the Dutch they formed a company to trade with the Indians. The company sent people to live in the new colony and traders to trade with the Indians.

6. In 1623 these people arrived in the colony they called **New Netherlands**, which is now the state of New York. The Dutch Governor, **Peter Minuit**, bought Manhattan Island from the Indians for $24 worth of beads and trinkets.

7. Sweden also sent colonists to the New World. They did not come looking for the Westward Passage. Sweden, which is a small country in northern Europe, wanted a colony to trade with the other colonies.

8. The Swedes landed in **Delaware** in 1638. They were led by Peter Minuit, who had been fired by the Dutch in 1631 and hired by the Swedes in 1637.

9. What the Swedes and Minuit did not know was that the Dutch were already in the area they claimed. The new Dutch governor moved quickly and took the land from the Swedish settlers peacefully.

Dutch East India Flag of Henry Hudson

39

10. The Dutch then began to have problems with the British. The British said that Cabot's exploration in 1497 gave them the rights to all the east coast, including New Netherlands.

11. In 1664 a war broke out between the two nations. The British sent a fleet of ships to New Netherlands and took the colony without firing a shot. New Netherlands became **New York**, named after the Duke of York. Land across the Hudson River became a British colony named **New Jersey** in honor of an island off the coast of England.

The Quakers

12. At about this same time in history, a man named **William Penn** lived in England. Penn was a member of a religious group called the **Quakers**.

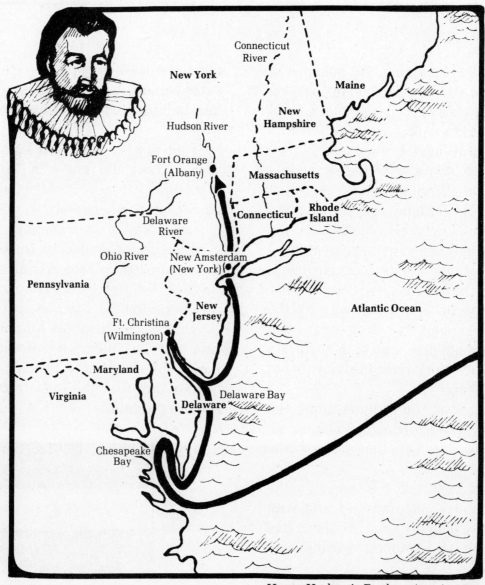

Henry Hudson's Explorations in 1609

In Pennsylvania the Quakers often shared their homes with the Indians.

13. The Quakers had no religious leaders. They believed every man was the equal of all others. All the members met to worship God as equals.

14. The Quakers could not worship in England because they did not follow the beliefs of the Church of England. Many Quakers were sent to jail for this reason.

15. William Penn was one of those who had been sent to jail for following his beliefs. The king of England owed Penn's father a lot of money. The king did not want to pay the money to Penn's father. Penn's father asked the king to give him land in America instead of money.

16. The king agreed, thinking that he was cheating Penn and his father. He did not believe the land was worth that much money.

17. In 1682 Penn and his fellow Quakers came to the New World. They named their colony **Pennsylvania** (Penn's woods).

18. Penn opened his land to Quakers from all over the world so that they could worship in peace. Thousands came from Germany, Scotland, Ireland, and England.

19. Although Penn was given the land by the king, he paid the Indians for all that the colony used.

20. Penn also was given Delaware after the English took it from the Swedes. The British governor, the Duke of York, did not want the problems of running the small colony. He gave it to Penn to govern. In 1704 Penn let it become a separate colony.

21. The last colonies to be settled in the New World were the southern colonies of

Maryland, **North Carolina**, **South Carolina** and **Georgia**.

22. **Maryland** was founded in 1634 by a group of English Catholics who could not practice their religion in England. Their leader, Lord Baltimore, sent about 300 settlers to the colony. They founded the settlement of St. Mary's, later to be named Baltimore for their leader.

23. In 1663 King Charles of England gave a grant of land "South of Virginia", to a group of his friends. They wanted to use the colony for their businesses. The friends named the colony Carolina in his honor.

24. The first settlement they founded was at Charlestown. But they found that many settlers from Virginia had come from that colony into the area that they owned and were already living there.

25. Arguments between the two groups broke out. In 1680 Carolina became two separate colonies — **North Carolina** and **South Carolina**.

26. The last of the original thirteen colonies was **Georgia**. In 1733 the king gave land to a man named James Oglethorpe. The king planned this colony as a place to get rid of people England did not want. He also wanted this colony to protect the other colonies from the French and Spanish to the south and west.

27. Oglethorpe brought many people to Georgia who had been in jail or who owed large sums of money that they couldn't pay. The colony was named after King George of England. The first settlement in the new colony was at Savannah.

The Thirteen English Colonies

28. By 1750 the English had thirteen colonies in America. Ten of them had always been

English Colonies In America

42

English colonies. New York and New Jersey became English colonies after a short war with the Dutch. Delaware had first been owned by Sweden and then became English.

29. The colonies were naturally divided into three different land areas — north, middle and south. People within each area soon found they had the same kinds of problems. They also found they needed and wanted many of the same things. For example, Massachusetts, Plymouth, Hartford and New Haven together made up an army to protect their villages when Indians attacked.

30. The southern colonies became much like the English colonies in the West Indies. Large farms called plantations, worked by cheap labor, turned out turpentine, indigo and tobacco.

31. The southern colonies were Georgia, North and South Carolina, Virginia and Maryland.

32. The middle colonies — Delaware, Pennsylvania, New Jersey and New York — were called the Bread Colonies. They had good soil and good rivers for water and transportation. The chief products of these states were grain and livestock.

33. The people in the New England colonies — Connecticut, Massachusetts, Rhode Island and New Hampshire — fished and built ships. They also carried on much of the slave trade.

34. The thirteen British colonies grew quickly. By 1775, more than three million people lived in those colonies.

Spotlight On Regional Differences

35. The three regions (areas or parts) of the early colonies developed in different economic (business and work) ways. This has had a great effect on American history, and was due to two factors — the different kind of land in each, and difference in climate.

36. The kind of land has a lot to do with what can be done in an area. The rocky soil of New England was not good for crops. It was hard for farmers to earn a living there. Since it was near the sea and large fishing banks, most New Englanders worked in fishing, shipbuilding and trading.

37. The middle and southern colonies had good soil. Grain and vegetables, cotton and tobacco could be grown, so they became farming areas.

38. The climate also had much to do with making the areas very different. The north was too cold and did not have a long growing season. Even if the land had been good for crops, the weather was wrong.

39. The south, on the other hand, had a warm climate and a long growing season.

40. As we can see, these differences in kinds of land and climate brought about differences in the way people made their living. The different climates also brought about differences in the way people lived and enjoyed themselves.

41. At times these differences also made people act and believe differently. We will see this in American history during the War Between the States.

42. The next chapter will show you what life was like in each of the three areas of the British Colonies. You will see it through the eyes of people who might have lived then and there. You will also find out what it was like to have lived in an area with few settlers — the wilderness beyond the thirteen colonies.

Understanding What You Read

1. Look at the chart below and then answer the following questions:

Settlement Of The Middle And Southern Colonies

Colony	Settlement	Leader	Date	Reason
New York	New Amsterdam	Peter Minuit	1626	Trade
Maryland	St. Mary's	Lord Baltimore	1634	Religious freedom
Delaware	Wilmington	Peter Minuit	1638	Trade
North Carolina	Albemarle	Group of businessmen	1653	Trade
South Carolina	Charleston	Group of businessmen	1670	Trade
Pennsylvania	Philadelphia	William Penn	1682	Religious freedom
New Jersey	Various settlements	Lord Berkeley	1664	Trade
Georgia	Savannah	James Oglethorpe	1733	Place for unwanted people and protection from Spain and France

a. The one man who was the leader of two different colonies was _____ ,

who led both _____ and _____ .

b. The two colonies that were founded for religious freedom were

_____ and _____ .

c. The colony that was founded as a place for unwanted people from England and to give the

colonies protection from other nations was _____ . It was founded by

_____ in the year _____ .

44

d. Two colonies were founded by groups of businessmen. Those colonies were _____ and _____ .

2. William Penn was the leader of a religious group called _____ . He brought

his people to the colony of _____ in the year _____ . (17)

He asked people from all over the world to join his colony. Thousands came from

_____ , _____ , _____ , and

_____ . (18)

3. The southern colonies were _____ , _____ ,

_____ , _____ , and _____ . (31)

4. The middle colonies were _____ , _____ ,

_____ , and _____ . (32)

5. The New England colonies were _____ ,

_____ , _____ , and _____ . (33)

6. **Map Study:** Look at the map on page 40 and then answer the following questions:

a. Which body of water in America did Henry Hudson first enter? _____ .

b. Hudson sailed along the coast of the following states: _____ ,

_____ , _____ , _____ and

_____ .

c. The Hudson River is in what is now the state of _____ .

d. The states of _____ and _____

are on the Chesapeake Bay.

Chapter 8
Life In The Colonies

1. Life in the thirteen colonies was often exciting, sometimes dangerous. But mostly, the people lived everyday lives just as we do today.

2. The four diaries you are about to read are similar to many diaries written by people who lived in the colonies around 1760. They will give you a better idea of what the colonists faced in their everyday lives.

Diary of Jeremiah Greene

3. My name is Jeremiah Greene, and I live in the colony of Massachusetts with my parents and my two brothers and sisters. We came here from England.

4. We had to leave England because of our religion. My family and I are Puritans. We could not practice our religion in England, but we can here in Massachusetts.

5. This morning, like most mornings, I went to school. We go to school six days each week and spend most of Sunday in church.

6. My school has only one room and one teacher. All the children in the colony come here to study. We learn to read and understand the Bible, write and do arithmetic.

7. My father works in a shipyard, building ships that are used for trade with other countries. He likes his work, but he does not like what the ships are sometimes used for.

8. He told us at dinner the other day that the ships usually take rum from New England to

At an early age boys in New England were apprenticed to become shipbuilders.

Africa. There the rum is traded for black slaves taken from the forest.

9. The black slaves are brought to the West Indies or to the south of America where they are traded for molasses. The molasses is brought to New England where it's used in making rum. Then the ship again goes to Africa.

10. My father also builds whaling ships that leave for the cold waters of the north to catch the giant whales, and smaller boats that catch fish closer to home. We eat lots of fish because the soil around here is not very good for growing crops.

11. When I get older I will be apprenticed to the same shipbuilder my father works for. I will have to go and live with the shipbuilder and his family for five years. He will teach me his trade, allow me to read from his books, and will give me food and clothing. He will pay me no money for the work I do for him.

12. I am looking forward to learning to be a shipbuilder.

Diary of Jonathan Franklin

13. My name is Jonathan Franklin, and I live in the colony of New York.

14. My parents came here from England. In England they worked on a farm belonging to a

In the middle colonies boys and young men worked long hours in the field.

man they hardly ever saw. Here in America we have our own farm.

15. The farm is a small one, but we grow wheat, rye, oats and barley. We all work very hard on the farm. Often my mother and older sisters work right along tending the crops.

16. Many of our neighbors are from other lands such as Germany, Sweden and Holland. We are all Americans now, I suppose.

17. There are no schools here in the New York colonies. One of the women in the town is teaching me and a few other boys how to read and write. My mother teaches many of the girls how to cook and spin wool on the spinning wheel.

18. I will probably spend my whole life right here on the farm. The roads are so bad traveling to see neighbors or going to church on Sunday is hard. We walk most places that we have to go.

19. When I get older I will probably take the farm over from my father. I would really rather go into the city and become an iron or leather worker there. Or, maybe I will go into the wilderness and earn my fortune.

20. Those jobs sound much more exciting than life here on the farm.

Diary of Deborah Prentice

21. My name is Deborah Prentice. I live in South Carolina with my parents and my brothers.

In the south indentured servants and black slaves worked together on plantations.

22. We live on a big plantation — a farm where we grow tobacco. But I'm not the daughter of the owner. My parents are indentured servants. They owed money in England and were brought by the people who own the plantation to work here in Carolina.

23. In about ten years they will be free to buy their own land and move out on their own. That is the difference between us and the black slaves who work here.

24. The slaves were bought by the owner of the plantation. They will probably never be free. Their children are born to slavery and can be sold away. I was free from birth.

25. I do work, however. I help my mother in the kitchen and carry water for cooking and washing. I've never learned to read and write, and probably never will. There's no need for a woman to know how to do those things as long as she can cook, make clothes and bake bread.

26. My father takes care of the tobacco sheds. The tobacco business makes a lot of money for the people who own this plantation.

27. Someday he will be free and we can start our own tobacco farm. Then we will be rich, too.

Diary of Jeremy Adams

28. My name is Jeremy and I live in the Mohawk Valley of New York. I live with my parents and my two brothers.

29. We all moved to what most folks call the wilderness because we did not like living in the city of New York. Besides, there is more chance for a man to be his own king here in the wilderness.

30. We live in a cabin made of logs. My father, my brother and I trap beaver and other animals. We sell the furs to traders for money.

31. But we don't need much. We grow our own food and my mother makes all the clothes. Some of our clothes are made from the skins of animals we kill.

32. Life is hard here. Everyone works hard, including my mother. When we lived in one of the settlements, the women did nothing but cook and make clothes. Here the women do everything right along side the men. My mother says she likes it much better this way.

33. Other people are coming this way and we will build a wooden fort around all our homes. I guess someday this will become a town like the one we left behind. Then we will have to move westward again. America is a big country and there is plenty of land for us.

Spotlight On Slavery

34. The first slaves were brought to the colonies in 1619 by the Dutch. These slaves were sold at Jamestown in Virginia Colony.

35. Slaves were brought to America in what is called the **Triangle Trade.** Rum was taken to Africa and exchanged for slaves. Slaves were exchanged for molasses. Molasses was then made into rum.

36. Because of the Triangle Trade, the number of slaves in the colonies grew quickly.

37. While there were slaves in every colony, slavery grew more quickly in the southern colonies than anywhere else.

38. Slave labor was well suited for the farm work of the south. The people needed on the plantations to grow rice and tobacco did not have to be educated. The work called for only the use of simple tools and could be done in large groups. There was little need for someone to tell them what to do.

39. The southern growers believed they could not get along without slaves. Many laws were passed to control the slaves.

Even in colonial times people were already moving West to find more land.

40. While indentured servants could become free after a period of time, the laws in the south made a person a slave for life.

41. Any children born to slaves became slaves from birth. They became the property of the person who owned their parents.

42. Slaves could not be taught to read or write under southern law. They could own no property since they were property themselves.

43. A slave could be sold any time his or her master decided to. Families were not respected. A child could be sold away from his or her mother. Husbands and wives could be separated at will.

44. By the end of the eighteenth century (1799), several hundred thousand slaves lived in the south.

45. There were fewer slaves in the north because the need for them was not as great as it was in the south. Slaves in the north were given better treatment and more protection.

46. In Massachusetts, slaves could own property, marry, and testify in court. An owner could not kill a slave, although he did have the right to punish his slaves.

47. Neither slaves nor free blacks, however, could vote or hold office in the north.

Understanding What You Read

1. Beside each statement write the area or region of America (New England, middle colonies, southern colonies, wilderness) where the diaries told us it might have taken place.

   a. I read the Bible in school each day. _____ (6)

   b. We grow wheat on our farm. _____ (15)

   c. The plantation I live on has many slaves. _____ (24)

   d. We live in a log cabin among the tall trees of the deep woods. _____ (30)

   e. We grow tobacco on our plantation. _____ (22)

   f. We trap beaver and sell the furs. _____ (30)

   g. I am going to learn to be a shipbuilder. _____ (11)

   h. Many of our neighbors come from countries other than England. _____ (16)

2. The main idea of this chapter is:
   a. to show how ships were built
   b. to show how people lived in various parts of Colonial America
   c. to show how to write a diary
   d. to show where slaves come from

   My answer is _____ .

3. **True Or False:** Decide if the following statements are true or false. If they are true, place a **T** in the correct answer space. If the statement is false, change the underlined word to make it true.

   _____ a. Many young people in New England went to school because they were Puritans who were supposed to know how to read the Bible. (4-6)

   _____ b. Rum from New England was used to trade for slaves from Africa. (9)

   _____ c. An apprentice had to work for no pay. (11)

   _____ d. A farm in the middle colonies might grow tobacco. (15)

_____ e. Slaves could one day be free. (22,27)

_____ f. Children of indentured servants had to become slaves themselves. (41)

_____ g. People who lived in the wilderness usually lived in log cabins. (30)

_____ h. Women who lived in big cities usually worked right alongside their families in hunting, trapping, and farming. (32)

_____ i. Slave labor was better suited to the north because large farms needed many workers. (38)

_____ j. Slaves had more rights in the south. (45)

Chapter 9
Update To History

The questions on this page are written so you will think about the meaning of this history for today's Americans.

1. How is your life as an American shaped by the region in which you live? Can you see that some differences are because of the country that once owned the colony or area in which you live? How? For example, does a person living in New Orleans (French) live, eat, or act differently than a person living in Texas (Spanish) or a person in New England (British)? Why do these differences occur?

_____

_____

_____

_____

_____

_____

2. Many people came to America looking for religious freedom. How does that affect the way the United States government deals with religion today? What problems do we have today concerning government and religion?

_____

_____

_____

_____

_____

3. Slavery started in the colonial period and grew in the south because slaves were needed to work the plantations. How did slavery in the colonial period affect you as an American today?

_____

_____

_____

_____

4. Why do you think we should study history? Do you think it is important for a person to know about the past? Why? Why not?

_____

_____

_____

_____

5. The first explorers that came to the New World were looking for a westward passage to the riches of the East Indies. Nobody ever found such a passage. Suppose such explorers were looking at America today. Would they be disappointed in what they had found? Why or why not?

_____

_____

_____

_____

Time Line Update: In the space below, draw a time line for all of the period covered in this unit. Begin with 1492, the voyage of Columbus and end with 1733, the beginning of the Georgia colony.

1492

1733

Unit 2
The Colonies Gain Their Freedom

Chapter 10
The Road To Revolution

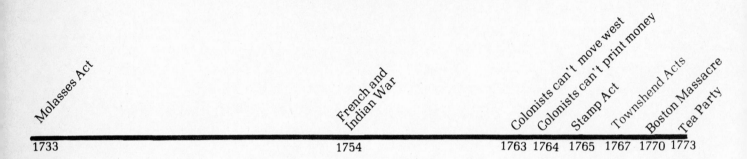

Molasses Act		French and Indian War		Colonists can't move west	Colonists can't print money	Stamp Act	Townshend Acts	Boston Massacre	Tea Party
1733		1754		1763	1764	1765	1767	1770	1773

1. It is true that the British colonies gave their people more freedom than the Spanish or the French. However, the British lawmakers made a number of laws that were to help businessmen in England more than the colonists in America.

2. One such act was the **Molasses Act** of 1733. This act helped the sugar plantation owners on the islands in the British West Indies. It put a tax on sugar and molasses coming from any other place. The cost of rum would go up if the colonists had to pay the extra tax on sugar and molasses.

3. The law also said that the traders in New England could trade only with these British islands. But the French and Dutch islands had bought lots of goods from the New Englanders. Many New England shippers and businessmen would have lost fortunes if they had only traded with the British islands.

4. Many New Englanders did not like the Molasses Act. They found ways of getting around it and the British did not always make people obey the law.

5. From 1754 to 1763 the British and the French fought a war over land in America. In America this was called the **French and Indian War**, because many Indians fought on the side of the French. They fought with the French because many French fur traders and missionaries lived with the Indians. In Europe this war was called the **Seven Years War**.

6. The British won the war. France lost Canada and all of the French territory east of the Mississippi River except for the city of New Orleans.

7. For England the war was a way to get more land for **expansion** (growing outward). For many colonists the war meant much more.

8. First of all, many colonists had fought alongside the British Army. They saw that the British Army was only made of men like themselves. They did not need the British Army for protection as much as they had before. American soldiers had learned to fight.

9. Secondly, the colonists saw that they would have to work together. More and more people were coming to America. They also wanted land. The colonists would have to work together to keep the land they had and also the land they wanted to move into across the mountains.

10. Since the English and the colonists had won the war, the French were not a danger to them now. They could safely move across the mountains and not be attacked by the French.

The King Tightens His Control

11. The British had no idea of moving out and leaving the colonists to themselves. In fact, King George III, the new king of England, thought that it was time to tighten his control on the colonies.

12. In the king's mind, there were good reasons for greater control over the colonies. The French had been defeated, but the Indians were still enemies of England and the British settlements. The war with France had also cost the English a lot of money. The king wanted the American colonists to pay for the war with higher taxes.

13. The king believed that all this was necessary. The colonists did not think so.

14. Shortly after the war ended the king put out a **proclamation** (law). It said that colonists could not move westward over the Appalachian Mountains.

15. This angered many Americans. They saw this land to the west as a place for their colonies to grow.

16. In fact, many colonies had already claimed land west of the mountains. Some settlers had already moved there. The **Proclamation of 1763** as it came to be called was not obeyed by all Americans.

17. Then, very quickly, the British passed several more laws which angered the colonists.

18. In 1764, a new law forbid the colonies from printing or using their own money.

19. In 1765, the **Stamp Act** was passed. Tax stamps had to be put on 54 kinds of papers, such as playing cards, newspapers, wills and licenses. The taxes colonists had to pay on these items went from one cent for newspapers to ten dollars for a college diploma. Payment had to be made in either gold or silver.

20. Many colonists began to speak out against the new taxes. Patrick Henry, a young man from Virginia, was one who spoke the loudest.

21. "**Parliament** (the British lawmakers) made these laws," Henry said. "But we have nobody to speak for us in Parliament. Therefore we cannot be taxed by them."

22. In October of 1765, nine colonies sent people to a meeting in New York City. The meeting was to talk about the Stamp Act.

23. The people at the meeting made a decision. Parliament had no right to tax the American colonies as long as the colonies had no

Colonists burn the British flag to protest taxes.

JOIN, or DIE.

representation (voice) in Parliament. "No taxation without representation" became the word of the meeting.

24. The people at the meeting sent Parliament a letter asking it to **repeal** (do away with) the Stamp Act.

25. Up until that time there had been little cooperation between the colonies. The meeting in New York was the first time a large number of the colonies acted together.

26. "There ought to be no New England man, no New Yorker, but all of us Americans," one man said at that meeting.

27. But the British did not repeal the Stamp Act. In fact, they put new taxes on the colonies.

28. In 1767 the British passed the **Townshend Act.** This act put taxes on tea, glass, paper and paint. These taxes affected every colonist living in America.

29. Many people were angered when the British would not change the Stamp Act or the new Townshend Act. Some refused to pay the taxes. Many refused to buy any goods made in England.

The Sons Of Liberty

30. Others decided to take action. They formed clubs called the **Sons of Liberty**. The motto (saying) of the Sons of Liberty was **Join or Die**.

31. The Sons of Liberty broke into the homes of tax collectors. They beat them and burned the hated tax stamps.

32. British troops were sent to some of the larger cities. The soldiers were sent to help the tax collectors do their job. Many were sent to Boston, where the anger seemed to be the greatest. They were without places to sleep. American colonists were told that they would have to let the soldiers live in their homes. This made the colonists even more angry with the British.

58

33. Many American traders smuggled goods in and out of American ports to keep from paying the British taxes. Americans often teased British troops in the streets by throwing rocks or snowballs at them.

34. Many American settlers moved across the Appalachian Mountains to the west. They did this even though the British had said they could not.

35. In these ways individual Americans protested against the British. But the colonies as a group also protested. Many colonies would not give any tax money to the British. Others refused to follow the rules of the British governor.

36. One town, Newburyport, Massachusetts, summed up the feelings of most Americans at a town meeting. The people of Newburyport voted to say:

37. *"That a people should be taxed at the will of another, be it a man or a nation, without their own permission to be taxed, is slavery, because, if that man or nation see fit, they may have everything taken from them."*

The Sons of Liberty throw British tea into Boston Harbor.

The First Shots

38. In 1770 the first real battle between the colonists and the British Army took place. In March of that year some British soldiers got angry at a crowd of colonists who were throwing snowballs at them in Boston.

39. This shooting was later called the **Boston Massacre**. It was not to be the last shots fired between the colonists and British soldiers.

40. For the next few years, between 1770 and 1773, there were only a few acts of violence in the colonies. Some British tax boats were burned. The British repealed many of the taxes the colonists did not like, but the tax on tea stayed.

41. However, in 1773, the peace ended. In that year the British told the British East India Company it could send tea to America without paying the tax. All other tea traders still had to pay the tax.

42. The British company now could sell tea in America much more cheaply than anyone else. Americans, angered at the new rules, refused to buy any tea. They also refused to unload tea from British ships in American ports.

43. The Sons of Liberty went even further. In an action later to be called **The Boston Tea Party**, a group of Sons, dressed as Indians, boarded a tea ship in Boston harbor. They threw all the tea into the water. The 342 chests of tea that were thrown overboard were valued at $75,000.

44. Many say the Boston Tea Party was the most important event that led to the start of all-out war between the colonies and the British — the Revolutionary War.

Spotlight On The Boston Massacre

45. The first shots in what was to be the Revolutionary War were fired in Boston in March of 1770 in the Boston Massacre.

46. Many British soldiers had come to Boston and other large American cities in the fall of 1768.

47. The city council of Boston refused to find housing for the soldiers. It also refused to give the British government money to pay for such housing.

48. The British were angered by the city's refusals. They ordered that British soldiers be housed in private houses in the city. Many families had to make room for the soldiers.

An engraving of the Boston Massacre by Paul Revere.

49. Anger ran high in Boston towards the British and their soldiers.

50. Here is what happened in Boston that winter day in the words of a man who watched it all happen.

51. *"The people in Boston were really angry at the British soldiers. The soldiers came and lived in our homes and ate our food. They bullied and punished citizens of Boston and were not punished for it.*

52. *I have heard a story that everyone in Boston believes. It is said that the British soldiers have pulled down the Liberty Pole in New York City. That pole was a symbol of our independence and right to govern ourselves.*

53. *But something which is even worse has happened. It was early in the evening when a party of British soldiers under the command of Captain Preston came walking down the square in Boston.*

54. *A group of 50 or 60 men, led by a black freeman named Crispus Attucks, began to shout at the soldiers to go home. Some of the younger boys in the crowd began to throw some snowballs at them. They had done this many times in the past.*

55. *But this time was different. Although I heard no order from the Captain, two of his men began firing at the crowd. Attucks fell first, then many others. The crowd ran. Five were left dead and many were wounded."*

56. The Captain and his men were put on trial. All but two were found not guilty. Those two men were found guilty of manslaughter and taken back to England for punishment.

Understanding What You Read

1. Match the British law with what it was meant to do to the colonies:

   a. Molasses Act (2)
   b. Stamp Act (19)
   c. Townshend Acts (28)
   d. Proclamation of 1763 (14,16)

   1. no settlement west of the Appalachian Mountains
   2. tax on papers and articles
   3. trade only with British Islands
   4. tax on tea and paper.

   My answers are: a. _____ , b. _____ , c. _____ , d. _____ .

2. By "No taxation without representation", the colonists meant that:
   a. they didn't want to pay any taxes to the British.
   b. the taxes they had to pay were much too expensive.
   c. they had no say in deciding what would be taxed and they didn't want to be taxed until they did have a say.
   d. they wanted the taxes to be higher.

   My answer is _____ . (21)

3. During the French and Indian War, the Indians fought on the side of the _____

   against the _____ and the _____ . (5)

4. Many Americans disobeyed the law and moved across the _____ to the west. (34)

5. The British let the _____ _____ _____ Company send tea to America without paying taxes. (41)

6. At the Boston Tea Party the _____ of _____ threw tea

   overboard valued at _____ . (43)

7. The Boston Massacre was the first time shots were fired by the _____ at a

   group of _____ . (53-55) The crowd in Boston was throwing

   _____ at a group of British _____ when they opened

   fire. (54)   One of the first to fall was the leader of the crowd, _____

   _____ . (55)

61

8. **Word Skills:** Solve the puzzle below using the clues provided.

Puzzle Clues

Across

1. British lawmakers
5. people who lived in American Colonies
7. item taxed by the British
8. the British ruler
9. the _ _ _ _ _ Act
11. The Americans threw these in Boston.

Down

2. French and _ _ _ _ _ _ _ War
3. The Americans were unhappy about British _ _ _ _ _ _ .
4. the first British Act: the _ _ _ _ _ _ _ _ _ Act
6. the _ _ _ _ _ of Liberty
10. place of the massacre and the tea party

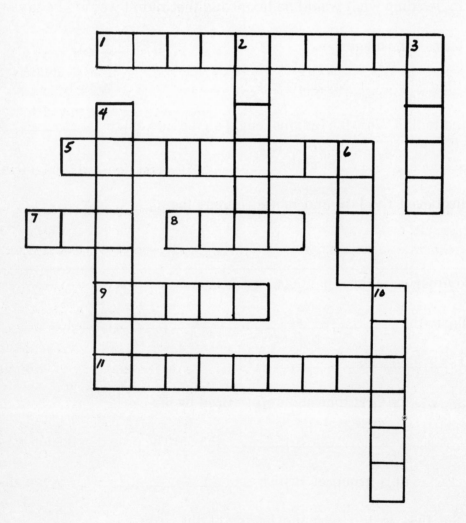

Chapter 11
War Comes Closer

Boston Tea Party

First Continental Congress, Intolerable Acts

Lexington and Concord, Breeds Hill

1773   1774   1775

1. Many people, both Americans and British, thought that the Boston Tea Party was wrong. Benjamin Franklin, a famous American patriot, called the tea party "an act of violent injustice". Some Boston businessmen offered to pay the British shipowners for the damages done by the Sons of Liberty.

2. But the British king was not about to let the Americans go unpunished for what they had done in Boston Harbor. The king had the British Parliament pass three new laws.

3. The new laws were so hard on the colonies that they were called the **Intolerable Acts**. (acts that could not be followed or allowed)

4. The Intolerable Acts closed the harbor at Boston to all shipping until the tea was paid for. They also said that people in America could no longer hold town meetings. The colonists would have to house British soldiers for as long as England wanted them to. Any British subject who committed a crime in America would be tried in England and not in the colonies.

5. The people of Massachusetts felt that they could not possibly obey the Intolerable Acts. With the port closed, no food could come into Boston. They would not be able to govern themselves without holding town meetings.

Few colonists wanted British soldiers living in their homes.

6. Massachusetts decided not to obey the laws. They also decided to ask the other colonies for help and support. Many of the colonies near Massachusetts sent food overland to Boston.

The First Continental Congress

7. All of the colonies except Georgia sent men to a meeting in Philadelphia. This meeting, called the **First Continental Congress**, opened in September, 1774.

8. The members of the Congress argued about what to do about the Intolerable Acts. They finally decided they must force the British to repeal the acts. The Congress decided to cut off all trade between England and the colonies until the acts were changed.

Flag of Virginia's Culpepper Minutemen

The Minutemen

9. By 1774, colonists all over America were arming themselves. In New England these men were called **Minutemen** because they could be ready to fight in a minute. They practiced fighting and marching with wooden guns.

10. But many men had real muskets. The countryside was alive with the sounds of men marching and firing their muskets.

11. The feelings of the Minutemen can be found in a letter from a Massachusetts man to his brother in England.

March, 1775

Dear John,

12. *As you probably already know, things are not good here in Massachusetts Colony. We are getting tired of being told what to do by our British rulers. Most men in the other colonies feel much the way we do.*

13. *There are still some — we call them Tories — who support the Englishmen. Tories believe that the king has the right to rule our lives. We don't.*

14. *We are told to pay high taxes to the British. Few pay the taxes. British soldiers live in our homes without our permission. Our port is closed and all our food must come from friends in other colonies. We can no longer make our own laws.*

15. *Something must be done. One of our most outspoken leaders, Patrick Henry, has best said what must be done. He was speaking before the Virginia House of Congress. Henry said "There is no longer any room for hope. If we wish to be free we must fight."*

16. *I have to agree with what Henry says, though I know what you must be thinking in England. You must believe that we are traitors to England. Perhaps we are, but we have no choice.*

17. *I have joined the Minutemen here in Massachusetts. We will fight to win our freedom if we must. As Henry said in ending his fine speech, "I know not what course others may take; but as for me, give me liberty or give me death."*

18. *I hope that not too many will die for the liberty we seek.*

Your Brother,

Thomas

An angry British soldier takes over a colonist's home.

19. In April of 1775 the British commander in Boston sent a group of soldiers to Concord, a village near Boston. They were to find a load of guns and powder (used for ammunition) which was supposed to be hidden there.

20. The British troops were also ordered to arrest two colonial leaders, Samuel Adams and John Hancock. Both men were said to be hiding in Lexington, which was on the way from Boston to Concord.

21. What happened at Lexington and Concord was told in a later letter from Thomas to his brother John in England.

May, 1775

Dear John,

22. *This may be my last letter for some time. As I told you in my other letter, I recently joined a group of Massachusetts Minutemen who are ready to fight against the British.*

23. *Last month a good friend, Paul Revere, rode to tell us that British soldiers were marching on the road to Concord. We formed ranks at Lexington. We stood while our leaders told the British that they could not pass.*

24. *The British soldiers began firing at us. There were too many of them and we had to retreat. We had only seventy men and they had hundreds.*

25. *The British moved on into Concord, where they burned some guns we had hidden there.*

26. *We formed again at Concord Bridge. This time we had more men. Some were well-trained in fighting. The British soldiers told us to go home before they fired on us. We would not move.*

27. *They shot at us and we fired back. Many were killed on both sides. The British ran for Boston. We fired at them from behind trees, walls and barns as they went.*

28. *I believe that a war began here at Lexington and Concord. It will not end until we are a free nation. I don't think that mail will be moving between our two nations until the war ends. You probably will not hear from me for some time.*

29. *Don't worry about me. I'll be all right. I'll join*

the rest of my men here in Boston. We will force the British rulers out of this city. Then we will force them to leave our nation.

30. *I am fighting for a cause that I believe in deeply.*

Your Brother,

Thomas

31. Many colonists joined the Minutemen outside of Boston. The American soldiers had little training and fewer weapons. They faced one of the best-trained and best-equipped armies of that time.

32. Later that year, the colonial army took a hill that overlooked Boston Harbor. The hill was called **Breed's Hill**, after its owner. The army thought they were on **Bunker Hill**, which was nearby. The famous battle is still named for Bunker Hill even though it was not fought there.

33. The battle began when the British commander sent soldiers up the hill to take it. The British soldiers marched right up the hill. They were sure that they would win easily over the untrained American soldiers.

34. The British came on. They were forced back by American muskets.

35. They regrouped and charged again. Again they were driven back by the colonial guns. They charged for a third time. By now the colonial minutemen were almost out of ammunition.

36. On the third charge the British took Breed's Hill, but at great cost. The colonial army had lost 140 men. The British army had lost nearly 1,000 killed or wounded.

37. At Breed's Hill the American soldiers proved that they were up to fighting the better-trained British army. It could be a long war.

Spotlight On The Two Sides

38. Who would win the Revolutionary War? Would America win its independence? If England won, the colonial leaders would be punished as traitors. England would again take control of the thirteen colonies.

39. To fight the strong British army, the colonies had to work together. "We must all hang together now, or we will hang separately," Benjamin Franklin said. Nobody laughed. The leaders of the revolution may very well have been hung if they had lost the war.

40. Most people, in fact, thought the British would win without much trouble. There were a number of reasons for that belief:

41. • The British government was the strongest in the world. The American government did not yet really exist.

42. • The British had lots of money to pay for war. The American government had none. It

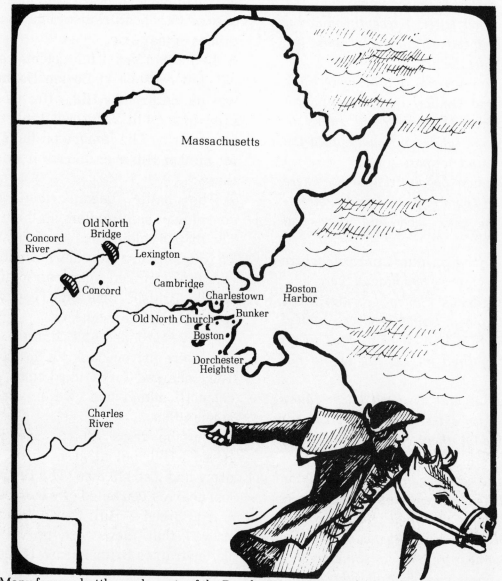

Many famous battles and events of the Revolutionary War took place in Massachusetts.

could only print its own money. This money would really be worthless if the colonists lost the war.

43. • The British army was the strongest in the world. The American army was made up of **militia** (citizen-soldiers) who were badly trained and badly armed. The British army had many officers, while the American army had few with any experience. Besides that, the British navy ruled the seas. The Americans had no navy at all.

44. The American army had some advantages, and other things turned out to be advantages as the war went on:

45. • The British had to fight a war 3,000 miles away from home. They had to ship men and supplies across the Atlantic Ocean.

46. • The British had to fight a war over a very large area. It went from New Hampshire and New York to Georgia, from the ocean to the Appalachian Mountains. To win, the British had to have men in all of that area.

47. • Time was on the American side. The colonists just had to hold out long enough. England might then lose because they couldn't bring soldiers over quickly enough.

48. • The war was not a popular one in England. Many people there had family and friends in America. The British army had trouble getting people to fight in the war.

49. • France helped turn the tide by sending money and trained officers to aid the colonists. Without help from other countries, all the other advantages might not have helped the Americans enough.

The Minutemen fighting the British at the Battle of Lexington.

Understanding What You Read

1. **Cartoon Reading Skills:** Look at the following cartoon and then answer the questions below:

a. Which does the cartoonist think is the better army, the British or the Americans?

_____

b. How does the cartoonist show what he thinks? _____

_____

_____

c. Do you agree with the cartoonist? Why or why not? _____

_____

_____

d. In the space below, draw your own cartoon showing one of the differences between England and America which you read about in the Spotlight section of this chapter (pg. 66). Then explain what you are trying to say with your cartoon.

Explanation: _____

_____

_____

2. Match the person or persons in the left column with what they did or said in the right column:

   a. Ben Franklin (1)   1. cut off trade between England and the colonies
   b. First Continental Congress (8) 2. warned that the British were marching
   c. Minutemen (28)   3. said "Give me liberty or give me death".
   d. Patrick Henry (17)   4. fought at Lexington and Concord
   e. Paul Revere (23)   5. thought the Boston Tea Party was wrong
   f. British commander in Boston (33) 6. sent men to take Breed's Hill

   My answers are: a. _____ , b. _____ , c. _____ , d. _____ , e. _____ , f. _____ .

3. The Intolerable Acts did **not** do which of the following:
   a. allowed British soldiers to live in private homes in America
   b. closed the port of Boston until the tea was paid for
   c. allowed America to become a free and independent nation
   d. stopped the American people from holding town meetings

   My answer is _____ . (4)

4. The first battles between American soldiers and British soldiers took place at

   _____ and _____ . (23-26)

Chapter 12
The Colonies At War

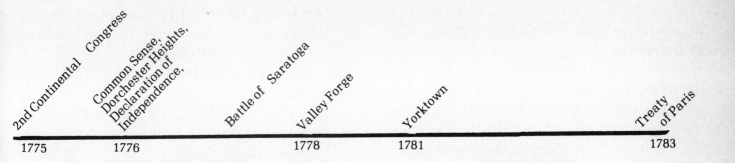

2nd Continental Congress

Common Sense, Dorchester Heights, Declaration of Independence,

Battle of Saratoga

Valley Forge

Yorktown

Treaty of Paris

1775   1776   1778   1781   1783

1. In May of 1775 a **Second Continental Congress** met in Philadelphia. Many of the representatives at the Congress still believed that the fighting around Boston was only a **New England War**. They did not think that the rest of the colonies would have to get involved.

2. Many still did not think of the colonies as a separate nation. They believed that England and America could work out their differences and once again be friends.

3. The Congress voted to ask each of the thirteen colonies to give war supplies and troops. They voted to ask France for help. They voted to make **George Washington** the Commander-in-Chief of the new army.

4. They picked Washington for two reasons. He was a trained solder, having fought in the French and Indian War. And he was from the south — from Virginia. The Congress wanted the southern colonies to come into the war. They believed that picking Washington would bring them into the war.

5. Even though many representatives to the Congress did not want an all-out war, the war seemed to get closer and closer.

6. The American army invaded Canada and tried to take Quebec. They failed. The British navy burned the port of Falmouth, Maine.

7. King George could not get enough British men to fight in America. He hired soldiers from the rulers of Germany. These soldiers, called **Hessians**, came to fight not for a cause, but for money.

8. The British paid the Prince of Hesse $500,000 a year plus $35 for each Hessian killed and $12 for each one wounded. The prince then paid the soldiers.

Continental Navy flag

9. In January of 1776 an Englishman named Thomas Paine who had come to America published a small book called **Common Sense**. It said that all kings in general, and especially George III of England, were bad. America must become a separate nation if Americans were ever to be free to make their way in the world.

10. **Common Sense** became a best-seller. Reading it made many Americans believe that

the time had come for America to become a free and independent nation.

11. By the spring of 1776 the Second Continental Congress made a decision. That decision was to write and sign a **Declaration of Independence**. This was to show England and other countries that Americans were determined to become a free nation. If the colonists lost the war, all the men who signed the declaration would hang. With this in mind, the Declaration of Independence was signed in July, 1776 in Philadelphia. (You will read more about the Declaration of Independence in Chapter 13.)

12. Many other Americans thought differently. About one-third of all Americans stayed loyal to the king and to England. They were called **Tories** or Loyalists. Many others would not take any side at all in the fight.

Early Battles

13. Many of the early battles of the Revolutionary War took place around New York City. Washington's army faced the British on Long Island. The Americans lost. They had to retreat first to New York City and then to Pennsylvania.

14. There were some early victories, however. (See map on page 74.) One was in March of 1776, four months before the signing of the Declaration of Independence. A group of freezing, hungry American soldiers and civilians had captured cannons in New York State. They pulled them 200 miles across snowy land and icy rivers to Boston.

15. The guns were brought up to Dorchester Heights, a hill overlooking Boston Harbor, at night. Two thousand people worked long and hard to get the guns in place and to build a fake fort to protect them.(See Spotlight on page 74.)

16. When the British awoke in the morning they looked up into the guns of Dorchester Heights. A few days later they sailed from Boston without a further fight.

17. In the winter of 1776, General Washington and his poorly-equipped men were camped in Pennsylvania. Then, on Christmas Eve, Washington and his men crossed the icy Delaware River. They attacked a group of Hessians at Trenton, New Jersey.

Flag of 1777

18. The Germans, celebrating the holiday with strong drink, were taken by surprise. They surrendered themselves with all of their weapons and equipment.

19. Two weeks later Washington led another surprise attack. This one was on Princeton, New Jersey. Again, the colonial army was successful.

20. The British army grew weaker as the American army grew stronger. In October of 1777 the Americans beat a large British force at Saratoga, New York.

21. The French had not been sure about helping the American side in this war. They waited until they thought the Americans could win.

22. The Saratoga battle proved this to them. They saw a chance to help defeat an old enemy by helping the Americans. They decided to supply money, arms and officers to help the Americans.

Valley Forge

23. The British army spent the winter of 1778 comfortably camped in Philadelphia. Washington's army spent a cold, hungry winter camped at Valley Forge, about 30 miles away. The French supplies and money had not yet come.

24. The American army was short on food and clothing. There were almost no medical supplies. The winter was a very cold one, even for Pennsylvania.

25. Many men deserted and went home. There was a lot of sickness. Many men lost fingers and toes to frostbite.

26. Then the Americans got money from France. The Congress bought guns, ammunition, clothing and good food for the men at Valley Forge.

27. Officers from other countries such as Lafayette from France, Von Steuben from Germany, and Kosciusko from Poland came to help train the American army.

28. By the end of winter, men were fighting in all thirteen colonies. There was even fighting in the Northwest Territory , the land beyond the mountains.

29. The main battles were still to be fought by Washington and his foreign helpers.

30. In 1780 British soldiers, led by General Cornwallis, went to Virginia. They wanted to take an American army led by the Frenchman Lafayette.

31. Cornwallis and his army camped at Yorktown on the coast. They were waiting for supplies to come from England by ship.

32. But the French fleet and a few ships of the new American navy kept the supplies from getting through to Cornwallis.

33. Washington and his army of American and French soldiers marched south from New York to meet Lafayette. The two armies met

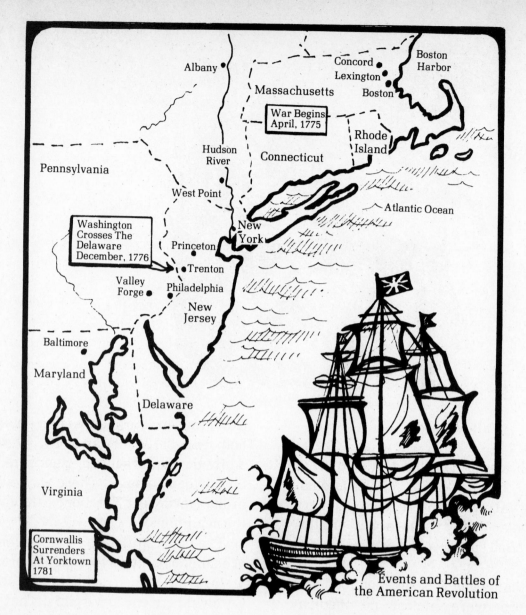

Events and Battles of
the American Revolution

and surrounded Cornwallis and his British soldiers.

34. Cornwallis surrendered his army to Washington. On October 9, 1781, after six long years, the Revolutionary War was over. America was a free and independent nation.

35. In 1783 the Americans and British signed a peace treaty in Paris, France. The treaty gave to America the right to be free and independent, to fish in certain waters, and to have set boundaries.

Spotlight On The Battle of Dorchester Heights

36. One of the more interesting and exciting battles of the Revolutionary War took place soon after the war began.

37. The battle, without a shot being fired, took place in Boston. But it really began in New York State at Fort Ticonderoga.

38. On May 10, 1775 a group of American soldiers from Vermont called **The Green**

Mountain Boys, attacked the British Fort Ticonderoga near Lake Champlain.

39. It was a daring raid. The Green Mountain Boys, led by Ethan Allen, surprised the fort. Allen knocked on the door of the fort. A sleepy commander asked what was going on.

40. Allen called out for their surrender. The commander asked in whose name.

41. "In the name of the Great Jehovah (God) and the Continental Congress," Allen shouted. The fort surrendered.

42. Fort Ticonderoga had forty cannons. They were badly needed by the Revolutionary Army in Boston, over two hundred miles away.

43. General Knox, an engineer, and a group of soldiers were sent to Ticonderoga to see if the cannons could be taken back to Boston.

44. Knox was not sure they could move the heavy guns to where they were needed. They would have to be carried by sled and wagon across the Berkshire Mountains and over many rivers and streams.

45. But Knox decided to try. He hired teamsters, drivers who had their own wagons and oxen or horses.

46. Knox and his Chain of Cannons left Fort Ticonderoga on December 17, 1775. The snow was deep and sleds were used to carry the heavy cannons. The sleds were pulled by the oxen and horses and pushed by Knox's men.

47. Luckily for the Americans, many of the bigger rivers were frozen. Crossing one, however, a cannon broke through the ice and was lost.

48. On January 24, 1776, more than a month after leaving Ticonderoga, they brought the cannons to Cambridge, outside Boston.

49. General Washington planned to use the cannons to help push the British out of Boston. He wanted to put them on Dorchester Heights, some hills overlooking Boston Harbor where the British ships were docked.

50. However, cannons, without anything around them for protection, would be of no use. They would be an easy target for British soldiers below.

51. Early in March, Washington called for help to put bundles of sticks together. Many people, including many women and young people, helped.

52. On March 4, 1776, 2,000 Americans marched up Dorchester Heights with the bundles of sticks. The cannons were brought up and set behind the flimsy fort.

53. The people were not sure what they were doing, but if Washington wanted it done they would do it. It was hard to see how a fort of sticks would stop the British army.

54. Washington hoped that the British in the harbor below would not be able to see how weak the fort was.

55. At daylight the British awoke. They saw a well built fort armed with many cannons looking down on them from above.

56. The Americans waited for the attack they were sure must come.

57. The days passed. March 6, 7, 8. Then a week. . .a week and a half. There was still no attack on Dorchester Heights.

58. Late in the day of March 16 there were signs of activity in the port. The Americans got ready for the attack. The British troops were forming up.

59. But they were going the other way. The British were boarding ships in the harbor.

60. By the next day all 6,000 British soldiers had left Boston.

61. The Americans from Dorchester Heights marched into the town. Boston was theirs, without firing a shot, thanks to the cannons from Ticonderoga and a fort made of sticks.

Understanding What You Read

1. Place the following historical events in the order in which they happened. The first event would be **1)**, and so forth.
   a. the Battle of Yorktown (30)
   b. The Battle of Dorchester Heights (52)
   c. the Treaty of Paris (35)
   d. Washington crossed the Delaware to attack Trenton (17)

   My answers are 1) _____ , 2) _____ , 3) _____ , and 4) _____ .

2. The Second Continental Congress voted to _____ and to _____

   _____ . (3)

3. The congress picked George Washington to lead the army because he was from

   _____ and he had fought in the _____ . (4)

4. _____ soldiers fought for the British. (7) King George paid _____

   _____ a year for them to fight. (8)

5. In 1776 Thomas Paine published a book called _____ . (9) In the book he said

   that all _____ were bad, especially _____ of

   _____ . (9)

6. The book **Common Sense** made many Americans believe _____

   _____ . (10)

7. People in America who stayed loyal to the king of England were called _____ . (12)

8. The French came into the war because they saw a chance to _____ an old
   enemy by helping the _____ . (22)

9. Three officers who came from other nations to help the Americans were _____

   from _____ , _____ from _____ ,

   and _____ from _____ . (27)

10. The Americans won the Battle of Yorktown with much help from the _____ . (30-33)

11. The Battle of Dorchester Heights was won without a shot being fired thanks to the _____

_____ captured at Fort Ticonderoga. (42) They were brought _____

miles to _____ (42). They were used in a fort made of _____ . (61)

12. **Map Skills:** Look at the map on pg. 74 and then answer the following questions:

a. In which state did the war begin? _____ .

b. Valley Forge is in the state of _____ .

c. Cornwallis surrendered in the state of _____ .

d. Washington crossed the _____ River in _____ .

e. The war began in the _____ _____ colonies and

ended in the _____ colonies.

Chapter 13
The Declaration Of Independence

1. On July 4, 1776, with fighting still going on, the leaders of the American colonies were meeting in Philadelphia. That day they signed the Declaration of Independence. They wanted to tell everyone — the American people and the world — why they thought that America must become a free and independent nation.

2. The words in the Declaration of Independence would be hard for many of today's Americans to read. Here's how it would sound if written in words we use today:

The Declaration of Independence

3. It sometimes becomes necessary for the people of one nation to break away from another nation which has ruled them. They must become free and equal on their own. It is then important to tell why that is being done.

4. We hold certain truths to be important and known to all people. That all men are created equal. That they are given certain rights that cannot ever be taken from them, such as life, liberty and the pursuit of happiness. That a government has to work hard to make sure that everyone keeps those rights. That a government can only rule for as long as the people it rules agree to be ruled by that government.

5. If a government fails to do this, the people have a right to form a new government. This is the case with the American colonies. It is time to change the government.

6. We say that the following facts prove that we must become a free and independent nation. They show why the government in England which rules us no longer has our agreement to be our ruler.

* The King has refused to approve laws necessary for the good of the colonies.

* He has stopped us from passing our own laws.

* He has taken away our right of self-rule.

* He has refused to allow us to spread our borders to new land.

* He has kept his army among us without asking our permission.

* He has protected his troops from punishment for crimes committed against us.

* He has burned our towns and taken the lives of our people.

* He has cut off our trade with the rest of the world by closing our ports.

* He has imposed taxes against us without our permission.

* He has brought large groups of foreign soldiers to our land.

7. We have tried over and over again to stop these things without going to war. We have failed at everything we have tried.

8. We therefore declare that these United Colonies are, and ought to be, free and independent states. And, that as free states, we have the right to act in the way which free states can act.

9. To this aim we pledge to each other our lives, our fortunes and our sacred honor.

Spotlight On The Declaration of Independence

10. When the Second Continental Congress met in Philadelphia early in 1776, the war had already begun. Many of the leaders wanted America to become a separate and equal nation.

11. Others did not want America to become a separate nation. They wanted to find a way for America to have some self-rule while still being colonies of England.

IN CONGRESS. JULY 4, 1776.

The unanimous Declaration of the thirteen united States of America,

When in the Course of human events, it becomes necessary for one people to dissolve the political bands which have connected them with another, and to assume among the powers of the earth, the separate and equal station to which the Laws of Nature and of Nature's God entitle them, a decent respect to the opinions of mankind requires that they should declare the causes which impel them to the separation. — We hold these truths to be self-evident, that all men are created equal, that they are endowed by their Creator with certain unalienable Rights, that among these are Life, Liberty and the pursuit of Happiness. — That to secure these rights, Governments are instituted among Men, deriving their just powers from the consent of the governed, — That whenever any Form of Government becomes destructive of these ends, it is the Right of the People to alter or to abolish it, and to institute new Government, laying its foundation on such principles and organizing its powers in such form, as to them shall seem most likely to effect their Safety and Happiness. Prudence, indeed, will dictate that Governments long established should not be changed for light and transient causes; and accordingly all experience hath shewn, that mankind are more disposed to suffer, while evils are sufferable, than to right themselves by abolishing the forms to which they are accustomed. But when a long train of abuses and usurpations, pursuing invariably the same Object evinces a design to reduce them under absolute Despotism, it is their right, it is their duty, to throw off such Government, and to provide new Guards for their future security. — Such has been the patient sufferance of these Colonies; and such is now the necessity which constrains them to alter their former Systems of Government. The history of the present King of Great Britain is a history of repeated injuries and usurpations, all having in direct object the establishment of an absolute Tyranny over these States. To prove this, let Facts be submitted to a candid world. — He has refused his Assent to Laws, the most wholesome and necessary for the public good. — He has forbidden his Governors to pass Laws of immediate and pressing importance, unless suspended in their operation till his Assent should be obtained; and when so suspended, he has utterly neglected to attend to them. — He has refused to pass other Laws for the accommodation of large districts of people, unless those people would relinquish the right of Representation in the Legislature, a right inestimable to them and formidable to tyrants only. — He has called together legislative bodies at places unusual, uncomfortable, and distant from the depository of their Public Records, for the sole purpose of fatiguing them into compliance with his measures. — He has dissolved Representative Houses repeatedly, for opposing with manly firmness his invasions on the rights of the people. — He has refused for a long time, after such dissolutions, to cause others to be elected; whereby the Legislative powers, incapable of Annihilation, have returned to the People at large for their exercise; the State remaining in the mean time exposed to all the dangers of invasion from without, and convulsions within. — He has endeavoured to prevent the population of these States; for that purpose obstructing the Laws for Naturalization of Foreigners; refusing to pass others to encourage their migrations hither, and raising the conditions of new Appropriations of Lands. — He has obstructed the Administration of Justice, by refusing his Assent to Laws for establishing Judiciary powers. — He has made Judges dependent on his Will alone, for the tenure of their offices, and the amount and payment of their salaries. — He has erected a multitude of New Offices, and sent hither swarms of Officers to harrass our people, and eat out their substance. — He has kept among us, in times of peace, Standing Armies without the Consent of our legislatures. — He has affected to render the Military independent of and superior to the Civil power. — He has combined with others to subject us to a jurisdiction foreign to our constitution, and unacknowledged by our laws; giving his Assent to their Acts of pretended Legislation: — For Quartering large bodies of armed troops among us: — For protecting them, by a mock Trial, from punishment for any Murders which they should commit on the Inhabitants of these States: — For cutting off our Trade with all parts of the world: — For imposing Taxes on us without our Consent: — For depriving us in many cases, of the benefits of Trial by Jury: — For transporting us beyond Seas to be tried for pretended offences — For abolishing the free System of English Laws in a neighbouring Province, establishing therein an Arbitrary government, and enlarging its Boundaries so as to render it at once an example and fit instrument for introducing the same absolute rule into these Colonies: — For taking away our Charters, abolishing our most valuable Laws, and altering fundamentally the Forms of our Governments: — For suspending our own Legislatures, and declaring themselves invested with power to legislate for us in all cases whatsoever. — He has abdicated Government here, by declaring us out of his Protection and waging War against us. — He has plundered our seas, ravaged our Coasts, burnt our towns, and destroyed the lives of our people. — He is at this time transporting large Armies of foreign Mercenaries to compleat the works of death, desolation and tyranny, already begun with circumstances of Cruelty & perfidy scarcely paralleled in the most barbarous ages, and totally unworthy the Head of a civilized nation. — He has constrained our fellow Citizens taken Captive on the high Seas to bear Arms against their Country, to become the executioners of their friends and Brethren, or to fall themselves by their Hands. — He has excited domestic insurrections amongst us, and has endeavoured to bring on the inhabitants of our frontiers, the merciless Indian Savages, whose known rule of warfare, is an undistinguished destruction of all ages, sexes and conditions. In every stage of these Oppressions We have Petitioned for Redress in the most humble terms: Our repeated Petitions have been answered only by repeated injury. A Prince, whose character is thus marked by every act which may define a Tyrant, is unfit to be the ruler of a free people. Nor have We been wanting in attentions to our Brittish brethren. We have warned them from time to time of attempts by their legislature to extend an unwarrantable jurisdiction over us. We have reminded them of the circumstances of our emigration and settlement here. We have appealed to their native justice and magnanimity, and we have conjured them by the ties of our common kindred to disavow these usurpations, which, would inevitably interrupt our connections and correspondence. They too have been deaf to the voice of justice and of consanguinity. We must, therefore, acquiesce in the necessity, which denounces our Separation, and hold them, as we hold the rest of mankind, Enemies in War, in Peace Friends. —

We, therefore, the Representatives of the united States of America, in General Congress, Assembled, appealing to the Supreme Judge of the world for the rectitude of our intentions, do, in the Name, and by Authority of the good People of these Colonies, solemnly publish and declare, That these United Colonies are, and of Right ought to be Free and Independent States; that they are Absolved from all Allegiance to the British Crown, and that all political connection between them and the State of Great Britain, is and ought to be totally dissolved; and that as Free and Independent States, they have full Power to levy War, conclude Peace, contract Alliances, establish Commerce, and to do all other Acts and Things which Independent States may of right do. — And for the support of this Declaration, with a firm reliance on the protection of divine Providence, we mutually pledge to each other our Lives, our Fortunes and our sacred Honor.

John Hancock

Button Gwinnett
Lyman Hall
Geo Walton.

Wm Hooper
Joseph Hewes,
John Penn

Edward Rutledge 1.

Thos Heyward Junr.
Thomas Lynch Junr.
Arthur Middleton

Samuel Chase
Wm. Paca
Thos. Stone
Charles Carroll of Carrollton

George Wythe
Richard Henry Lee
Th Jefferson
Benja Harrison
Thos Nelson jr.
Francis Lightfoot Lee
Carter Braxton

Robt Morris
Benjamin Rush
Benja. Franklin
John Morton
Geo Clymer
Jas. Smith
Geo. Taylor
James Wilson
Geo. Ross
Caesar Rodney
Geo Read
Thos M:Kean

Wm Floyd
Phil. Livingston
Frans. Lewis
Lewis Morris

Richd. Stockton
Jno Witherspoon
Fras. Hopkinson
John Hart
Abra Clark

Josiah Bartlett
Wm. Whipple
Saml Adams
John Adams
Robt Treat Paine
Elbridge Gerry
Step. Hopkins
William Ellery
Roger Sherman
Saml Huntington
Wm. Williams
Oliver Wolcott
Matthew Thornton

12. Still others were not sure what they wanted.

13. On the seventh of June the issue came to a head. Richard Henry Lee of Virginia stood and put a **resolution** (idea to be voted on) before the convention.

14. "The united colonies are and ought to be free and independent, "Lee said. "We should break completely with England."

15. Many of the delegates were shocked. This was really the first open talk of independence.

16. Some delegates, many of them from the middle colonies and the south, shouted "No, no."

17. The convention decided not to vote on that matter until July 1st. They set up a committee to write a declaration of independence from England. The committee was made up of John Adams of Massachusetts. Benjamin Franklin of Pennsylvania, Roger Sherman of Connecticut, Thomas Jefferson of Virginia, and Robert Livingston of New York.

18. Franklin was sick at home that day. The other four men went to visit him at his house. They had a short meeting and decided that one man should write the declaration. The others would then look at it after it was written.

19. Thomas Jefferson was given the job because he was a good writer and because he was from the south. Many in the south and the middle colonies did not trust anyone from New England.

20. Jefferson wrote for three weeks. He worked alone, had his meals in his room and would not let anyone visit him.

21. When he had put down the last words he showed it to the rest of the committee. They liked what Jefferson had written. On Friday, the 28th of June, the declaration was read to the Congress.

Thomas Jefferson, one of the Founding Fathers, signs the Declaration of Independence.

22. The Virginia Resolution to break with England was again brought before the Congress.

23. After hours of discussion, the congress agreed to break with England. The delegates then discussed the declaration. They argued over the words Jefferson had written. They could not agree with all that the declaration said.

24. The arguments went on and on. By late in the day of July 4th, the delegates were tired. Some were shouting and many were afraid there would be fights. It was a very hot day and flies from the stable next door flew around the room.

25. At last the final vote was taken. The declaration was approved by the Second Continental Congress. A large bell rang out the news to the people of Philadelphia. This bell was later to be called the Liberty Bell.

26. Some of Jefferson's words were changed before the voting. A statement against slavery was taken out, so that the delegates from the south would vote for the declaration.

27. With the words written by Thomas Jefferson, Americans declared they lived in an independent nation. Now they had to win the war to get their freedom.

Thomas Jefferson presents the Declaration of Independence to the Second Continental Congress.

Understanding What You Read

1. The Declaration of Independence was written to tell the world:
   a. why more British soldiers should be sent to America.
   b. how good the King of England was to the American colonies.
   c. why America believed it should be a free and independent nation.
   d. what George Washington thought about the American soldiers.

   My answer is _____ . (1)

2. The Declaration of Independence says that when a ruler no longer has the permission of the people to rule, the people have the right:
   a. to kill the king.
   b. to start a war.
   c. to write declarations.
   d. to form a new government to rule them.

   My answer is _____ . (5)

3. The Declaration of Independence says that all men are _____ _____

   (4) and have certain rights that cannot be taken away from them, such as _____ ,

   _____ , and the pursuit of _____ . (4)

4. Some of the reasons the Americans were angry at the king are stated in the Declaration of

   Independence. Three of these are: _____ , _____ ,

   and _____ . (6)

5. Did all of the delegates at the Congress want to be free from England? (11) _____

   What did they want for the colonies? (11)_____

6. The committee to write the declaration was made up of _____ , _____ ,

   _____ and _____ . (17)

7. The Declaration of Independence was written by one man named _____

   (19) and was approved by the Second _____ (25)

   on _____ _____ , 1776. (24)

82

Chapter 14
Update To History

The questions on this page are written so you will think about the meaning of this history for today's Americans.

1. The people who fought the Revolutionary War and those who wrote the Declaration of Independence saw America as a certain kind of nation, with a certain way of life. Do you think America is today what the **Founding Fathers** wanted? Why or why not?

_____

_____

_____

_____

_____

_____

2. The Declaration of Independence says that all men are created equal. Now, 200 years later, are all Americans equal? Explain your answer.

_____

_____

_____

_____

_____

_____

3. Do all people in America today have the right to "life, liberty and the pursuit of happiness"? Explain your answer.

_____

_____

_____

_____

_____

4. Some of the reasons for the Revolutionary War and the breakup with England were unfair taxes and unfair laws. Do you think that today's Americans have any of the same problems? Do you think that a revolution would be the answer to today's problems? Explain your answer.

_____

_____

_____

_____

_____

5. The Declaration of Independence always speaks of "men", but not "people", or "citizens". Do you think the men who wrote the Declaration were thinking of women as equals when they wrote it? Explain your answer.

_____

_____

_____

_____

_____

_____

Time Line Update: In the space below, draw a time line for the entire period covered in this unit. Begin with 1754 with the French-Indian War and end with 1781—the end of the Revolutionary War.

_____

1754   1768   1781

Unit 3
The Problems Of The New Nation

Chapter 15
The New Government Begins Work

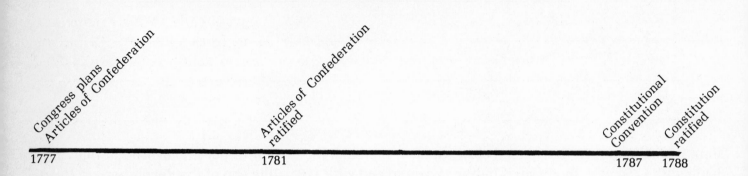

1777   1781   1787   1788

1. America's problems did not end with victory in the Revolutionary War. The people of America were now free from England, but they were not sure what kind of government they wanted.

2. While the war was going on, the Second Continental Congress acted as the government. They made laws, appointed officers in the army, made loans, and did all the things a government can do.

3. The Congress had to look ahead to the end of the war. They had to make decisions about the government of America when it became an independent nation.

4. Many of the colonies did not want a strong national government. They wanted to make many of their own laws.

5. In 1777 the Congress made a plan for governing the nation after the war. The plan, called the **Articles of Confederation**, would become law as soon as all thirteen colonies approved it.

6. The Articles of Confederation called for the states to be loosely joined together, with each state making many of its own laws. The Articles called this a **League of Friendship**.

7. A Congress was formed to govern the new states, with each state having one vote.

8. The colonists did not allow Congress to have many powers. Congress could declare war in the name of the Confederation, but it could not raise or pay an army or navy. There was no department or person set to carry out the laws made by Congress. There were no national courts. Congress had no control over trade with other nations or even trade among the states themselves. Congress had no power to tax anyone. It had to ask the states for any money it needed.

9. Some of the colonies approved the plan right away, others took longer. It was not until 1781 that all thirteen colonies **ratified** (approved of) the Articles of Confederation. By that time, the war was over and the colonies had become states.

10. Each of the thirteen states wanted to protect its own rights and freedoms. They didn't want a strong central government to take any of these rights away from them. This idea of states' rights would cause many problems later in American history.

11. Congress was very weak under the Articles of Confederation. Many members of Congress did not even bother to go to meetings. There were hardly enough members present to vote on the Treaty of Paris to end the Revolutionary War.

Sometimes men used their fists and not their heads at the Congress.

12. Other nations, such as Spain and England, saw the weakness of the American government. They quickly moved to take advantage of that weakness.

13. The Spanish stopped American farmers and fur traders from working on and around the Mississippi River.

14. England would not take its troops out of the Northwest Territory, though they had agreed to close their forts and send their men home.

15. Pirates in the Mediterranean Sea off the northern coast of Africa stopped and searched American ships. They took what they wanted from the cargoes.

16. The new government was not able to do anything about these problems. Its hands were tied by the states and the rules of the Articles of Confederation.

17. By 1787 one thing seemed clear to most Americans and to people in Europe as well. A stronger government than the one set up under the Articles of Confederation was needed. The new nation needed a stronger government or it could not last.

Constitutional Convention

18. In 1787, Congress called for a convention of representatives from each of the 13 states. It was to be held in Philadelphia. The people at the convention were to change the Articles of Confederation.

19. The convention was to open on May 14, but poor roads and spring storms kept the representatives from coming. It took almost two more weeks before the convention could start. Of the 73 men chosen to attend, only 55 came. Rhode Island sent no one to the convention.

20. The men worked for four months to write a new Constitution to present to the states. The work was not easy. Many of the people at the convention still believed that a strong central government was bad. They thought that a loose union of the states was necessary. They wanted the states to have the final say on most issues.

21. Others believed that a strong central government was necessary to keep the United States free and independent. They believed that the nation as a whole was more important than any of the separate states.

22. One of the biggest arguments at the convention was between the larger and the smaller states. The larger states wanted representation by **population** (the number of people in a state). That would mean that the states with more people would have more representatives in Congress.

23. The smaller states were afraid that under that system they would be ruled by the bigger states. They wanted the representation in Congress to be equal. That is, they wanted the

same number of representatives from the smaller states as from the larger.

24. The arguments grew heated. Fights broke out. Then a **compromise** was reached. Each side got part of what they wanted. There would be two houses of Congress. One would have representation based on population (the House of Representatives). The other would have an equal number of representatives from each state (the Senate).

25. The members of the Philadelphia convention held their last meeting and signed the new Constitution on September 17, 1787.

26. The people at the convention had written the Constitution. They had argued over what was in it and then approved it, but it could not become law yet.

27. Now conventions in each state would meet to **ratify** (approve) the new Constitution. Nine of the thirteen states had to ratify the Constitution before it could become law.

Ratification Of The Constitution

28. The men at the Philadelphia convention had decided that only two-thirds of the states would have to ratify the Constitution. They knew that some of the states would never agree to it.

29. Rhode Island was so strongly against a central government that it did not even send a delegate to Philadelphia. The people who wrote the Constitution were afraid that Rhode Island and a few other states might never vote to ratify.

30. Delaware was the first to ratify the Constitution. Their state convention voted 30-0 to ratify on December 7, 1787.

31. In other state conventions, the votes for and against ratification were very close.

32. In Massachusetts the vote was 187-168 for ratification. In Virginia the vote was 89-79. In New York the vote was 30-27.

33. The ninth state to ratify the Constitution was New Hampshire. By a vote of 57-47 that state ratified the Constitution on June 21, 1788. It then became the law of the land.

34. In the end, all thirteen colonies did ratify the Constitution. The last to do so was Rhode Island, which passed it by a 34-32 vote on May 29, 1790. That was almost two years after it had already become the law.

35. The new Constitution called for three branches of government. They were: a **legislative** branch to make the laws, an **executive** branch to carry out the laws, and a **judicial** (courts) branch to decide if the laws were fair and legal.

36. The new central government had many powers that it had not had under the Articles of Confederation. It had the power to set and collect taxes. It could control trade between the United States and other nations, and between the states themselves. The government could print money.

37. At the same time, many rights were still left for the states.

38. The Constitution that was ratified on June 21, 1788 is the same one which governs America today, almost 200 years later.

Spotlight on The Authors of the Constitution

39. Some of the same people who had approved the Declaration of Independence in 1776 worked on the Constitution in 1787.

40. Benjamin Franklin was there, as were James Madison and Roger Sherman of Connecticut.

41. Alexander Hamilton of New York and Charles Pinckney of South Carolina were also there. They had not helped with the Declaration of Independence, but helped a great deal with the Constitution.

42. The chairman of the convention was George Washington.

43. Washington and Madison were both from Virginia. Most historians today believe that the Virginians were the most important members at the convention.

44. Washington, who was trusted by all, kept the fights to a few, even in the hottest of times.

45. Madison, only thirty-six at the time of the convention, was the man behind the **Virginia Plan.** This plan was for a new government, not just a rewriting of the Articles of Confederation. It was a blueprint that was to be accepted by most of the delegates.

46. Benjamin Franklin was over 80 years old at the time of the convention. He had to be carried to and from all the meetings. He could not take part in the discussions, but he kept the convention from breaking up many times.

North America in 1783

When tempers grew hot and fists flew, his good will and good stories calmed things down.

47. There were three main arguments at the convention. They were: 1) the representation of each state in the Congress; 2) the control of trade and other business interests; and 3) slavery.

48. The argument over representation (see pg. 88.) was finally settled by having two houses of Congress. An upper house would have the same number of representation from each state. The lower house would have representatives based on the population of each state.

49. Alexander Hamilton was one of the people who helped work out this compromise.

50. The second problem was the control of trade. Many people in the New England states and some of the middle states were in the shipping business. They wanted the central government to be able to pass laws to protect their business against foreign shippers.

51. The southern states, on the other hand, did not want to have to pay more for shipping their goods to foreign markets. A compromise was worked out in this area, as well.

52. The question of slavery came before the convention. The members did not debate whether slavery should be allowed, but how the slaves should be counted as part of the population.

53. Slaves were not thought of as people in the population, but as the property of their masters. Most of them were living in the south.

54. Taxes were paid according to how many people lived in each state. The northern states wanted to count slaves when deciding how much to tax a state. They did not want to count the slaves when deciding how many representatives could be sent to Congress.

55. The south, on the other hand, wanted the slaves counted in deciding how many representatives they would have. They didn't want the slaves counted for taxes.

56. Another compromise was worked out. A **three-fifths rule** was decided on. That is, five slaves would count as three people for deciding how many representatives and how much tax would be collected in each state.

57. The south also got a promise. The central government could not keep them from bringing in slaves for twenty years. The government would also charge a tax of no more than $10 a head on slaves.

58. The south had wanted the Constitution to state that slavery was all right. Instead, they accepted the twenty-year promise.

59. In the end, our **Founding Fathers** wrote a Constitution that made a strong **federal** (national) government with some rights left to the states.

Understanding What You Read

1. What is the main idea of this chapter?
   a. America was ruled very well under the Articles of Confederation.
   b. The Articles of Confederation called for a strong central government.
   c. The Articles of Confederation did not work well in governing the new nation and a new form of government was needed.
   d. Most people did not want to see the Articles of Confederation work.

   My answer is _____ . (17)

2. Why were some colonists not sure they wanted a strong government? _____ . (4)

3. Some of the weaknesses of the Articles of Confederation were _____ and

   _____ . (8)

4. The Spanish took advantage of the weakness of the American government by_____

   _____ (13).

5. The English took advantage of the new American government by _____

   _____ (14).

6. At the convention the larger states wanted representation based on _____ (22).

   The smaller states wanted each state to have an _____ (23) number of

   representatives. A compromise was found. It called for _____ houses of Congress,

   one to have representation based on _____ and the other to have an

   _____ number from each state. (24)

7. Why were the delegates afraid Rhode Island would not ratify the Constitution? (29) _____

   _____

8. In order to ratify the new Constitution, _____ (27) of the thirteen states had

   to vote in favor of it. The first state to ratify the Constitution was _____ (30).

The ninth was _____ . (33) That state ratified the Constitution, making it law,

on _____ . (33)

9. The three main arguments at the convention were over 1) _____ ,

   2) _____ , and 3) _____ . (47)

10. The south wanted the Constitution to allow _____ . (58) But the northern

    states refused. The south was promised that there would be no action against slavery for

    _____ years. (57)

11. **Map Skills:** Look at the map on pg. 89 and then answer the following questions:

    a. The new border between America and her neighbors was the _____ River.

    b. Much of the land to the west of America was owned by _____ .

    c. The land north of the new nation was owned by _____ .

    d. The only land east of the Mississippi River owned by another nation was owned by _____

       _____ .

    e. The land around the Rio Grande River was owned by _____ .

    f. Some land on the west coast was claimed by three countries, _____ ,

       _____ , and _____ .

    g. Which country owned the most land in the Americas? _____

Chapter 16
The First President
Begins His Work

1. The government that had operated under the Articles of Confederation was replaced by the new government set up by the Constitution.

2. An election was held in November of 1788. The members of the new government were elected. The new government was supposed to take power in March of 1789.

3. Because of bad roads, the new representatives were late getting to New York City, the new nation's first capital. The Congress didn't do any business until April.

4. One of the first things that Congress did was to tell George Washington he had been elected as the first President of the United States of America.

5. On April 30, 1789, Washington took the oath of office in New York City.

6. The old government had left the new one a pile of troubles with foreign nations, 70 unpaid clerks and an army of 672 men.

7. Money was one of the biggest problems facing Washington and his **administration** (the people who help the President). How would they raise money for the government to run?

8. The government owed millions of dollars to people and other nations. This had been borrowed during the Revolutionary War.

9. Washington appointed Alexander Hamilton to be Secretary of the Treasury, the man in charge of raising money.

10. Hamilton had been with Washington during the Revolutionary War. He had won a medal for bravery at the Battle of Yorktown. He also took part in writing the Constitution.

11. Hamilton told Congress that there were two good ways to get money. The government could borrow money or collect taxes.

12. Congress passed a law putting taxes on all trade goods coming into the nation. A tax on foreign goods is called a **tariff.**

13. Congress also taxed some American goods, such as whiskey. America borrowed money by selling bonds to foreign nations and to rich Americans.

14. Hamilton wanted to set up a central National Bank to take care of the money problems of the nation. He said it would be easy to send money from a branch of the bank in one state to another branch in another state.

15. He also wanted the bank to be able to lend money to the national government if it was needed.

16. Thomas Jefferson, Washington's Secretary of State, was against the idea of a National Bank. He believed that the Constitution did not say it was all right and therefore it should not be done.

George Washington takes office as President.

17. He was also afraid that such a bank would control the **economy** (how a country makes money). He thought it would help rich Americans and hurt the small farmers and businessmen.

18. Hamilton won, and a National Bank was formed. It helped to make American business and the United States stronger in the eyes of the world.

Whiskey Revolt

19. Not all of Hamilton's ideas worked out as well as the National Bank. Many farmers in Pennsylvania made whiskey from grain. They did not like the tax on whiskey which Hamilton recommended and the Congress had passed.

20. Many farmers refused to pay the tax, and some attacked the tax collectors.

21. Washington had to send 12,000 **militiamen** (soldiers) from four states to Pennsylvania. The soldiers stopped the farmers and arrested some of them.

22. Two of the leaders of the farmers were found guilty of treason. However, Washington pardoned them both. They were allowed to return to their homes without being punished.

The First Political Parties

23. During this time, the first political parties began to form. Today the two main parties in the United States are the Democrats and the Republicans. In the days after the Revolutionary War the two parties were the **Federalists** and the **Democratic-Republicans.**

24. The Federalists were led by Alexander Hamilton. Hamilton did not trust the common people. He called **democracy** (the people's right to rule) a "poison".

25. Hamilton wanted the government to be run only by those who were educated and owned land. The others, he thought, were not smart enough to take part in choosing or running a government.

26. Hamilton wanted a strong federal government, courts, and an army and navy to "keep order".

The new government faced a revolt of grain farmers.

27. Thomas Jefferson was the leader of the Democratic-Republicans. He believed that the central government should leave many powers to the states.

28. He believed that the workers and farmers should have a loud voice in choosing and running the government. Jefferson wanted to educate everyone so that they could better take their place in America.

29. Washington held office as President for two four-year terms. By the time he left office the United States was a strong, up-and-coming nation.

Spotlight On George Washington

30. Most people grow up learning about George Washington. He's called **The Father of Our Country,** and **America's Best President**.

31. One of the best-known stories in American history is about Washington as a boy. In the story he chopped down one of his father's cherry trees with a small hatchet.

32. When asked by his father, Washington was reported to have said, "I cannot tell a lie. I did it with my hatchet."

33. Some people look at this story as proof that the good child grew up to be the great man.

34. But is the cherry tree story really true? Most historians are not sure.

35. The story first came to light in a book written by a minister in the Church of England, Mason Locke Weems, in 1806.

36. Weems said that he first heard the story from "an aged lady who was a distant relative of Washington's who, when a girl, spent much of her time in the family."

37. Ever since that time historians have been trying to find out if the story is true or a myth.

38. There is little proof that the cherry tree story ever really happened. There are many facts known about Washington, however.

39. He was born in Virginia in 1732, the son of a rich planter. Like other rich children in the Virginia colony, Washington went to school, rode horses, and learned about plantation life.

40. He stopped going to school at fourteen. He then became a surveyor, a man who measures land.

41. He took part in the French and Indian War and became an officer.

42. After the war he returned to his home at Mount Vernon, Virginia. He became a farmer, and thought that his days of government service were over.

43. When the First Continental Congress was called in 1774, Washington was a delegate from Virginia.

44. After the Battle of Bunker Hill he was appointed Commander-in-Chief of the American army. He led the colonial soldiers to victory, then returned to his home in Virginia to take up farming again.

45. Five years later he was again a delegate to the Continental Congress. He was then made chairman of the Constitutional Convention.

46. Washington was elected to be the first President of the United States of America.

47. Whether the cherry tree story is true or not, Washington grew into a man who made his mark on American history.

Library of Congress

George Washington, the first President of the United States.

95

Understanding What You Read

1. The first President of the United States was _____ . (4)

2. One of the first problems of the new administration was:
   a. getting an army to fight the French and Spanish.
   b. raising money to support the new government.
   c. starting a bank.
   d. building ships.

   My answer is _____ . (7)

3. Congress passed a law putting a tax on all foreign goods. Such a tax is called a _____ . (12)

4. Farmers in Pennsylvania did not like the government because it:
   a. set up a national bank.
   b. drafted many of them into the army.
   c. made New York City the new capital.
   d. put a tax on whiskey.

   My answer is _____ . (19)

5. Alexander Hamilton and Thomas Jefferson were on opposite sides in the new government because of their beliefs. Answer these questions by telling whether Jefferson or Hamilton would have been in favor of the statement:

   a. America needs a central bank to help it do business. _____ (14)

   b. Everybody should be educated so they can help run the government. _____ (28)

   c. I am the leader of the Democratic-Republicans. _____ (27)

   d. Democracy is a poison. _____ (24)

   e. I am the leader of the Federalists. _____ (24)

   f. Only those who are educated and own land should have a say in running the government.

   _____ (25)

   g. I want the states to have most of the power. _____ (27)

h. I want the central federal government to have most of the power. _____ (26)

i. I want the farmers and workers to be able to run the government. _____ (28)

6. **Word Search Puzzle:** Find the hidden words in the puzzle below:

BANK	Y E K S I H W R Q A
CONGRESS	F N A G B C A E C B
DEMOCRATIC	E O C O D O S P I C
FEDERALIST	D T E V F N H U T D
GOVERNMENT	E L F E F G I B A F
HAMILTON	R I G R I R N L R H
REPUBLICAN	A M H N R E G I C J
TARIFF	L A K M A S T C O L
WASHINGTON	I H N E T S O A M N
WHISKEY	S I A N J K N N E P
	T L B T M N O P D R

Chapter 17
Update To History

The questions on this page are written so you will think about the meaning of this history for today's Americans.

1. The question of whether the states or the federal government should have the most power runs throughout American history. It began with the people who wrote the Constitution and continues today. What do you think? Should the federal government be able to tell the states what to do? Should the states have the right to do as they see fit?

_____

_____

_____

_____

_____

_____

_____

2. The Constitution written 200 years ago was not fair to many people. For example, it did not give voting rights to slaves, Indians or women. That was changed by later amendments to the Constitution. Do you think that, in the Black and Women's Movements today, we are still seeing problems that began in the 1700's? Why?

_____

_____

_____

_____

_____

_____

3. Do you think that Hamilton was right in believing the common people could not take part in government? Was Jefferson right that everyone should take part? Explain your answer.

_____

_____

_____

_____

_____

_____

Time Line: Complete the following time line for the entire unit. Begin with 1777 and the drawing up of the *Articles of Confederation*, and end with 1789, when Washington took office as President.

1777   1789

Unit 4
The Constitution
Chapter 18
The Constitution — An Introduction

1. It is important for all Americans to know and understand the Constitution. It is the basic law under which each and every one of us lives.

2. First, let's look at the **Preamble,** the very first part of the Constitution. Preamble means "to walk before".

3. The Preamble to the Constitution tells you what the Constitution aims to do. That is, the Preamble tells you what is going to be in the Constitution.

4. To help you understand what the Preamble means, here are the meanings of some of the words in it:

tranquility: peace
defence (defense): to protect oneself
posterity: those who come after us
ordain: make part of

The Preamble reads:

5. *We the people of the United States, in order to form a more perfect Union, establish Justice, insure domestic Tranquility, provide for the common Defence, promote the general Welfare, and secure the Blessings of Liberty to ourselves and our Posterity, do ordain and establish this Constitution for the United States of America.*

6. To understand what the Constitution says and means, you must understand a little about the men who wrote it. Those are the men we call the Founding Fathers. You have read about some of these men in the last chapters.

7. You also need to understand their ideas about laws. When they wrote the Constitution they were thinking about all the laws that would be needed for the country. They were thinking about the rights of individual people when they made such laws as those which help a person who has been arrested. They were thinking of the country as a whole when they set up the Supreme Court for all Americans.

8. They didn't want a government so strong that it would take away the rights of the people. On the other hand, they didn't want one so weak that it could not rule.

9. They made a federal government, with the power divided between the states and the central government. There are certain things that only the states can do, certain things that only the central government can do, and other things that can be done by both.

10. Only the central government can make money or declare war. Only the state governments can have police. Both can have courts, but the courts rule on different matters.

11. The Founding Fathers made a representative form of government. That is, the people don't vote directly on the laws that are made. The people elect representatives to sit in Congress, and those representatives make the laws that govern us.

12. Finally, they formed a system of **checks and balances.** This system makes sure that none of the three branches of government (executive, legislative and judicial) gets too strong. It was their belief that if one branch of government got too powerful it would control all of the government.

13. Under this system, the President may not make laws. If he would like a certain law to be passed, he must ask Congress to do it for him. Congress may or may not listen to what he wants.

14. Congress makes all the laws of the country. The President may **veto** (say no to) any law passed by Congress. After a veto, that law can take effect only if two-thirds of the members of Congress vote for it again.

15. The judicial branch decides if laws or acts made by Congress are in line with the Constitution. If not, they can declare a law **unconstitutional**. It will then no longer be the law.

16. In those ways, each branch of government keeps a check on the others. No branch can act alone to make and carry out acts that would take away rights or harm the people or the nation.

17. After the Constitution was passed, many people wanted the rights of Americans spelled out more clearly than they were in the Constitution. "Just what rights do Americans have?" was the question they were asking.

18. To answer that question, Congress passed **amendments** (changes) to the Constitution. The first ten amendments, passed in 1791, are called the **Bill of Rights**. You will read more about the Bill of Rights in Chapter 22.

All kings, out! We don't want them.

Understanding What You Read

1. The _____ to the Constitution tells what the Constitution is trying to say. (2)

2. In a federal government, the powers are divided between the _____ and a

   strong _____ . (9)

3. To make sure that no one branch of government would become too strong, the writers of the

   Constitution built in a series of _____ and _____ . (12)

4. If the Congress passes a bill and the President refuses to sign it that is called a _____ . (14)

   After that, two-thirds of the Congress must vote if it is to become a _____ . (14)

5. If a law is decided to be _____ (15) by the judicial branch it can no longer
   be a law.

6. A representative form of government is one in which:
   a. all the people vote directly for new laws themselves.
   b. the people vote for representatives who make the laws for them.
   c. no laws are necessary.
   d. the President makes the laws.

   My answer is _____ . (11)

7. Match the word with its meaning:

   a. tranquility (4)   1. those who come after us
   b. defense (4)   2. to say no to
   c. posterity (4)   3. peace
   d. ordain (4)   4. change
   e. judicial (15)   5. make part of
   f. unconstitutional (15) 6. not according to the Constitution
   g. amendment (18)   7. protecting oneself
   h. veto (14)   8. relating to courts

   My answers are: a. _____ , b. _____ , c. _____ , d. _____ ,

   e. _____ , f. _____ , g. _____ , h. _____ .

8. If a President wants a law passed, he or she must:
   a. pass it alone.
   b. ask the courts to pass it.
   c. ask Congress to pass it.
   d. ask the American people to pass it.

My answer is _____ . (13)

9. **Chart Reading:** Look at the chart below and then answer the following questions.

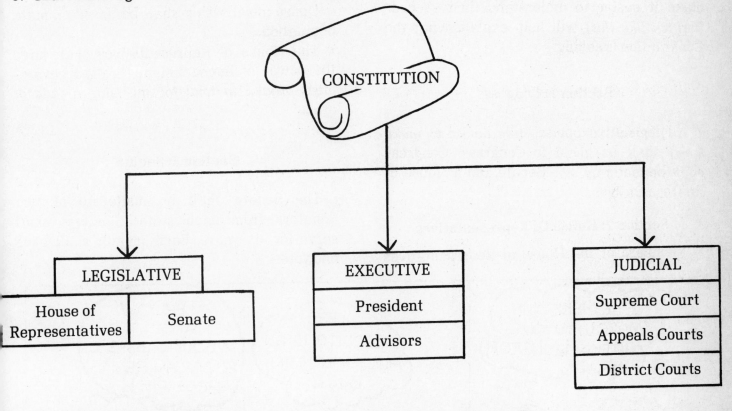

   a. The three branches of Government set up by the Constitution are the _____,

   _____ and the _____ .

   b. Which two bodies make up the legislative branch? _____ _____ .

   c. The person who heads the executive branch is the _____ .

   d. Which is the most important of the three courts in the judicial branch? _____

   e. Which are the lowest courts in the judicial branch? _____?

Chapter 19
The Legislative Branch

1. The legislative branch of government makes the laws that govern all Americans. Article I of the Constitution sets up the legislative branch. Here is what the Constitution says about the legislative branch.

2. Most of the words are those in the Constitution. Some have been changed to make it easier to understand them. Words (*written like this*) will help explain what the Constitution is saying.

Section 1: Congress

3. All legislative powers (*the power to make laws*) shall be given to Congress. Congress shall be made up of a Senate and a House of Representatives.

Section 2: House Of Representatives

4. Members of the House of Representatives shall be chosen every second year by the voters in the states they represent.

5. To be a representative, a person must be at least 25 years of age. He or she must have been a citizen of the United States for at least seven years. A representative must live in the state from which he or she is chosen.

6. House membership shall be based on state population.

7. The House of Representatives shall have the power of **impeachment** (*bring a government official to trial for misusing a federal office*).

Section 3: Senate

8. The Senate shall be made up of two Senators from each state. Senators shall serve for six years. Each senator shall have one vote.

Senator Braghorn decides to get a bill started in Congress.

9. One-third of the total number of senators shall be elected every two years.

10. To be a senator a person must be at least 30 years of age. He or she must have been a citizen for nine years. A senator must live in the state from which he or she was chosen.

11. The Vice President of the United States shall be the President of the Senate. The Vice President cannot vote on Senate business unless there is a tie vote by the Senators.

12. The Senate shall act as a court in trying all impeachment cases.

Section 4: Election And Meeting Of Congress

13. The times, places and manner of holding elections for Representatives and Senators shall be set by each of the states. Congress, by law, can change the state's rules.

14. The Congress shall meet at least once each year. Such meetings are to be on the first Monday in December.

Section 5: Organization And Rules Of Each House

15. Each house shall be the judge of the elections and qualifications of its own members.

16. Each house may decide how it is to operate and the rules it must follow.

17. Each house shall keep a record of its proceedings (*what it does*).

18. Neither house, without the permission of the other, shall, during the session of Congress, adjourn (*stop working*) for more than three days. The place they are meeting can not be changed.

Both the House and Senate vote yes on the bill and the President signs it into law.

Section 6: Congressional Privileges And Restraints

19. Senators and Representatives shall be paid for their time. They shall, in all cases except Treason, Robbery, and Breach of the Peace, be free from arrest while Congress is in session.

20. No Senator or Representative shall, during the time he serves, be appointed to any civil office. No person holding any office under the government shall be a member of either house.

Section 7: How Bills Become Laws

21. All bills to raise money for the government must start in the House of Representatives. Other bills can start in either house.

22. Each bill must be passed by both the Senate and the House of Representatives. Then it must go to the President.

23. If the President agrees with a bill he signs it and it becomes a law. If he does not agree, he must send it back to the house that started it, stating why he does not agree.

24. If two-thirds of the members of that house pass the bill a second time, it then goes to the other house. If two-thirds of the members of that house now pass the bill, it becomes law without the President's agreement.

25. If any bill is not returned by the President within ten working days after it has been sent to him, it becomes a law.

Section 8: Powers Given To Congress

26. To make and collect taxes, and to pay debts (*what it owes*) for the common defense and general welfare of the United States.

27. To borrow money on the credit of the United States.

28. To control commerce (*trade*) with other nations, among the states, and with the Indian tribes.

29. To make uniform (*regular and equal*) laws allowing people to become citizens.

30. To coin (*make*) money and control the value of that money. To make standard weights and measures.

31. To provide for the punishment of counterfeiters (*people who make fake money.*)

32. To establish post offices and toll roads.

33. To promote the progress of science and the arts. It may give for limited times, the rights (*copyrights and patents*) to authors and inventors for their writings and inventions.

34. To create and run courts below the level of the Supreme Court.

35. To declare war and to make rules concerning the capture of enemies on land or sea.

36. To punish pirates and others who commit crimes on the high seas.

37. To raise and support an army and navy.

38. To call out the militia (*National Guard*) to stop invasions or insurrections (*rebellions*).

39. To provide for organizing, arming and leading a militia.

40. To control an area within the United States that shall be the seat of government, not to be more than ten miles square. (Now Washington, D.C.)

41. To make all laws which shall be necessary and proper for carrying out the above powers.

Section 9: Powers Denied To The Congress

Congress may not:

42. Interfere with the slave trade before 1808.

43. Take away the **habeas corpus** (*individual legal*) rights of citizens except in cases of war or rebellion. At those times the public safety might require taking away these rights.

44. Pass **ex post facto** laws (*laws that punish people for doing something before it was against the law*).

45. Make a tax against any one group or individual.

46. Make a tax against goods moving from one state to another.

47. Favor one port over any other.

48. Spend money unless it is approved by Congress.

49. Grant any title of nobility (*King, Count, etc.*)

Section 10 Powers Denied to the States

No state shall:

50. Enter into any treaties.

51. Set any duties (*taxes*) on imports or exports (*goods coming in or going out*).

52. Wage war unless invaded.

How Congress Works

53. To sum up this chapter, the Congress today is made up of two houses. There is a Senate with 100 members (two from each of the 50 states) and a House of Representatives with 435 members. The number of representatives from each state depends on its population.

54. At present, California has 43 representatives because it has the largest population in the United States. States with smaller populations such as Delaware, North Dakota and Alaska have only one representative each in the House. Each of these states, however, has two members in the Senate.

55. The main purpose of Congress is to make the nation's laws. Either house may start a bill on the way to becoming a law. However, bills to raise money have to start in the House of Representatives.

56. The way a bill becomes a law is complex. Look back a few pages to pgs. 104-105. You will see in pictures how a bill moves from its beginning to the time it is signed by the President and becomes a law.

57. If the President does not sign a bill and sends it back to Congress with the reason he does not like it, it has been vetoed. Then two-thirds of the members of both the Senate and the House have to approve it before it can become law over the President's veto.

58. Let's follow a bill through the House and the Senate and then to the President with an imaginary example. A member of the House proposes to make it unlawful to sell widgets. The bill is sent to a committee of the House to be discussed and written out. After a few weeks of discussion, the committee brings it back to the House for a vote. The House votes for it, 250-185.

59. The bill then goes to the Senate. It is again sent to a committee for discussion. The committee decides they would not change anything in the bill. The Senate then votes, 53-47, for the bill.

60. The President does not like the bill because he likes a widget with dinner each night. He vetoes the bill. He sends it back with a note telling Congress how important widgets are for America.

61. The Congress decides to try to pass the bill over the President's veto. They vote again. This time 67 Senators (⅔ of 100) and 290 Representatives have to vote in favor of the bill for it to become law.

62. If they do so, the bill becomes a law even though the President likes a widget with his dinner. If they do not, the President's veto stands and it is still legal to sell widgets.

Understanding What You Read

1. **Chart Reading:** Look at the chart and then answer the following questions.

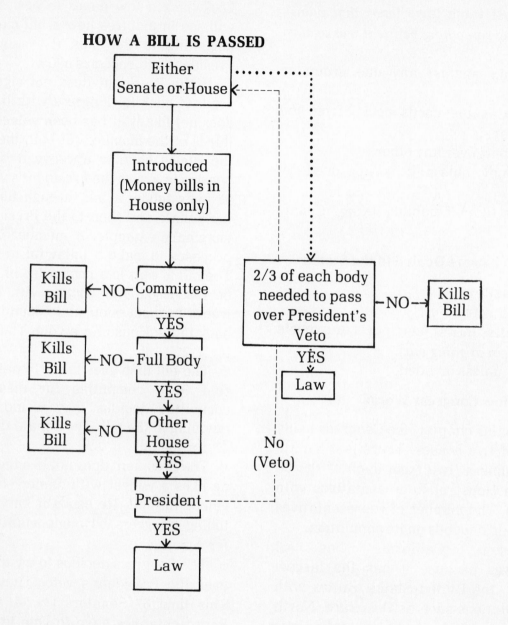

HOW A BILL IS PASSED

a. A bill can be introduced either in the _____ or the _____ .

b. A money bill must be introduced in the _____ .

c. Both houses of Congress must pass a bill before it goes to the_____

   for his or her _____ .

d. The two ways that a bill can become a law are passage by both _____ and

signed by the _____ , or veto by the President and passage

by _____ of both _____ .

e. A bill may be killed by _____ , or

_____ , or _____ ,

before it even goes to the President.

2. The main reason for the legislative branch of government is to:
   a. make sure the laws are carried out.
   b. make the laws.
   c. start wars.
   d. elect the President.

My answer is _____ . (1)

3. Which of the following is **not** a right of the federal government?
   a. to declare war
   b. to raise and collect taxes
   c. to set the time and place for elections
   d. to establish a post office

My answer is _____ . (26-41)

4. A bill becomes a law when it is passed by _____ (22) and signed by

the _____ . (23)

5. If a President vetoes a bill, _____ members of the Senate and _____
   members of the House must pass it to have it become the law. (24)

6. The Senate is made up of _____ from each state (53) while the House of

Representatives is made up of _____ members. (53) The number from

each state depends on its _____ . (53)

Chapter 20
The Executive Branch

1. The executive branch of the government is given the job of seeing that the laws made by Congress are carried out. It also can recommend laws to Congress to be passed.

2. Article II of the Constitution sets up the executive branch. Here is what the Constitution says about the executive branch.

Section 1: President and Vice President

3. The executive power of the government shall be given to the President of the United States of America. He shall hold his office for a term of four years.

4. Each state shall appoint, as it sees fit, a number of Electors. This number is equal to the number of Senators and Representatives it may have in Congress. No Senator or Representative may serve as an Elector. (*Electors will be discussed later in this chapter.*)

5. (*This part discusses how the Electors vote for the President and Vice President. It has been replaced by the 12th Amendment and will be discussed later in this chapter.*)

6. Congress may set the date and time for choosing Electors.

7. The President must be born in the United States. He or she must be at least 35 years of age, and have been living in the U.S. for at least fourteen years.

8. In case the President cannot serve for any reason, the Vice President takes his or her place. If both the President and Vice President cannot serve, Congress passes a law which appoints someone to fill the office until the next election.

9. The President shall be paid for his job.

10. The President must take the following oath before taking office.

11. *I do solemnly swear that I will faithfully execute the Office of the President of the United States, and will, to the best of my ability, preserve, protect and defend the Constitution of the United States.*

Section 2: Powers Of The President

12. The President shall be the Commander-in-Chief of the army and navy of the United States. He also leads the militia of the states when they are called on to serve the government. He can ask his advisors for ideas about any subject he wishes. He can pardon criminals.

13. The President can, with the advice and approval of Congress, make treaties with other nations. He or she can appoint representatives to other nations, appoint Supreme Court judges, and any other person necessary to do the work of the government.

Section 3: Presidential Duties

14. The President shall, from time to time, give to the Congress information on the **State of the Union** (*how things are going in the country*). The President shall recommend any laws he or she thinks are good and necessary. He or she will make sure that any laws made by Congress are carried out.

15. The President, Vice President, and all other officers of the United States shall be removed from office by impeachment. They may be impeached for treason, bribery, or other high crimes and misdemeanors (*minor crimes*). (To impeach means to bring charges in the Senate against one of these officers. The Senate then acts as a court and tries the case.)

How The Executive Branch Works

16. To sum up this section of the Constitution, the President is head of the executive branch. His job is to make sure that the laws of the United States are carried out.

17. There are many departments and offices in the executive branch. Each department is headed by a member of the President's **Cabinet** (group of advisors and managers). This person is responsible to the President. He or she must also see that money given by the Congress is spent correctly.

18. For example, money given to the nation's schools by Congress is controlled by the Health, Education, and Welfare Department. The Secretary of that department must see that the money given to the department by Congress is spent correctly.

Electoral College

19. There is one section of the Constitution which is very hard to understand. It is about the election of the President and Vice President.

20. There are really two separate Presidential elections. The people vote every four years on the first Tuesday after the first Monday of November for President and Vice President. Anyone over the age of 18 who is a U.S. citizen can vote in that election.

21. The winner of the total vote in this election is said to be the winner of the **Popular Vote.**

22. However, the President and Vice President are really elected by a group of people called electors. (See paragraphs 4-6 on pg. 110.)

23. There are 535 such people (one for each Senator and Representative). They are generally elected by the people in each state.

24. Each state has the same number of electors as they have Senators and Representatives. For example, California has two Senators and 43 Representatives. California then has 45 electoral votes and can choose 45 electors.

25. After the Popular Vote in November, the 535 electors vote. They give the electoral votes from their states to one candidate or the other. The one who has the most electoral votes wins the election.

26. In most cases, the electors vote for the same candidate that the people of their states voted for. But there is no law that they have to vote that way. They can vote for anyone they want, no matter how the people of their states voted.

27. It might happen that no candidate gets more than one-half of the votes of the electors. The House of Representatives would then vote for the President from among the top three vote-getters. The Senate would vote for the Vice President.

28. There have been a few times in history when different candidates won the popular and the electoral votes. They will be discussed later in this series of books.

29. The Congress has tried many times to change the Electoral College system. So far, no change has been made.

Understanding What You Read

1. The main purpose of the executive branch of the Government is to:
   a. make new laws.
   b. choose new judges.
   c. make sure the laws made by Congress are carried out.
   d. choose new Vice Presidents.

   My answer is _____ . (1)

2. The President and Vice President are really elected by:
   a. the Senate.
   b. the House of Representatives.
   c. the voters of America.
   d. the 535 electors in the Electoral College.

   My answer is _____ . (25)

3. The President serves for a term of _____ years. (3)

4. Each state has a total of electors equaling the number of their _____ and

   _____ . (4)

5. If, for any reason the President can't serve he is replaced by the _____ . (8)

6. To become President a person must be born in _____ , at least

   _____ of age and have been living in the U.S. for _____ years. (7)

7. Some of the duties of the President are: 1) _____ , 2) _____

   _____ , 3) _____ . (13)

8. The President gives information on the state of the Union, which is _____

   _____ (14) to the Congress.

9. The President and Vice President are really chosen by the _____ . (22)

10. At some times in our history different candidates have been picked by the _____
    vote and the Electoral College. (28)

113

11. Complete the puzzle below.

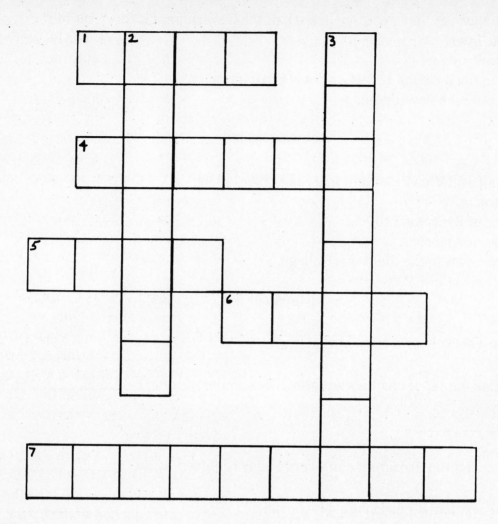

Puzzle Clues

Across

1. A President serves for a four-year __ __ __ __ .
4. There are two people from each state in this body.
5. A President must take an __ __ __ __ of office.
6. The people __ __ __ __ for the President.
7. The head of the executive branch of government.

Down

2. This person is chosen by the voters to elect a President.
3. The President is in charge of the __ __ __ __ __ __ __ __ __ __ branch of government.

114

Chapter 21
The Judicial Branch

1. The judicial branch of the government is made up of the **federal** (or national) **courts** of the United States.

2. Article III of the Constitution gives the judicial branch its power. This branch is made up of the Supreme Court and any lower courts that Congress may set up.

3. Judges in the federal courts decide whether the laws made by Congress and rules made by the executive branch are **constitutional.**

4. They also decide who is right in law suits brought by people against states, or by one state against another.

5. There are also state courts in each state, but these are not part of the federal court system. We will look only at the federal courts.

Section 1: Federal Courts

6. The judicial power of the United States shall be given to the Supreme Court and to as many lower courts as Congress might set up. The judges in these courts shall serve for life.

Section 2: Jurisdiction

7. The federal courts are given the power to rule on all questions about the Constitution.

8. The courts can also rule on all laws of the United States and on treaties made with other nations.

9. It shall have power in any case in which people from other nations are a party. It shall have power in all cases where the United States is one of the parties.

Section 3: Treason

10. Treason shall mean going to war against the United States or helping those who are at war against the United States.

11. No person shall be found guilty of treason unless there are at least two witnesses against him, or he confesses in court.

How The Judicial Branch Works

12. The Constitution gives us only the beginning of a court system. The Constitution left it to Congress to add other courts it thought were needed.

13. Congress later added **district courts** around the nation. They divided the country up into districts and set up a court for each district.

14. They also added **courts of appeal**. These are courts where people can go for another ruling if they don't agree with the **verdict** (decision) given by a lower court.

15. There are now 93 district courts and 11 courts of appeal around the nation. There are also special courts that take care of such things as taxes.

16. To see how the federal court system works, let's say that Ms. Jones has a complaint about the company she works for. She believes that she was not given a better job because she is a woman. This is a **violation** (not following the law) of the Constitution.

17. She could **sue** the company that would not give her the better job in a federal district court. After the court has made a decision, either of the parties (Ms. Jones or the company) can ask for another ruling from a court of appeals.

18. That court would study the case and make a ruling. If the appeals courts thinks the district court made a mistake it can change the ruling.

19. Such a case might even go to the Supreme Court. That court has the right to **hear** (rule on) only cases it wants to hear.

20. The Constitution does not spell out all the rights and duties of the Supreme Court. This was left up to the court itself. The court has said that it has the right to rule on all laws made by Congress.

21. The nine **justices** (judges) of the Supreme Court can decide that a law passed by Congress is against something written in the Constitution. They can then declare that law **unconstitutional**. This is one more of the checks and balances in our government.

22. For example, let's say that Congress makes a law saying that women cannot vote. The 19th Amendment to the Constitution says that women have the right to vote. Therefore, the Supreme Court would declare that law unconstitutional. It could not then be carried out by the executive branch.

Other Articles in the Constitution

23. There are a number of other articles (parts) in the Constitution.

24. Article IV says that citizens of one state must be treated like citizens of all the others. It also promises to protect the states from invasion or violence.

In the early days of our country, court was sometimes held outdoors.

25. Article V discusses how to **amend** (change) the Constitution. Amendments can be started in two ways. A vote by two-thirds of both houses of Congress can start an amendment. Or, the legislatures of two-thirds of the states can start an amendment.

26. In either case, the amendment must be ratified (agreed on) by three-fourths of all the states. Therefore, 38 of the 50 states must ratify an amendment before it becomes part of the Constitution.

27. Article VI states that all federal laws take **precedence** (first call) over all state laws. If a federal law and a state law disagree with each other, the federal law is the one that must be followed.

Understanding What You Read

1. The branch of the government that controls the federal courts is the_____ branch. (1)

2. There are three main kinds of courts in the federal court system. They are _____ , (6)
   _____ , (13) and _____ (14).

3. People who have a case that involves the Constitution can sue in a _____ court. (7)

4. The Supreme Court has the right to declare laws made by Congress to be _____ . (21)

5. Amendments can be started by the _____ or by a vote of _____ . (25)

6. In order for an amendment to become a part of the Constitution, _____ states have to ratify it. (26)

7. If a federal law and a state law disagree with each other, the _____ law is the one that is obeyed. (27)

8. Match the word with its meaning:

   a. judicial (3)   1. highest court in the U.S.
   b. Supreme Court (6)   2. against the Constitution
   c. treason (10)   3. judges
   d. unconstitutional (21)   4. change in the Constitution
   e. justices (21)   5. helping those at war against the U.S.
   f. amendment (25)   6. ruling on laws

   My answers are: a) _____ , b) _____ , c) _____ , d) _____ , e) _____ , f) _____ .

9. The main idea of this chapter is that:
   1. the U.S. does not need courts.
   2. the Constitution set up a judicial branch of government to rule on laws.
   3. state courts and federal courts do the same thing.
   4. people can appeal court decisions.

   My answer is _____ . (2-3)

10. **Chart Reading Skills:** Look at the chart below and then answer the questions.

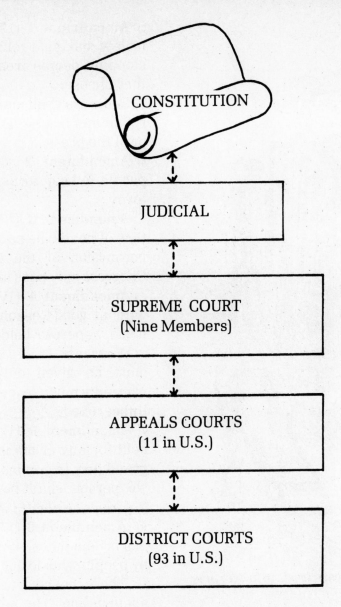

1. Which is the highest court in the United States? _____

2. If cases begin in the district courts, which is the highest court they can go to? _____

3. How many appeals courts are there in the U.S.? _____

4. How many Supreme Courts are there? _____

5. How many district courts are there? _____

Chapter 22
The Bill Of Rights And Other Amendments

The Bill of Rights gives Americans freedom in everyday life.

1. As you read in the past chapter (pg. 117), amending the Constitution is not an easy job. Yet it has been done 26 times since the Constitution was first written over 200 years ago.

2. The first ten amendments were passed in 1791. Many persons at that time wanted the rights of the people clearly written out. People would then know just what their rights were. The **Bill of Rights**, as the first ten amendments are called, were then added.

3. **Amendment 1** (1791): Congress shall pass no law making a religion. It cannot pass a law stopping people from practicing any religion they choose.

4. Congress shall make no laws taking away or reducing (*making less*) the freedom of speech or of the press.

5. **Amendment 2** (1791): The right of the people to keep arms (*guns*) shall not be taken away.

6. **Amendment 3** (1791): No soldier shall, in time of peace, be placed in a home without the permission of the owner. In time of war, Congress may pass laws making this possible.

7. **Amendment 4** (1791): There shall not be, without good reason, searches of a person's home, papers or belongings.

8. Warrants (*permission*) for such searches must be given only for good cause. The warrants must describe the person or place to be searched.

9. **Amendment 5** (1791): No person shall be held for any crime unless made to do so by a **grand jury** (a *group of citizens who hear a case.*) No person shall be made to give evidence (*information about the crime*) against himself.

10. **Amendment 6** (1791): The accused person in a criminal case has the right to a quick trial by people who do not favor either side.

11. The accused must be told of the charges against him. He has the right to face the witnesses against him and to have a lawyer in his defense.

12. **Amendment 7** (1791): In any case where the argument shall be for more than twenty dollars, there shall be a trial by jury (*twelve people chosen from the accused's community.*)

13. **Amendment 8** (1791): Not more than a necessary amount of bail (*money given to the court to make sure that a person shows up for trial*) shall be set. No cruel or inhuman punishment shall be given.

14. **Amendment 9** (1791): Even if a right is not stated in this Constitution such a right can still be enjoyed by the people.

15. **Amendment 10** (1791): The powers not given to the United States by the Constitution, nor kept from the states, are hereby given to the states, or to the people.

16. **Amendment 11** (1798): The federal courts cannot take cases that deal with a law suit brought against one state by the resident of another state. Nor can they hear a case brought by people of other nations against a state.

17. **Amendment 12** (1804): (*This amendment was discussed earlier in Chapter 20 (pgs. 112-113). It is about the election of the President and Vice President by the Electoral College.*)

18. **Amendment 13** (1865): There shall be no slavery in the United States.

19. **Amendment 14** (1868): No state shall make or carry out a law which takes away any rights of their people as citizens of the United States.

20. Nor shall any state deprive (*take away*) any person of life, liberty, or property without fairness. No person shall be denied equal protection under the laws of the United States.

21. **Amendment 15** (1870): All males over the age of 21 shall have the right to vote. (*This included former black slaves.*)

22. **Amendment 16** (1913): Congress shall have the right to set up an income tax.

23. **Amendment 17** (1913): Senators (*two from each state*) shall be elected by the people for six years. Each Senator shall have one vote.

24. **Amendment 18** (1919): The sale of alcoholic drinks in the United States shall be stopped. (*This was called* **Prohibition.** *This amendment was later repealed by the 21st Amendment.*)

25. **Amendment 19** (1920): Women over the age of 21 shall have the right to vote.

26. **Amendment 20** (1933): The terms of President and Vice President shall end at noon on the 20th day of January in the year in which such terms end.

27. **Amendment 21** (1933): The 18th Amendment is repealed (*done away with*) making it legal to sell alcoholic drinks again.

28. **Amendment 22** (1951): The number of terms a President may serve is limited to two (*eight years in all*).

29. **Amendment 23** (1961): The people living in the District of Columbia (*Washington, D.C.*) shall have the right to vote for the President and Vice President.

30. **Amendment 24** (1964): People cannot be forced to pay a tax without being able to vote.

31. **Amendment 25** (1967): If a President is removed from office, dies or resigns, the Vice President shall take over that office.

32. To fill the office of Vice President, the President shall appoint a person to take that office. That person must be approved by the majority of both houses of Congress.

33. **Amendment 26** (1971): All people over the age of 18 shall have the right to vote.

34. Other amendments are now being voted on for **ratification** (approval) in the states. One, the **Equal Rights Amendment (ERA)**, may soon become the 27th Amendment to the Constitution.

Understanding What You Read

1. Look at the chart below and then answer the following questions:

How The Constitution Is Amended

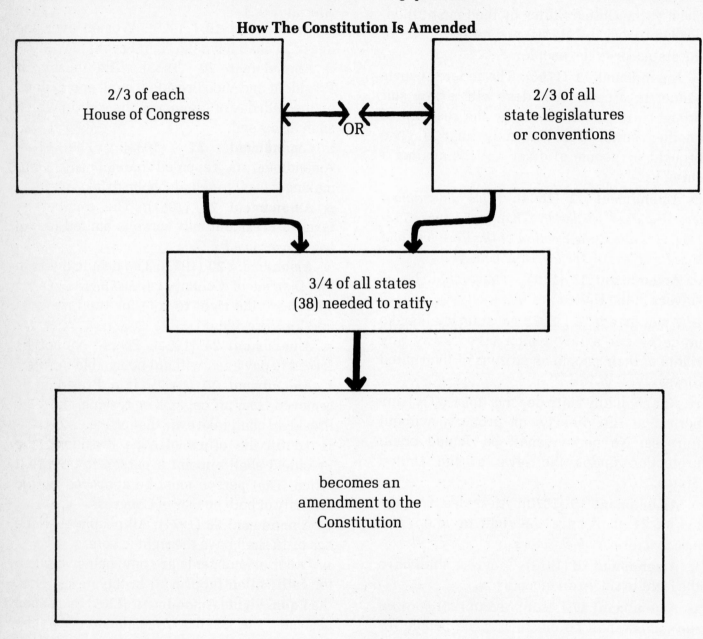

2/3 of each
House of Congress

OR

2/3 of all
state legislatures
or conventions

3/4 of all states
(38) needed to ratify

becomes an
amendment to the
Constitution

a. To start an amendment on the way to being part of the Constitution, 2/3 of either_____

_____ or of _____ must call for the amendment.

b. Once the amendment is proposed, _____ of the states must ratify it in order for it to become a part of the Constitution.

2. The first ten amendments, passed in 1791, are called _____

   _____ . (2)

3. The Bill of Rights gives Americans basic rights such as_____

   _____ , (3) _____ , (4)

   and _____ . (7)

4. Three amendments gave the right to vote to new groups of Americans. The _____

   Amendment gave the right to vote to _____ . (21)

   The _____ Amendment gave the right to vote to _____ . (25)

   The _____ Amendment gave the right to vote to _____ . (33)

5. The Constitution has been amended _____ times since it was first approved. (1)

6. The one amendment that was later repealed (done away with) by another amendment was the

   _____ . (24) It stopped _____ . That

   amendment was later repealed by the _____ Amendment. (27)

7. The _____ Amendment limits the number of Presidential terms to _____ . (28)

Chapter 23
Update to History

The questions on this page are written so you will think about the meaning of this history for today's Americans.

1. Many people say the American Constitution is the best of its kind ever written, yet it allowed for slavery, and denied rights to slaves, women and Indians. It also gave the real power to choose Presidents to the Electoral College. Do you think the Constitution, as it was written, was a good blueprint for governing America? Explain your answer.

_____

_____

_____

_____

_____

_____

2. What rights set forth in the Bill of Rights are still creating problems today? Look in today's newspapers. You will see problems involving freedom of speech and freedom of the press, for example. How do these problems relate to the way the Bill of Rights was written? Explain your answer.

_____

_____

_____

_____

_____

3. Women, Indians, Blacks, Chicanos, all have their own "movements". They are demanding equal rights as citizens of the United States. Were they ever given these rights? Are they asking for rights which were not given to them in the Constitution? Explain your answer.

_____

_____

_____

_____

_____

_____

4. Many people think the Electoral College system of selecting the President is wrong. Do you agree? If so, what would you do to change it?

_____

_____

_____

_____

_____

Unit 5
Our Nation Grows

Chapter 24
The New Nation Reaches For New Land

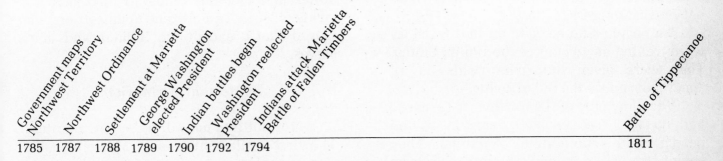

Government maps Northwest Territory — 1785
Northwest Ordinance — 1787
Settlement at Marietta — 1788
George Washington elected President — 1789
Indian battles begin — 1790
Washington reelected President — 1792
Indians attack Marietta / Battle of Fallen Timbers — 1794
Battle of Tippecanoe — 1811

1. After the Revolutionary War, America was a free nation. It was free to make its own laws and to decide its own future.

2. Many things had angered the Americans when they lived under British rule. One of these was the law keeping them from moving westward.

3. Now that they were free, Americans wanted more than ever to move into the new territory west of the Appalachian Mountains. They felt crowded in the growing cities of the thirteen states. They wanted land and freedom to spread out.

4. Many people began moving towards the territory west of the mountains. The American movement west would not stop at the Appalachians, however. It would one day carry Americans all the way to the Pacific Ocean — and beyond.

5. Part of the land Americans were moving to in the late 1700's was known as the **Northwest Territory** (See the map on pg. 129.) America had won this land from the British in the Revolutionary War. This land was north of the Ohio River and east of the Mississippi River. Today, parts of Ohio, Michigan, and Illinois are in the old Northwest Territory.

6. In 1785 the federal government sent men to **survey** (map out) the land in the Northwest Territory. These surveyors divided all of the land in the territory into **townships** (land where a town could be built).

7. They made each township six miles long by six miles wide. The surveyors then divided each township into four equal parts. One part was set aside for public buildings such as schools and courthouses. The rest of the land was to be sold to people who wanted to move to the township.

The Northwest Ordinance

8. In 1787 the men in Congress began to worry because there were no rules for governing the newly-settled land. They passed an act called the **Northwest Ordinance.** They hoped to make 3 to 5 states from the land of the Northwest Territory.

9. The Northwest Ordinance said that Congress had the right to appoint a governor to make rules for each new area where people settled. He would govern until there were "5,000 free male settlers" over the age of 21 living in the area.

10. When the population became that large the settlers could start their own legislature and make their own laws. They would then be a **territory.** That territory could later become a state.

11. The legislators from that territory could go to Congress and watch what went on. They could speak for the territory, but they could not vote in Congress.

12. The people who moved into that territory were treated as citizens of the United States. They were given the same rights as all Americans under the Bill of Rights.

13. When any part of the Northwest Territory had 60,000 "free people" living in it, the people could write a state constitution. They could then ask to be made a state. The term "free people" in the Northwest Ordinance did not include black slaves or Indians. They would have no say in governing the new states.

14. Some of the people who moved to the Northwest Territory brought slaves with them. However, when new states were formed, no more slaves could be brought into them.

15. The Northwest Ordinance was important. It planned a way for this land to be made into states and join the Union. It also gave the rights of American citizens to all settlers who moved there, except the Indians and black slaves.

Settlement At Marietta

16. Many settlers moved to the new territory. The first settlement was at Marietta, Ohio. The journal you are about to read is like ones which were written by settlers at that time. It describes what really happened and what the settlers thought.

17. **"June, 1788:** We have finally reached our

Fort Washington was typical of the forts built in the new Northwest Territory.

Library of Congress

new home. Our leader, General Putnam, calls this land a perfect place to make our settlement. We will call our settlement Marietta. It is where two rivers, the Ohio and the Muskingum, join.

18. We have pulled our flatboat, the Mayflower, up on the shore. It was a trusty boat, bringing us all the way down the river to this spot. Now, we shall break it up and use the logs to build our cabins.

19. I understand that we are the first settlement in the Northwest Territory. There are 48 people in our settlement. We have traveled very far. I hope that now we have found a place to call our home.

20. **August, 1788:** The land has been good to us since we came here. It is easy to grow crops in this soil. Our first crops of corn and wheat have begun to ripen. We will keep what we need and send the rest to markets farther south on the river. The rivers will be our lifeline to the outside world.

21. **September, 1788:** We have built our first cabins here at Marietta. They are made from

North America In 1783

the logs of our flatboat. Our farms are small, the land cleared of rocks and trees by hard work. We do not need much to live here.

22. Our cabin has only one room with a dirt floor. We cook on a fireplace that will also heat the cabin in the coming winter. We eat whatever we grow and the meat of animals we hunt in the forest around the settlement.

23. Most of our days are spent farming and clearing new land. We need more land to grow crops and more logs to build bigger homes. The forest is slowly giving way to farmland.

24. This has caused one problem. The Indians, who I suppose have lived on this land forever, do not like us cutting down the forest. They live in the forest and hunt game there. I hope they soon realize that we are here to stay and the land belongs to us to do with as we see fit.

25. **September, 1792:** We have been here in Marietta for four years. As General Putnam promised, this place has been good to us. The winters are hard and cold, but no worse than in our old home, Massachusetts.

26. Our crops have been good. Thousands of other settlers have followed us to this land. Some have stayed. Others have moved further along the river towards Canada.

27. We continue to have trouble with the Indians. A large Indian army, under the command of a Miami Indian by the name of Little Turtle, has defeated our armies twice in the last two years. We must have a stronger force to beat those savages.

28. As more settlers come, more land has to be cleared. That means the Indians must lose more hunting land. I suppose the Indians hate to see their land destroyed. I can understand that. But now it is our land and we are making it more valuable by farming it. More of us will come and more land will be taken.

29. **July, 1794:** The Indian attacks on our land have become more than we can stand. The Indians burn our homes and crops and have murdered some of our people.

30. We have asked our leaders in Congress for more help. Let us hope it comes quickly. The red man must be shown that he no longer has a place on our land.

31. A fur trapper tried to explain to us why the Indians fight. He said that the Indians believe that the land belongs to everyone, just as the air does. To the Indian hunters the land is their life.

32. Our people do not believe as the Indians do. The land should be used to grow crops and to house people. It belongs to whoever has a deed to it. The Indians must understand that. Or, they must be forced to go elsewhere.

33. **September, 1794:** Our Indian problems are over. President Washington and Congress sent General Anthony Wayne and his troops to fight the Indians. His army was too much for Little Turtle and his army of Indians. They fought at a place called **Fallen Timbers.** It was given that name because the land had recently been cleared, and dead trees lay all over the battlefield.

34. Little Turtle and his men have promised to move off our land and go westward, across the Mississippi River.

35. **April, 1795:** Most of the Indians are gone now. We hope that is the end of the Indian problem in the Northwest Territory. More and more settlers are moving to the northwest.

36. Some Indians are still here, but they cause us no trouble. We hear from traders that the Indians think a leader will come soon to bring all the tribes together and take back the land. That is foolishness. The land is ours now, and it will be forever."

Spotlight On The Northwestern Indians

37. The journal you have just read shows only one side of the story of the fight between the white settlers and the Native American Indians.

38. The Indians, of course, would have a different story to tell.

Settlers in the west had trouble with Indians who lived and hunted in the forests.

39. Many tribes lived in the area called the Northwest Territory. The Kickapoo and the Illinois lived in the southern part of the territory. In the central part of the territory were the Miami, the Potawatomi, and the Chippewa. In the northern part of the territory were the Ottawa, the Winnebago, and the Sauk-Fox.

40. These Indians were **semi-nomadic.** That means that the tribes moved camp a few times during the year to follow the **game** (animals) that they hunted for food. When they moved camp, however, they would move around within one large area. They thought of all the land where they hunted as theirs.

41. The white settlers found this hard to understand. They could see the Indians needed land for their camps and villages. They knew the Indians needed land for growing crops.

42. They could not understand when the Indians said that they needed the thousands of miles of forest land which they used only for hunting.

43. President James Monroe later summed up the feeling of the settlers. In 1817 he wrote "The hunter needs much more land to keep him going than is good for the progress of the settler. The Indian must give in to the settler."

44. At the end of the Revolutionary War a series of battles between the Indians and the American Army took place. The Miami Indian, Little Turtle, won battles in 1790 and 1791.

45. In 1794 the American army, under the command of General Wayne, won a major battle. Many settlers thought the **Battle of Fallen Timbers** marked the end of the Indian problem, but it did not.

46. After 1794 the Indian tribes signed treaties with the U.S. government. These treaties gave the Indian land to the Americans.

47. In the early 1800's a new Indian leader came upon the scene. **Tecumseh** was a young chief of the Shawnee.

48. Tecumseh moved around the country, speaking with other Indians. His dream was to build an Indian nation that was stronger than the United States. He argued that no tribe had the right to sell their land to the government.

49. "Why not sell the air, the clouds, and the sea?" he asked. "Did not the Great Spirit make them all for the use of all of his children?"

50. Tecumseh wanted to make the Ohio River the border between the white man and the Indian. His talk excited young Indians from Florida to the Canadian border. Many joined him and his brother, Tenskwatawa.

51. The brothers made their camp at Tippecanoe. This was a large Indian settlement on the banks of the Wabash River.

52. In November of 1811, while Tecumseh was away from camp, Tenskwatawa led an attack on an army led by General William Henry Harrison. Without their leader, Tecumseh, the Indians lost the battle. The great movement for an Indian nation had ended.

53. Tecumseh later joined the British during the War of 1812, and was killed in Canada.

54. There were a few Indian uprisings in the Northwest Territory after that, but a way of life had ended for the Indians. They were soon pushed across the Mississippi River to the west. They would never again hunt on the land they continued to think of as their own.

Understanding What You Read

1. The main idea of this chapter is that:
   a. the Northwest Territory had Indian problems.
   b. many settlers moved to the Northwest Territory after the Revolutionary War.
   c. Congress was worried about the people living in the Northwest Territory.
   d. General Putnam moved to the Northwest Territory.

   My answer is _____ . (3-5)

2. The Northwest Territory was made up of land north of the _____ and east of the

   _____ . (5)

3. One-fourth of each township in the Northwest Territory was set aside for _____

   _____ . (7)

4. The act of Congress passed to govern the Northwest Territory was called the _____

   _____ . (8)

5. Three groups of people had no say in governing the Northwest Territory. One such group was

   women. The other two were _____ and _____ . (13)

6. One of the major problems faced by the settlers was the _____ . (24)

   These people did not want the settlers to come because they thought the land _____

   _____ . (31)

7. The Indians were defeated in 1794 at the battle of _____ . (33)

8. Many Indian tribes lived in the Northwest Territory. Some of these were the _____ ,

   the _____ , the _____ , the _____ , the _____ ,

   and the _____ . (39)

9. The Indian leader who wanted to bring all tribes together was named _____ . (47)

10. **Map Study:** Look at the map on pg. 129 and then answer the following questions.

    a. Two nations owning land touching the Northwest Territory were _____

    and _____ .

    b. The western boundary of the Northwest Territory was the _____ River.

    c. The _____ _____ made up part of the northern boundary of the Northwest Territory.

Chapter 25
Expansion And Exploration

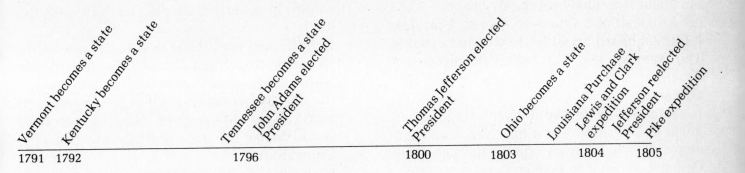

Vermont becomes a state — 1791
Kentucky becomes a state — 1792
Tennessee becomes a state — 1796
John Adams elected President — 1796
Thomas Jefferson elected President — 1800
Ohio becomes a state — 1803
Louisiana Purchase — 1804
Lewis and Clark expedition — 1804
Jefferson reelected President — 1805
Pike expedition — 1805

1. The Northwest Territory was not the only area being settled by Americans in the late 1700's. Many settlers passed right by the Northwest Territory. They headed farther west, into the center of the American continent.

2. It was said that in the spring of 1788 a person could stand at one place on the Ohio River and watch the crowds go by. During that spring more than 300 boats, carrying over 6,000 people, 3,000 horses, 500 head of cattle, 600 sheep and 150 wagons passed by.

3. We will read more about these western settlements later.

4. Between 1790 and 1800 two other areas were settled, also. They were in what is now Tennessee and Kentucky. The people in those territories quickly asked to be admitted to the Union — to become a part of the United States.

5. The people in Kentucky and Tennessee applied for statehood under the rules of the Northwest Ordinance. They were able to do this, even though they were not in the Northwest Territory.

6. As you read in the last chapter, Congress had written the Northwest Ordinance to govern the Northwest Territory. Later, Congress decided to use these rules for other territories as well. That is how Tennessee and Kentucky could come into the Union under the Northwest Ordinance.

7. Kentucky became a state in 1792, and Tennessee in 1796. That was the year John Adams was elected as the second President of the United States. Vermont, in northern New England, had been made a state in 1791. There were now 16 states in the United States of America.

8. In 1803 Ohio became a state, the 17th to come under the American flag. At that time Thomas Jefferson was President. He had been elected in 1800.

9. The farmers in the new states, like those in the Northwest Territory, depended on the rivers for transportation. They used the rivers as highways to move from one place to another and for getting products to market.

10. Many products from those states, such as furs, grain, whiskey and tobacco, were sent down the river highways to New Orleans. From there the goods were shipped to markets in Europe.

Jefferson Buys Louisiana

11. New Orleans, the main link in the transportation chain, did not belong to the United States.

12. Spain had taken New Orleans, and the rest of Louisiana, from France in 1762. In 1800, Spain secretly sold the land back to

135

France. **Napoleon**, the ruler of France, wanted the land for a French **empire** in the Americas. (An empire is a large amount of land held and ruled by a country.)

13. Although the sale was secret, President Jefferson heard about it. He worried about it. The Spanish had not been friendly to the American settlers sending goods through New Orleans.

14. Even so, Jefferson thought, the French might be worse. He knew that Napoleon might stop all goods from going through New Orleans, in order to weaken the new nation.

15. Jefferson thought he might be able to buy the port of New Orleans from the French. Napoleon was fighting with other nations in Europe and he needed money to keep those wars going.

16. President Jefferson did not know one very important thing. Because of his problems in Europe, Napoleon had given up the idea of an empire in America. He didn't really want the land.

17. Jefferson sent three men to France to ask Napoleon to sell New Orleans. The Americans were surprised to find that Napoleon wanted to sell New Orleans and all of the French land west of the Mississippi. Such a purchase would double the amount of land owned by the United States.

18. Jefferson did not know what to do. He wanted the land for the United States. The price, at only 15 million dollars, was a good one for so much land. However, nowhere in the Constitution did it say that the President had the right to buy land.

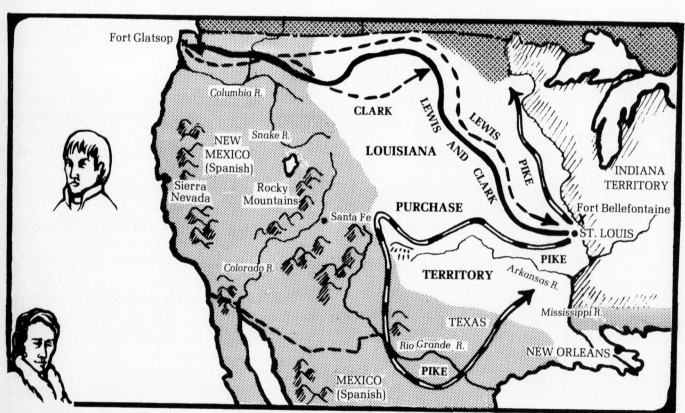

The Louisiana Territory and Its Explorers

19. Jefferson believed a President had to do what the Constitution said he could do. Some of his advisors argued that he could not buy the land. Others argued that the President would have to use powers that were not written in the Constitution.

20. Jefferson sent the question to Congress. The Senate agreed that Jefferson could buy the land. They approved the Louisiana Purchase in October of 1803. The United States took over the land in December of that year. (See the map on pg. 136.)

21. Many Americans were happy about the purchase. They saw the land as a new place for America to grow. Others were not as happy. They thought the President was doing things he was not allowed to do. They worried that America would get too big to rule. They said that the land was only worthless forests and mountains.

22. Most agreed, however, that getting the port of New Orleans was important to America. Little was known about the rest of the area for which the United States had just paid fifteen million dollars.

Lewis and Clark Head West

23. Jefferson wanted to find out more about the land west of the Mississippi River. He sent two young army officers, **Meriwether Lewis** and **William Clark** on a trip to the new land.

24. The two men were to find out all they could about the new land. They were to look for the beginnings of the Missouri River, and a way through the Rocky Mountains to the Pacific Ocean.

25. Jefferson also asked them to learn all they could about the Indians in the new territory. They were to find out about the plants and animals and to explore for **minerals** (coal, oil, gas, gold, silver, etc.). They were to make maps of all they found.

26. Lewis and Clark took 27 other men with them on their trip. They started from St. Louis in May of 1804. (See the map on pg. 136.)

27. They traveled 1,600 miles up the Missouri River until they reached what is now South Dakota. There they met an Indian woman named **Sacajawea**. (See the Spotlight on pg. 138 for more about her.) She came from a tribe that lived in the west, and Lewis and Clark hired her and her husband to guide them to the Rocky Mountains.

28. With Sacajawea's help they reached the Rocky Mountains and found the beginnings of the Missouri River. Traveling by wagon, canoe, and on foot, they crossed the mountains and found the Columbia River. They followed that river to the Pacific Ocean.

29. Lewis and Clark each took a different route for the trip back home. They returned in 1806, their mission completed. Only one man from their party had been lost. He died of illness, not from Indian or animal attacks.

The Indian woman Sacajawea was of great help to Lewis and Clark.

30. The two explorers had made detailed maps and brought back useful information on the Louisiana Territory and the land west of the Rockies. They were surprised by the richness and beauty of the land they had found. Their descriptions and reports were written up in newspapers all over the country. Many people decided to go to the new land.

Pike's Explorations

31. In 1805 another young officer, **Zebulon Pike**, was sent to explore the Mississippi River. He found where the river began. Later, he traveled westward across the plains to the Rocky Mountains and into the southwest.

32. Pike traveled to Santa Fe in New Mexico. he talked with the Spanish settlers there and found out what goods they would like to have from the Americans. He opened up trade between Santa Fe and the Americans in the east.

33. On his travels to the southwest he found a high peak that today bears his name — **Pike's Peak**.

Spotlight On Sacajawea

34. One of the first Native American heroines was a woman called Sacajawea (or Sacagawea).

35. She has become one of the most famous Indians of all time. Artists have painted many pictures showing her with Lewis and Clark. There are a number of statues of her around the nation.

36. Sacajawea was born around 1787 in the camp of the Snake Indians (a branch of the Shoshone Tribe.) The camp was probably in what is now the state of Idaho. When she was about 14 or 15 a war party of Indians from South Dakota attacked her tribe. She and an older girl were captured. The older girl

escaped. Sacajawea was taken to the area we call South Dakota by her captors, Hidatsa warriors.

37. She was taken in by a French fur trader named Charbonneau who traded with the Hidatsa. At the age of 18, Sacajawea became the trader's second wife. That was in 1804, shortly before Lewis and Clark reached the area in South Dakota where she lived.

38. Sacajawea and her French husband were asked by Lewis and Clark to guide their trip through the Shoshone territory. Her husband was the one who was hired as a guide, but the journals of the trip show that Sacajawea was of greater help to Lewis and Clark.

39. Sacajawea knew the territory, could speak the language, and could persuade her people to help the travelers. Many say that without her knowledge and help, the trip would have fallen short of its goal.

40. Lewis and Clark realized this, but it seems that Sacajawea never knew the part she was playing in American history.

41. "If she has enough food to eat and a few trinkets to wear, I believe she would be happy to be anywhere," Lewis wrote of her after the trip.

42. Sacajawea's life after the trip is a bit of a mystery. A journal written by a fur trader in 1812 says "This evening the wife of Charbonneau (the French fur trader), a Snake squaw, died of fever. She was aged about 25 years."

43. Yet, in 1875 a missionary among the Indians in Wyoming came across an old Indian woman who said she was Sacajawea. When she died, a statue was put up for her. Many experts believe that she was the real Sacajawea.

44. Whatever the true story, nobody will deny that Sacajawea helped to explore the new nation of America.

Understanding What You Read

1. The United States bought the Louisiana Territory because:
   a. Jefferson planned to buy all that land.
   b. Jefferson wanted the port of New Orleans only, but was offered the whole territory.
   c. The United States won it in a war with France.
   d. Jefferson wanted to give it to Sacajawea and her followers.

   My answer is _____ . (15-17)

2. Jefferson was not sure he could buy the Louisiana Territory for the United States because

   _____

   _____ . (18-19)

3. Three men who explored the Louisiana Territory for the United States were _____

   _____ , _____ , and

   _____ . (23,31)

4. **Map Skills:** Look at the map on pg. 136 and then answer the following questions:

   a. St. Louis is a city on the _____ River.

   b. The explorers who crossed the Rocky Mountains were _____ and

   _____ .

   c. The explorers who traveled along the Columbia River were _____ .

   d. The explorer who traveled the farthest south was _____ .

   e. The explorers who went to the Pacific Ocean were _____ and

   _____ .

   f. The explorer who traveled to Mexico before returning to the U.S. was _____ .

   g. Lewis and Clark took different routes for their return trip. The explorer who took the more

   southern route was _____ .

   h. On his trip, Pike explored land belonging to _____ .

5. **True or False:** Decide if the following statements are true or false. If the statement is true, place a **T** in the space beside the letter. If the statement is false, change the **underlined** word to make it true.

_____a. The U.S. bought Louisiana from <u>France</u>. (15,20)

_____b. The 17th state to enter the Union and become part of the United States was <u>Vermont</u>. (8)

_____c. Many American farmers sent their products through the port of <u>New Orleans</u> to European markets. (10)

_____d. The President who bought Louisiana for the United States was <u>President Washington</u>. (20)

_____e. The President sent Lewis and <u>Pike</u> on a trip to find a way through the Rocky Mountains to the Pacific Ocean. (23-24)

_____f. <u>Sacajawea</u> was an Indian woman who helped guide the explorers. (27)

_____g. The U.S. bought Louisiana for <u>25 million</u> dollars. (18)

_____h. <u>Tennessee</u> became a state in 1792. (7)

_____i. Lewis and Clark traveled as far west as <u>St. Louis</u>. (28)

_____j. Napoleon was the ruler of <u>Spain</u>. (12)

Chapter 26
The Wasted War Of 1812

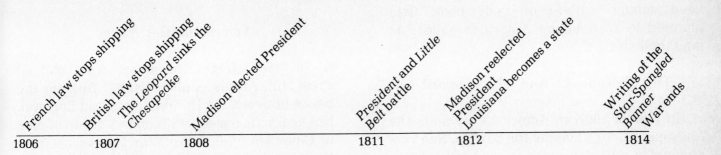

| 1806 | 1807 | 1808 | 1811 | 1812 | 1814 |

French law stops shipping — 1806

British law stops shipping / The Leopard sinks the Chesapeake — 1807

Madison elected President — 1808

President and Little Belt battle — 1811

Madison reelected President / Louisiana becomes a state — 1812

Writing of the Star-Spangled Banner / War ends — 1814

1. America grew larger and stronger as people moved westward. Many people moved away from the crowded eastern cities to open new land for trapping, trading and farming. New cities grew up along the river highways of the nation.

2. Events in Europe were soon to slow down the rapid growth of the United States. England and France were at war (1803-1815). France had the strongest land army in Europe. England had the strongest navy in Europe.

3. The United States told both sides that it wanted to stay out of the war. That became harder and harder to do with each passing month.

4. America's cargo ships were carrying goods to both France and England, and American shipowners were making a great deal of money in that way. Neither England nor France wanted the United States to sell goods to the other.

5. In 1806 Napoleon, the ruler of France, passed a law that any ship trading with the English would be taken by the French. That law made it impossible for any ship trading with England to also trade with France.

6. The British answered in 1807 by passing a law which said that all ships trading in Europe had to stop in England first. That law made it impossible for any ship to trade with France without also trading with England.

7. American shippers were in trouble. They could no longer trade with the European nations. Any ship trying to trade with both France and England could be captured by either the French or the British. British warships stood off American ports to make sure the laws were carried out.

The British Kidnap Americans

8. The British navy had trouble keeping sailors. Life on the British ships was very hard. Men could be whipped by their officers without a hearing. Even small "crimes" like smoking were punishable by whipping. The pay was low. Many men refused to serve in the navy. Others **deserted** (left) when they reached American ports.

9. Some of the British sailors who deserted from their own navy signed up to sail on American ships. The pay was better and the life was easier.

10. The British did not like the fact that they were losing sailors. They began stopping American ships on the high seas and taking sailors.

11. The British officers claimed that the sailors they took were deserters from their own navy. Most were not. The British just came aboard and took the strongest sailors for their own ships. About 9,000 American sailors

became British sailors in that way.

12. Americans complained to the British government about the **impressment** (taking) of American sailors. Because the British did not have enough sailors of their own, they planned to keep taking American sailors to man their ships.

The Chesapeake And The Leopard

13. In June of 1807 an American warship, the *Chesapeake*, was leaving for Europe. She was stopped by a British gunboat, the *Leopard*.

14. The captain of the *Leopard* demanded to board the American ship to search for British deserters. The American captain was afraid that he would lose some of his men, even if there were no British deserters on his ship. He refused to let the British come aboard.

15. The British ship fired on the *Chesapeake*, killing three Americans and wounding eighteen others. Then the British boarded the American ship and took off four American sailors claiming they were British deserters. Then they sailed away.

16. The American people were angered by the *Chesapeake* attack. Many wanted to go to war with England to keep them from taking any more American sailors.

17. President Jefferson did not want war. He asked Congress to pass a law saying that American ships could no longer trade with any nations. American ships were to stay in port. This is called an **embargo.**

18. Jefferson felt that such an embargo would make both England and France stop fighting. He believed that they both needed American goods to keep the war going.

19. Jefferson was wrong. Both the British and the French found other places to get the goods they needed.

20. The embargo on American goods to European nations did not even slow the war. All it did was put thousands of American

sailors out of work. It cost American shipowners thousands of dollars in lost profits.

Americans Get Angry

21. In 1808 **James Madison** was elected President. Madison also wanted to keep the peace between the United States and England. Not everyone agreed with him. A group of men in Congress, called the **War Hawks** because they wanted war with England, pointed out that the British were asking for war.

22. The War Hawks were angry at the impressment of American sailors by the British. They were also sure that the British were causing trouble for America in other places.

23. The War Hawks claimed that the British were causing the Indian attacks on the settlers in the Northwest Territory. They said that the British in Canada were paying the Indians and giving them guns.

24. Many Americans agreed with the War Hawks and wanted a war with England. The kidnapping of sailors and the British action in the Northwest Territory made them angry. They also wanted a war for other reasons.

25. Farmers in the northern part of the United States wanted the fertile land of British Canada as a place to **expand** (move outward).

26. Fur traders wanted the British out so they could take over the fur trade in Canada.

27. Farmers in the south wanted to get some of the land owned by Spain in Florida. Spain was a friend and **ally** (helper) of England. A war would give the southern farmers an excuse to take away "enemy" land.

28. Only one area in the United States was against a war. That area was the northeast. Most of the shipping and trading done by New England was with the British. The people in New England did not want to lose all that

business, even though many of the sailors taken by the British were from New England.

War Breaks Out

29. In May of 1811 an American ship, the *President*, attacked and defeated a small British warship, the *Little Belt*. Many Americans were happy that the war was coming. They wanted to show the British that America would not back down to anyone.

30. It had been 37 years since America had fought a war. Most of the soldiers who had fought in the Revolutionary War were, in 1812, too old to do the job any longer. The 6,000 man American army was not well trained. They were spread out all over the territories fighting Indians and guarding settlers.

31. Many of the New England states refused to supply any soldiers to the army. In fact, some of the New England states said they would leave the Union if the war did not end quickly.

32. The American army hoped to win the war quickly. It met with little success. A large force was sent to capture Canada. It was beaten easily by the British army.

33. However, some ships of the American navy had early victories. Oliver Perry won a big battle on Lake Erie. The *Constitution* won a victory over a large British warship in the Atlantic. The *Constitution* earned the name **Old Ironsides**, because the British

Commodore Perry won a major victory on Lake Erie in the War of 1812.

cannonballs seemed to bounce off the wooden sides of the ship.

34. The British landed a force in Maryland and marched to Washington. The President and Congress were forced to run from the city. The British burned the Capitol, the President's home and other government buildings.

35. A British fleet sailed up Chesapeake Bay to Baltimore, Maryland. The British ships bombed Fort McHenry. The fort refused to give up. The British ships fired at it all night long.

36. A young American lawyer named **Francis Scott Key** was on board one of the ships. He was trying to get the British to free an American who was held prisoner. He watched the battle all night long. In the morning he wrote a poem which has since become *The Star Spangled Banner*, our national **anthem** (song).

37. Neither side really wanted the war. It slowed down and ended in 1814. Word about the ending of the war did not get to the port of New Orleans in time. General "Andy" Jackson and his backwoodsmen beat a large British force there after the war had ended.

38. Nobody really won the war. Nobody really lost. Only the question of the border between the United States and Canada was settled.

39. The treaty ending the war did not cover impressment or the British actions in the Northwest Territory. Everything was the same as it had been before the war began. In that sense, the War of 1812 was a wasted war.

40. Many in the United States took a new pride in the nation and the war heroes, Perry and Jackson. Many thought that the war had earned America a new respect in the world. They felt they had gained something from it.

Spotlight On The Star-Spangled Banner

41. The wasted War of 1812 did bring America the song that has become our national anthem.

42. Francis Scott Key was a young American lawyer. He was on a mission to ask for the release of an American who was held prisoner, Dr. William Beanes. He went to the British fleet on the Potomac River.

43. Key spoke to the British admiral and showed him letters from British prisoners telling how well they were being treated. If the doctor could be set free, Key said, he would make sure that the good treatment of the British would continue. The admiral

Francis Scott Key wrote the *Star Spangled Banner* while he watched the British fire at Fort McHenry in the War of 1812.

agreed, but told Key that he and Dr. Beanes must stay on board the *Surprise* until after the attack on Baltimore.

44. It was from the deck of the *Surprise* that Key and the doctor watched the firing on Fort McHenry in Baltimore harbor. The firing went on all night. Just before morning the firing stopped. Key thought the fort had fallen to the British. He was wrong. At first light he saw the American flag which he called "the star-spangled banner", still flying over the fort.

45. He wrote a poem that began "Oh, say, can you see, by the dawn's early light, what so proudly we hailed at the twilight's last gleaming. . ."

46. The poem was written on the back of a letter that he had in his pocket. He continued to write as he was rowed ashore by the British. He rewrote part of it in his room that night.

47. Key's poem was printed in a handbill entitled "The Defence of Fort McHenry". Later it was set to the music of an old English song.

48. In 1931 it was officially adopted as the national anthem of the United States. People felt it showed that the United States would stay alive, no matter what.

49. In recent years many people have suggested changing the national anthem to *America*. They say that the *Star-Spangled Banner* is too warlike, as well as too difficult to sing. They think that *America* is a more peaceful song.

50. Our national anthem might someday be changed, but the poem written by Francis Scott Key has become one of the most familiar songs in history.

General "Andy" Jackson and his backwoodsmen defeated a large British force at the port of New Orleans.

Library of Congress

Understanding What You Read

For questions 1-8, circle the letter which is the correct answer.

1. The word **events** as used in **paragraph 2** means:
   a. war
   b. things that were happening
   c. stories that people were reading

2. The word **deserted** as used in **paragraph 8** means:
   a. took for their own
   b. left without permission, ran away
   c. signed up

3. The word **impressment** as used in **paragraph 12** means:
   a. taking men and forcing them into service
   b. looking good
   c. fighting against

4. The word **refused** as used in **paragraph 14** means:
   a. agreed to do something
   b. would not agree to do something
   c. was not sure what to do

5. The word **expand** as used in **paragraph 25** means:
   a. to move outward
   b. to stay where they are
   c. to go home

6. The word **ally** as used in **paragraph 27** means:
   a. a nation that fights alongside another nation
   b. an enemy
   c. two nations that don't like each other

7. The word **prisoner** as used in **paragraph 36** means:
   a. a person held by the enemy during a war
   b. a person who writes poems
   c. a person who captures other people

8. The word **border** as used in **paragraph 38** means:
   a. the place where two ships fight
   b. the place where a war takes place
   c. an imaginary line drawn between two nations

9. Some of the following statements are **facts**. That is, they really happened. Some of the statements are **opinions**. That is, they tell how someone thought or felt about something that happened. Place an **F** in the correct space if the statement is a fact, **O** if it is an opinion. The first one is done for you.

___**O**___a. America should not have gone to war in 1812.

_____b. British ships were impressing American sailors into the British navy.

_____c. The British were wrong for impressing American sailors.

_____d. Many sailors deserted from British navy ships.

_____e. The embargo cost American shippers thousands of dollars in lost profits.

_____f. The British ship was wrong for firing on the Chesapeake.

_____g. The War Hawks in Congress were men who wanted the United States to go to war with England.

_____h. People in the New England states lost shipping business during the war.

_____i. One battle was fought after the war had already ended.

_____j. *America* would be a better national anthem than *The Star Spangled Banner*.

Chapter 27
Sectional Differences

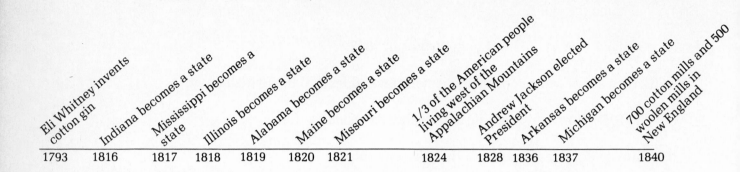

Eli Whitney invents cotton gin	Indiana becomes a state	Mississippi becomes a state	Illinois becomes a state	Alabama becomes a state	Maine becomes a state	Missouri becomes a state	1/3 of the American people living west of the Appalachian Mountains	Andrew Jackson elected President	Arkansas becomes a state	Michigan becomes a state	700 cotton mills and 500 woolen mills in New England
1793	1816	1817	1818	1819	1820	1821	1824	1828	1836	1837	1840

1. By the 1820's it was clear that three major sections of the nation were developing. It was also clear that these sections were very different from each other in way of life and even in way of thinking. The larger the country grew, the greater the differences became.

2. **The Northeast:** The northeast was turning more and more to industry and factories in what was called the **Industrial Revolution.**

3. The Industrial Revolution was a time of changing how people worked and lived. Machines were taking the place of hand tools. The steam engine and the electrical engine were taking the place of work animals and water power.

4. Transportation and communication were becoming faster and cheaper all the time. Factories sprang up. New industries began operation.

5. Textile factories, making cloth for clothing and other goods, grew rapidly in New England. By 1840 there were 700 cotton mills and 500 woolen mills in New England. More than fifty thousand people worked in these factories.

6. Cities grew up around the factories. More and more people came to live in cities, although there were still many small farms around.

7. In 1822 a Congregational minister named Timothy Dwight traveled around New England. Here is some of what he had to say about the life of the people there:

8. "It is easy to live comfortably in New England. Any man who wants to work the least bit can earn $125 to $250 a year. Such a man can easily buy himself a large farm in the new territories or a small one in New England.

Cities grew up around factories in New England.

148

Even someone who does not want to work hard can earn enough to buy a small house and to live a comfortable life.''

9. Dwight pointed out that New Englanders in the large cities ate too much and drank too much. They spent much time in such sports as football (British rugby), cricket, and skating in the winter.

10. Traveling for the purpose of visiting friends and neighbors was common. Music and dancing lessons were given to the children.

11. The New England winters were hard. They were particularly hard for the farmers trying to make a living farming the hard, rocky soil.

12. These New England farmers began to develop a certain way of life. It was a few-words-said and fewer-dollars-spent way of living. That is, they did not enjoy talking a lot and they were careful how they spent their money.

13. **The South:** The south produced the cotton that was made into cloth in New England. Since the textile mills in New England were growing at a quick pace, more and more cotton was needed.

14. In 1793 an inventor, Eli Whitney, made it easy for the south to produce much more cotton. Whitney invented a machine called the **cotton gin.**

15. Before Whitney's invention, it had taken a field hand one day to take the seeds out of one pound of cotton. A hand-run cotton gin could remove the seeds from fifty pounds of cotton a day. A water-powered gin could clean a thousand pounds of cotton in a day.

16. Black slaves, brought from Africa, had been working the land in the south since before the Revolutionary War. As the demand for cotton grew, more and more slaves were needed to plant, hoe, pick and gin the crops.

17. It was profitable to use slaves to grow the cotton. The slave was bought and was never paid any wages. All the owner had to give a

slave was a small cabin, some food and a suit of clothing. Slaves could not quit. Their children became the property of their owner. In time of hardship they could be sold like any other piece of property.

New Orleans became a center of social gatherings and fashion for rich southern plantation owners.

18. The climate in the south was much like the climate in Africa. The slaves were used to working in the hot southern sun.

19. The lower south became a one-crop area. That crop was cotton.

20. Timothy Flint was a man who visited the plantations in Louisiana around 1820. Here is some of what he had to say:

21. "The planters of the south are, for the most part, rich and very happy to take in travelers. Wherever I went I got some drink and a good meal.

22. "These plantation owners live in big homes overlooking thousands of acres of cotton land. The fact that they are rich is due, I suppose, mostly to slavery.

23. "In any case, they spend money more easily than any other group I have seen on my travels around the United States. Most of their spare time is taken up with balls (dances) and parties.

24. "The men dress handsomely, the women dress in the latest fashion. It is a life one could easily get used to."

25. The life of the slaves on the southern plantations was not so pleasant, however. That life was hard, with long work hours and little time for rest.

26. **The Northwest Territory:** After the War of 1812 and the defeat of the Indians at Fallen Timbers, more people moved to the Northwest Territory.

27. Ohio had become a state in 1803. Soon Michigan, Illinois, Indiana and Wisconsin became states.

28. Land was cheap and good for growing many crops. People came from many parts of the nation. From the south came poor whites who wanted land of their own. From the east came people who wanted a place away from the growing cities. From the northeast came people who wanted better land to farm. They came by the thousands.

29. As the land became settled and the number of farms grew, small cities to support them also grew. The cities had stores, lumber mills, saloons, and everything else that went with "civilization".

30. Life in the northwest was unlike that in the other sections of the country. People on outlying farms lived in rough cabins. Water had to be brought from streams or rivers.

Small towns grew up around farms in the northwest.

Heat came from open fireplaces.

31. Even life in the larger cities of the northwest was unlike life in the cities of the east.

32. Frances Trollope came to America in 1828. She wrote unfavorably about what she saw in the river city of Cincinnati, Ohio:

33. "This city has none of the things needed for good living. There is no way of getting water easily. The garbage from the city is placed in the middle of the street. Then the pigs of the city are set loose on it, and soon it is gone.

34. "The men do nothing but . . . talk of the price of goods and **produce** (fruits and vegetables). The women have nothing to do but look at each other to see what the other is wearing."

35. America was changing. The population of the United States was no longer **concentrated**

(the greatest, the heaviest) along the eastern seaboard. In fact, by 1824, one-third of America's population lived west of the Appalachian Mountains.

36. As the three sections of the nation developed differently, so did the thinking of the people who lived in those sections. Many people began to give their loyalty to their section, rather than the United States as a whole.

37. New Englanders thought of themselves as "Yankees", Southerners as just that, and people in the territories as Westerners.

Spotlight On The Common Man's President

38. Feelings of sectional loyalty had an effect on the Presidential elections. The first six Presidents had come from either Massachusetts or Virginia. By the 1820's people in other parts of the nation wanted a President to come from one of their states.

39. The President who did that won the election of 1828. His name was **Andrew Jackson**.

40. Jackson was a frontiersman and an Indian fighter. He was a hero of the War of 1812, where he had led the American troops in the Battle of New Orleans.

41. Jackson was from Tennessee. He had served in Congress from that state. He was elected as the "common man's" President.

42. People thought that Jackson was not a "high-class" type of President such as Washington, Jefferson and Adams. He was not very well educated and spoke like a man on the street.

43. Jackson believed that all citizens had the right to hold office and to vote. The fact that he had little schooling led many people to think that he was stupid. But he was not. He had taught himself to read at an early age and was a successful lawyer and judge before becoming President.

44. As an Indian fighter and a westerner, Jackson did not like Indians. He saw them as a threat to the westward movement of American settlers. He made thousands of Indians leave their homelands. He ruled that no Indians could live east of the Mississippi River. At that time the Mississippi was America's western boundary.

45. In the next chapter you will read about one group of Indians who had to leave their homes. They were the Cherokees and their story is a famous one in American history.

From the Esmark Collection of Currier & Ives

This old picture shows people ice skating in Central Park in New York City.

Understanding What You Read

1. Use the information from the chapter to fill in the chart below.

Section	Products	Way Of Living
Northeast		
	Cotton	
		Rough life, much hardship, more democratic

2. By the 1820's, three major sections of the country had developed. They were the _____ , (2)

   the _____ (13) and the _____ . (26)

3. In the Industrial Revolution the _____ _____ and the _____

   _____ took the place of work animals and water power. (3)

4. The New England winters were very hard for _____ trying to make a living
   from the rocky soil. (11)

5. Eli Whitney invented the _____ _____ , which helped the south produce
   more cotton. (14)

6. By 1824 _____ of America's population was living west of the Appalachian
   Mountains. (35)

7. Andrew Jackson was elected President in 1828 as the _____

   President. (41)   He believed all citizens had the right to _____

   and to _____ . (43)

152

8. **Word Search:** Find the hidden words listed in the puzzle below and circle them.

SECTIONALISM

FACTORY

CITY

YANKEE

DEMOCRACY

UNION

NORTHEAST

SOUTH

NORTHWEST

FARM

VOTE

SLAVE

COTTON GIN

```
C F B C D E F F G H N S
I S K L M N A O P Q O E
T L U M A I C X U Y R C
Y A N K E E T X N A T T
B V D D V E O F I C H I
V E T E O H R I O J W O
K K L N T O Y P N Q E N
S R T I E S O U T H S A
C O T T O N G I N V T L
D E M O C R A C Y W E I
X F A R M B X Q Y Z O S
A N O R T H E A S T P M
```

Chapter 28
America Expands And Changes

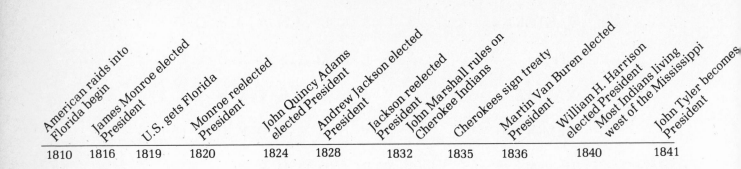

American raids into Florida begin	James Monroe elected President	U.S. gets Florida	Monroe reelected President	John Quincy Adams elected President	Andrew Jackson elected President	Jackson reelected President	John Marshall rules on Cherokee Indians	Cherokees sign treaty	Martin Van Buren elected President	William H. Harrison elected President / Most Indians living west of the Mississippi	John Tyler becomes President
1810	1816	1819	1820	1824	1828	1832	1835	1836	1840		1841

1. *I've got a mule and her name is Sal,*
Fifteen miles on the Erie Canal.
She's a good old workhorse and a good old pal,
Fifteen miles on the Erie Canal.
We've hauled some barges in our day,
Filled with lumber, coal, and hay.
And we know every inch of the way,
From Albany to Buffalo,
Fifteen miles on the Erie Canal.

2. That song was sung by the men who drove the horses along the Erie Canal in upstate New York. In the early 1800's many canals were built in America. They were used to connect towns and settlements as America grew.

3. More and more Americans were moving westward. At first, the settlers stayed near the rivers, because the rivers were an easy

Canals were an easy means of transporting people and goods between the east and west.

means of transportation for both people and goods.

4. Soon the land near the rivers became crowded. People had left the east to find room to grow, but the river towns were becoming as crowded as the towns they had left behind.

5. Settlers started moving farther away from the rivers. They had to use the dirt roads cut through the forest to move goods to market. Those settlers wanted good routes that would connect their settlements to the rivers. They wanted to be able to use rivers for all their travel, because it was cheaper and quicker.

6. People looked for a way to bring a river to settlers living far from one. They also looked for a way to connect rivers, so that overland travel would not be necessary.

7. The answer was the canal. Canals are man-made "rivers" used to move goods and for quicker travel.

Canal System, 1840

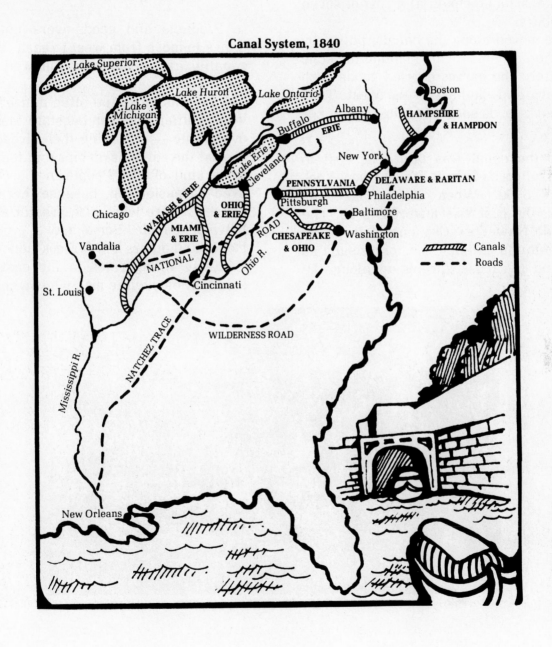

8. Perhaps the best-known of the canals was the Erie Canal mentioned in the song above. The Erie Canal ran 363 miles from Albany, New York on the Hudson River, to Lake Erie (See the map on pg. 155.) Its average size was forty feet wide and four feet deep. For its time, it was an engineering marvel.

9. The canal was dug by men with shovels and scoops. Horses were used to pull some of the bigger scoops. It took eight years (1817-1825) to build the 363-mile canal, at a cost of seven million dollars.

10. Barges moved along the canals, pulled by mules or horses which walked along the edge of the water. The barges carried goods such as furniture and clothing to the west. They brought back goods such as grain and lumber to the east.

11. Before the canal was built, the cost to bring a ton of goods from Buffalo to New York City was $100. When the canal was completed, the cost was lowered to $8. The canal made New York City one of the most used ports in the nation. Other cities such as Albany and Syracuse sprang up along the canal.

12. After the success of the Erie Canal, other states started canal projects of their own. Soon, major canals were built in Ohio, Pennsylvania, and other states. Smaller canals were built all over the nation. These canals allowed more people to move west and western products to move to markets in the east.

Ideas Move East

13. Products and goods were not the only things to move from west to east. Ideas about equality and democracy followed the same route.

14. Life was hard and often dangerous in the west. Settlers were in constant fear of losing everything — including their lives. Everyone shared the same hardships and fears and the same kind of life. People in the east mostly lived an easier life, because there was less danger. There were also greater differences between people. Some had a great deal of money and others had far less money.

15. Early voting rules in the eastern states said that only white men who owned property

This is how one artist saw life on the Mississippi River in the 1800's.

could vote. Those who had made the rules believed that men of wealth and property were more able to decide who should lead the government. Most of the eastern states followed those rules.

16. But, in the west, everybody lived more or less like everyone else. People didn't think they were better than their neighbors, whether they owned property or not.

17. Community problems were often argued out in town meetings where all the men in town had their say and their vote. Women were still not allowed to have a vote, nor were black men or Indians.

18. Most of the new states on the frontier, as they entered the Union, allowed all white men over the age of 21 to vote.

19. Factory workers and others in the eastern states heard of the voting rules in the new states. They wanted the same voting rights as the western settlers.

20. Many of the eastern states began to change their rules to allow all white men over the age of 21 to vote, even if they did not own property. The changes brought more **democracy** (rule by all of the people) to America.

Americans Push West

21. America continued to expand her borders. After American raids into Florida between 1810 and 1813, the Spanish decided to sell that land to the United States. A treaty with Spain was signed in 1819 giving Florida to the United States.

22. As America pushed her borders farther west, the Native Americans continued to lose their land.

23. At one time, 20,000 Cherokees were forced to move from their homes in Georgia to what is now Arkansas and Oklahoma. More than 4,000 of the Indians died on the long march.

24. By 1840 few Indians lived east of the

Some Indians escaped to the mountains when their homes and farms were taken away.

Mississippi. Those who did either lived on **reservations** (pieces of land set aside by the government where they had to live) or hid in the Florida swamps.

Spotlight On The "Trail of Tears"

25. The Cherokee Indians of the early 1800's were intelligent and hard-working people.

26. Most of them read books and American newspapers. They wore "white man's" clothing and lived like the white man. Many of the Cherokees lived in log cabins and some lived in large houses.

27. A Cherokee named Sequoyah made an alphabet for his language, so that it could be read and written as well as spoken. In 1826 the tribe held a convention and drafted a tribal constitution. In 1828 an Indian newspaper called the *Cherokee Phoenix* was published in Georgia, the tribe's homeland.

28. As early as 1802 the state of Georgia and the federal government had signed an agreement about the Indians. It stated that the

Indian land belonged to Georgia rather than to the Indians. Many people in Georgia wanted the good land the Indians lived on.

29. The federal government said it would help to get the Indians off their land as soon as it could be done "peacefully". Nothing was done to remove the Indians until 1829 when President Jackson had a "removal bill" introduced in Congress. The bill said that all Cherokee Indians would have to move to reservations in Oklahoma.

30. Many people in Georgia were happy about the bill to remove the Cherokees. They saw a chance to get the land cheaply if the Indians were made to move.

31. One song sung by whites in Georgia said:
All I want in this creation
Is a pretty little girl
And a big plantation
Way up yonder in the Cherokee nation.

32. Georgia began passing laws against the Indians. First the state took the Indians' land and began to break it into small pieces to be given to white settlers.

33. Then all contracts between the Indians and white people were **cancelled** (ended). Nobody who owed money to an Indian had to pay. The Cherokees were not allowed to hold meetings. They could not testify in court against white people.

34. Some white people attacked and burned Indian homes. They took away the Indians' livestock and belongings.

35. The Chief of the Cherokees, John Ross, took his case to the United States Supreme Court. He claimed that the state of Georgia had no right to do what it was doing to his people.

36. John Marshall, the Chief Justice of the Supreme Court, made a ruling in 1832. He agreed with the Indians and ordered the state of Georgia to stop. President Jackson refused to obey the court.

37. "Marshall made the decision," Jackson said. "Let him enforce it."

38. The Indian leaders were arrested and their homes were taken away. The *Phoenix* was closed down by U.S. soldiers.

39. In 1835 two Cherokees who were not elected leaders of the tribe signed a treaty with the federal government. That treaty arranged for the Indians to move away from Georgia. They were to be gone within two years.

40. Chief Ross said that the treaty was no good, because no elected leader had signed it. More than 16,000 Cherokees signed a **petition** (paper asking for something) asking that the treaty be cancelled. They sent it to the federal government, but President Jackson refused to see it.

41. Between 1836 and 1838 some Cherokees moved to the Oklahoma Territory. 15,000 remained in Georgia.

42. In May, 1838, 10,000 American troops were sent to Georgia. They were to remove the Cherokees from the land they had lived on for as long as anyone could remember.

43. The Indians were taken from their homes and farms and put into makeshift prisons until the trip west could begin. Many Indians got sick in the crowded prisons. White men, trying to make even more money from the Indians, sold them bad whiskey and food.

44. When the weather cooled, the move westward began. Groups of Indians were forced in chains to move first by flatboat and then on foot.

45. At times they traveled through deep snow. The Cherokees were not used to snow. They had only the clothing on their backs and were not able to keep warm.

46. Some of the Cherokees managed to escape to North Carolina and hid in the mountains. Their families still live there today.

47. More than 4,000, including Chief Ross' wife, died on the trip. Over one-fourth of the tribe died on the *Nuna-da-ut-sun'y*, the Trail Tears.

Understanding What You Read

1. Canals were _____ "rivers". (7)

2. The _____ Canal ran from Albany to Lake Erie, a distance of _____ miles. (8)

3. One idea that was brought from the west to the east was that_____

_____. (18)

4. The treaty between Spain and the United States in 1819 gave the United States

_____. (21)

5. The Cherokee Indians were not at all like Indians are shown on TV today. List a few ways in which they were different. (26,27)

_____

_____

_____

6. Many people think the Cherokees were treated unfairly by the white men. Do you agree or disagree? Reread the Spotlight on pgs. 157-158 before you answer. Explain your answer.

_____

_____

7. **Map Study:** Look at the map on pg. 155 and then answer the following questions:

   a. The _____ Canal, the _____ Canal and the
      _____ Canal connect the Great Lakes to the Ohio River.

   b. How many canals connect to the Ohio River? _____

   c. Which canal is farthest east? _____

   d. Which canal is farthest west? _____

8. **Word Search:** Find the hidden words listed in the puzzle below and circle them.

CANAL

SETTLERS

JOURNEY

ERIE

JACKSON

RIVER

FRONTIER

MARKET

WEST

INDIANS

SHOVEL

CHEROKEES

JOHN ROSS

```
A E B C D E J F G H I A
J R K L M N O O P Q R C
S I T U V W U X W Y Y H
S E T T L E R S E A J E
B C D D A E N F S C O R
R I V E R H E I T J H O
K K L N A O Y P O Q N K
C R T U M A R K E T R E
A Y J A C K S O N V O E
N S H O V E L P U W S S
A I N D I A N S Y Z S B
L B F R O N T I E R W C
```

Chapter 29
Life On The Frontier

1. The dictionary says the word "frontier" means "the edge of a country next to a wilderness where no people yet live".

2. The frontier of the United States was pushed westward time after time after the Revolutionary War. There was always a new place to make a home in the wilderness. And there were always men willing to risk whatever it took to bring "civilization" to the new land. (See the map below for early trails to the west.)

3. Modern Americans get their ideas about life on the American frontier from television and movies. They see Daniel Boone or Davy Crockett fighting against "bad guys", wild animals and Indians. The frontiersmen always win the fight.

4. In reality, life there was very rough and hard. Many people did not survive the hardship. Here are the words of a man who went to the Mississippi River Valley around 1820. He tells what he really saw. Some of his words have been changed to help you understand them better.

5. "When we look around this unsettled land and think that we are hundreds of miles from any law, it is a wonder that there are so few crimes around here.

6. "It is true that some backwoodsmen are gamblers, **swindlers** (cheats) and outlaws, but fewer than you might think. Most are good people trying to stay alive in a very rough land.

7. "The manners of the people who live here on the frontier are rough, as is their dress. The frontiersman wears a long beard. He and his family wear many bear and deer skins as clothing. Even furniture in the log homes is made of wood and animal skins.

8. "The man carries a knife wherever he goes. When in the woods he carries a rifle as well.

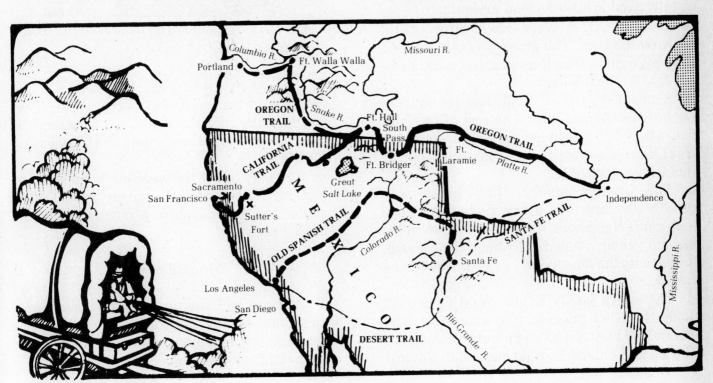

Early Western Trails

Even women and children use rifles with skill to keep off animals or Indians. When hunting or at home, the man usually travels with a pack of dogs.

9. "The people on the frontier need all of these things to stay alive. There are still bears, panthers and unfriendly Indians here. A person's life depends on how well he or she can use those things which civilized people might well run away from."

Frontier Settlements

10. A typical frontier settlement was started near a river. The river would provide transportation for the settlement.

11. First the frontier family would cut down some small trees. They used them to build a fence around the land they were going to clear.

12. Then the family would cut down all of the trees inside the fenced-in area. Often this took months. The trees were stripped of their bark and split in two. During this time the family usually lived in an open lean-to shelter.

13. Once the trees were down, grass would grow on the land. The grass was used to feed the cattle and other **livestock** (farm animals) brought by the family.

14. A small log cabin could then be built on part of the cleared land. The rest of the land was used for growing crops. The cut-down trees were used for building material and as fuel to heat the cabin.

15. The frontier family's first house was usually no more than a box made from trees and mud. Neighbors would come from miles around to help a new family build their house. In this way the house could go up in as little as two days.

16. The entire family would spend their days doing the work necessary to stay alive. The men would hunt, clear and plant the land. The women and children would make the clothing,

Life was rough and hard for travelers on the early trails to the west.

tend the crops, cook and carry water. They had to make sure the fire in the fireplace did not go out, and do any other work necessary for life.

17. The only fun of the week might be a trip on foot to a neighbor's house or to the local settlement for church or a meeting. It was a hard, rough life.

Mountain Men

18. As hard as living in a frontier community was, some men lived even harder lives in the mountains, trapping beaver and other animals. They were called **mountain men**.

19. A mountain man lived alone with only the animals and Indians for company. Most of them liked it that way. Some did not see other people for months on end.

20. They carried with them only their traps, and traveled on horses or small rafts along the rivers. They lived off the land, eating whatever they could find, often wild animal meat. There was constant danger from wild animals and from Indians. They also had to fight the cold and snow of the western winters.

21. Some of the mountain men became explorers and guides who opened up new territory for settlers. Jim Bridger, for example, was the first white man to see Utah's Great Salt Lake. He also helped another mountain man, Jed Smith, find the South Pass through the Rocky Mountains. That pass was later used by settlers moving from the east to California.

Mountain men explored and opened up new territory for settlers.

22. Bridger was also one of the great tellers of **tall tales** (stories that are too wild to be true) in American history. Sitting around at night, watching the campfire die out, Bridger would tell **tenderfeet** (those who had come to the wilderness for the first time) all sorts of half-true, half-fiction stories.

23. One of Bridger's favorite stories told of a lake near the Grand Canyon that was freezing cold at the bottom and boiling hot at the top. He told the tenderfeet that a person could catch a fresh fish at the bottom but by the time he got it out of the water it was cooked by the boiling water at top.

24. Davy Crockett was perhaps the most famous frontiersman of all. His real adventures in Congress and at the Alamo should have been enough for the life of any man, but not for Davy Crockett. He liked to **brag** (make things seem bigger and better) about what he could do. This was his favorite brag:

25. "I'm that same David Crockett, fresh from the backwoods, half-horse, half-alligator, a little touched with the snapping turtle. I can wade the Mississippi, leap the Ohio, ride upon a streak of lightning, and slip without a scratch down a honey locust (a very rough-barked tree).

26. "I can whip my weight in wild cats, and if any gentleman pleases, for a ten dollar bill, he may throw in a panther. I can hug a bear too close for comfort, and beat any man opposed to President Andy Jackson."

27. The frontiersmen and mountain men bragged, and lived tough lives. They also opened the wilderness to thousands of settlers who would follow in their tracks.

Spotlight On Our Folklore

28. Many of the stories from frontiersmen and mountain men have come down through history as our national **folklore** (traditional

stories, sayings, tales and songs about a nation and its people). Many of these folktales are passed from one generation to another by word of mouth.

29. Stories about **Paul Bunyan**, the giant north woodsman who was helped by a giant blue ox named Babe, are still heard today. It was said that Paul was able to fell whole forests of trees with his giant ax. The trees would then be pulled away by Babe.

30. Nobody knows for sure whether Bunyan really lived or not. There could have been a man of normal height who was really good at cutting down trees. Each time the story was told, he probably became bigger in the story until today he is known as a giant.

31. Many of the American folklore stories have to do with the making of natural landmarks, such as the Grand Canyon and the Great Lakes.

32. One story tells how the Great Lakes were made. The story goes that one day Babe decided to run away from Paul Bunyan. The ox ran north, heading for Canada.

33. When Bunyan got close to the Canadian border he did not want to go any further. He stopped and stamped his giant feet in anger. The force of his giant shoes formed the Great Lakes.

34. Babe came back when she saw how angry Bunyan was. The two shared a giant drink of water. They spilled out what was left from their waterskins and filled the Great Lakes with water.

35. Real people such as frontiersman Davy Crockett and flatboatman Mike Fink also are a part of our folklore. Not many people today believe that Crockett really killed a bear when he was only three. We don't believe that Mike Fink really used alligators to pull his boat up the Mississippi River. However, we have all heard and enjoyed these stories.

An old print shows pioneers traveling through the Rockies to the west.

Understanding What You Read

1. Life on the frontier was:
   a. easier than life in the east.
   b. very hard for all who lived there.
   c. fun for farmers.
   d. only for mountain men and frontiersmen.

   My answer is _____ . (4)

2. One man who traveled to the Mississippi River Valley thought that backwoodsmen and settlers were:
   a. rougher than they had to be.
   b. tough, but only because they had to be to live on the frontier.
   c. killers
   d. worse than wild animals and Indians.

   My answer is _____ . (6)

3. The word *frontier* means the _____
   _____ . (1)

4. Jim Bridger and Jed Smith found a pass through _____
   _____ which allowed settlers to move to _____ . (21)

5. Folklore is _____
   _____ . (28)

6. Two men who are real but have had folklore stories made up about them are _____
   _____ and _____ . (35)

7. Try to make up your own folklore story. Start with a hero who really lived and make up a story about him doing something really exciting. You might want to use a TV character or a sports hero. You could also make up a story about how some natural landmark was created by some

   long-ago hero. _____
   _____
   _____
   _____

8. **Map Study:** Look at the map on pg. 161 and then answer the following questions:

a. The city that was the starting point for both the Oregon and the Santa Fe trails was

_____ .

b. The trail that went south was _____ .

c. The Oregon Trail split in two at Fort Hall. Where did the two branches of the trail go?

_____

_____ .

d. The trail west that went the farthest north was the_____

_____ .

e. The Oregon Trail followed the _____ River, _____

River, and _____ River.

f. The Oregon Trail used the _____ Pass
to get through the Rocky Mountains.

g. The three cities at the end of the westward trails were _____ ,

_____ , and _____ .

h. Look at the part of the map which is shaded. To which country does this land belong?

_____

Chapter 30
Update To History

The questions on this page are written so you will think about the meaning of this history for today's Americans.

1. The War of 1812 has been called a "wasted war" because the United States did not really gain anything from the war. Compare the War of 1812 with recent wars in which our country has been involved. Did the United States gain anything? Explain your answer.

_____

_____

_____

_____

_____

_____

2. As America grew, the problem of sectionalism (people being loyal to their section of the country rather than to the nation as a whole) became greater. What problems did sectionalism cause in the 1800's? Do sectional loyalties still exist? How do they affect you?

_____

_____

_____

_____

_____

_____

3. It has often been said that Americans are a "restless people". Since the early days of the United States, Americans have moved around a great deal in the country. How do you think this "restlessness" would help a country grow? Do you see signs of restlessness around you in today's Americans? If so, how do you think it affects the way they live?

_____

_____

_____

_____

_____

_____

_____

Time Line Update: Complete the following time line for the entire unit. Begin with the Northwest Ordinance in 1785, and end with 1838, when troops were sent to Georgia to remove the Cherokees.

1785

1838

Unit 6
America In The Middle 1800's

Chapter 31
The Fight For Texas

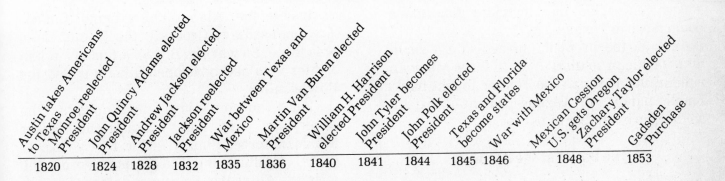

1820	1824	1828	1832	1835	1836	1840	1841	1844	1845	1846	1848	1853
Austin takes Americans to Texas	Monroe reelected President	John Quincy Adams elected President	Andrew Jackson elected President	Jackson reelected President	War between Texas and Mexico	Martin Van Buren elected President	William H. Harrison elected President	John Tyler becomes President	John Polk elected President	Texas and Florida become states	War with Mexico	Mexican Cession U.S. gets Oregon Zachary Taylor elected President	Gadsden Purchase

1. In 1820, the first American settlers came to Texas, which was then a part of northern Mexico. These first Americans came with a man named Moses Austin. Austin had received permission from Mexico to bring the Americans to Texas. They came to settle the area, to farm and to raise cattle.

2. A year later, in 1821, the people of Mexico rebelled against Spain and won their freedom.

3. Moses Austin died soon after he arrived in Texas. His son, Stephen Austin, carried on as leader of the Americans there. They had been allowed to come to Texas under certain rules. Only a limited number of settlers could come into Texas, and slavery was forbidden. The Mexicans also said that all the Americans coming to Texas had to become Roman Catholics.

4. Austin agreed, and by 1830, there were over 20,000 Americans living in the Texas section of Mexico.

5. After moving to Texas, many of the settlers refused to follow the Mexican rules. Many of them were Protestants and they didn't want to become Catholics. They did not want to become Mexican citizens.

6. The settlers also wanted to use slaves to

General Santa Anna led the Mexican army against the Americans in Texas.

169

farm their land, but slavery was against the law.

7. In 1830 the Mexicans began to get worried about the Americans in Texas. The Americans refused to obey the Mexican laws and said that Texas should become part of the United States. At that time the Mexican government ruled that no more Americans could move to Texas.

8. In 1835 the problems turned into a small war. Mexican soldiers tried to force Mexican rule on the Texans. The Texans fought back. Small bands of Texans fought Mexican soldiers in a number of battles.

The Battle of the Alamo

9. One of the most famous battles in American history was in February, 1836. The Mexican leader, **General Antonio Santa Anna,** crossed the Rio Grande River to fight the Americans. His 2,000 soldiers marched to the city of San Antonio where 188 Americans were holding out in an old Spanish mission church. The mission was called the **Alamo**.

10. Inside the Alamo were many famous Americans. Davy Crockett, the frontiersman was there. So was Jim Bowie, a famous Indian fighter who had developed a knife called the **Bowie knife.**

11. For thirteen days and nights the Americans held out against the larger Mexican force. Finally, after two weeks of brutal fighting, the Mexicans overran the mission. All of the American defenders were killed. "Remember the Alamo" became a

Mexican troops defeated Americans at the San Antonio mission called the Alamo.

170

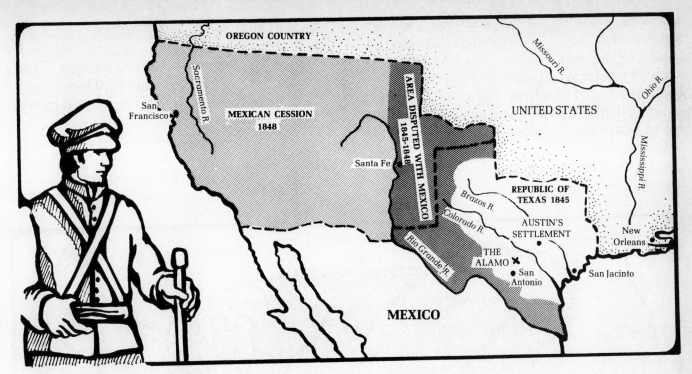

Texas and the Mexican Cession

saying of all Americans in Texas and many in the United States.

12. Two weeks later, at Goliad, Santa Anna fought another battle with Americans. He took 400 prisoners, and had them all killed.

13. On March 2, 1836, the Texans declared their freedom from Mexico. They called themselves the **Lone Star Republic. Sam Houston** was named the leader of the Texan army. He planned to continue the fight against the Mexicans.

14. The small Texan army did not do well against the larger, better-equipped, better-trained army of Santa Anna.

15. Then in April, 1836, Houston and the Texan army surprised the Mexican army near the San Jacinto River. The Americans won the battle.

16. Santa Anna was captured and forced to sign an agreement that Texas could be free of Mexico. As soon as he was let go, however, Santa Anna said he would not **recognize** (follow the rules of) the agreement.

Houston Goes To Washington

17. The Texans recognized it. They formed a government with Sam Houston as the president of the republic. The government sent Houston to Washington to ask that Texas be allowed to join the Union.

18. The leaders in Congress were not sure whether they wanted Texas as a state. First of all, taking Texas into the Union would cause problems with Mexico.

19. Secondly, the government was trying to keep a balance between **slave states** (states that allowed slavery) and **free states** (states that did not allow slavery.) Texas would surely become a slave state. Many Congressmen from free states did not want another slave state in the Union.

20. This argument in Congress went on for the next nine years. It was in March, 1845, that Congress took Texas into the Union as the 28th state.

21. As many people had thought, making

Texas a state made Mexico very angry. Mexico was also worried that the United States might want even more Mexican land, such as California. It still belonged to Mexico, but many Americans lived there.

22. President Polk sent some men to Mexico to try to settle the problem peacefully. He was willing to buy Texas and California from the Mexicans. The Mexicans refused to see the men Polk had sent.

capital of Mexico.

25. In February, 1848, a peace treaty was signed between the two nations. Texas became a part of the United States. The Rio Grande River was to be the border between the two nations.

26. The United States also got California and all of the land that was called New Mexico. (See the map on pg.171.) Mexico was paid 15 million dollars for the property. The United

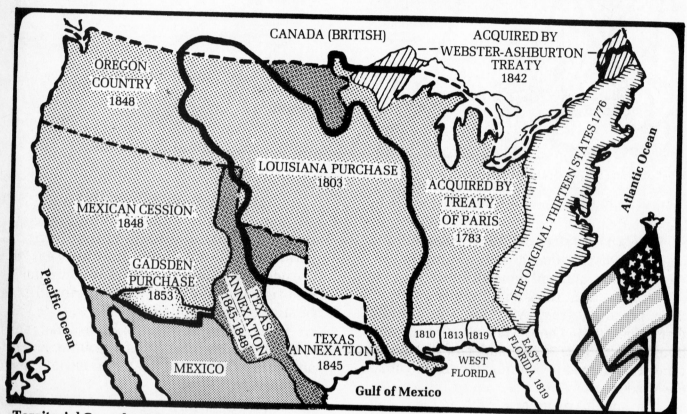

Territorial Growth of the United States

23. Both sides claimed the land between the Nueces River and the Rio Grande River as their own. It was there in 1846 that American and Mexican troops fought. Then Congress declared a war between the two nations.

24. The Mexican army was no match for the American army. In September, 1847, American troops captured Mexico City, the

States was now one nation from the Atlantic to the Pacific Ocean.

27. Twenty-eight years had passed since Austin first took settlers to Texas. Six Presidents, Adams, Jackson, Van Buren, Harrison, Tyler and Polk had held office during the long struggle between Texas and Mexico.

Spotlight On Manifest Destiny

28. Newspaper editors often write **editorials.** An editorial gives the editor's ideas and thoughts about different events that are happening. In 1845 an editor by the name of John Louis O'Sullivan wrote this editorial for his paper, the *Democratic Review:*

29. *"About the question of taking Texas into the Union . . . it is certain that other nations (Mexico) have come into the question without it being their business. They are trying to stop our power, limit our greatness, stop the completion of our Manifest Destiny to move across the nation given to us by heaven for our growing population."*

30. O'Sullivan was saying what many Americans were saying that year. They felt that it was America's **Manifest Destiny** (right) to take whatever land it wanted on the American continent to become part of the United States. Some people even went further, claiming that the lands of Canada and Latin America should be in the United States.

31. President Andrew Jackson had agreed with this idea. "We have a mission to extend the area of American freedom," President Jackson said when he was in office.

32. Not everyone agreed, however. "America already has more land than she could ever need," these people said. "Why should America seek more land in the west? Most of the land she now owns there is thinly settled. All the land between the Mississippi River and the Rocky Mountains is still completely empty."

33. But the westward movement continued. Many, like Editor O'Sullivan, saw the move westward as a patriotic duty of Americans. To make sure the United States kept the land won from Mexico, people had to live on it.

34. The Spanish and Mexicans still owned land on the American continent. The British were talking about claiming California for their own. Many Americans did not want this to happen.

35. Some saw the move westward as a religious act. "God gave us this land and we should populate all of it," one minister said.

36. Eventually, America's Manifest Destiny to hold all the land between the Atlantic and the Pacific Oceans came about. (See the map on pg. 172.)

37. Texas became a state in 1845. From 1845 to 1848 more land was **annexed** (taken) from the Mexicans. The Mexican Cession of 1848 gave the United States the New Mexico Territory, the Utah Territory and California.

38. In 1842 a treaty with England, the Webster-Ashburton Treaty, gave the United States some land around Lake Superior and in Maine. England gave much of Oregon to the United States in 1848. The last small piece of land to come to the United States was the Gadsden Purchase of 1853, a corner of New Mexico and Arizona.

39. By 1853 the United States of America had become a nation from sea to sea and Manifest Destiny had come true.

Understanding What You Read

1. **True Or False:** Decide if the following statements are true or false. If the statement is true, place a **T** in the correct answer space. If the statement is false, change the underlined word to make it true.

_____ a. <u>Mexico</u> said Austin could bring only a limited number of Americans to Texas. (3)

_____ b. All the American settlers in Texas had to become <u>Protestant</u> according to Mexican law. (3)

_____ c. One of the problems that arose between the Texans and the Mexicans was that the Americans wanted <u>slavery</u> to be allowed in that area. (6)

_____ d. The <u>Mexicans</u> were defeated at the Battle of the Alamo. (9-11)

_____ e. "Remember the Alamo" became a <u>Texas</u> saying. (11)

_____ f. The new Texas Republic was called the <u>Sam Houston</u> Republic. (13)

_____ g. Texas was the <u>25th</u> state to be admitted to the Union. (20)

_____ h. Texas became a state in <u>1845</u>. (20)

_____ i. The U.S. got Texas and <u>California</u> after the war with Mexico. (26)

_____ j. Many thought it was <u>Mexico's</u> Manifest Destiny to take over the whole continent. (30)

2. The Texan army captured Santa Anna in a battle at _____ _____ . (15-16)

3. By **Manifest Destiny**, Editor O'Sullivan meant that America had the right to _____

_____ . (30)

4. The main idea of the Spotlight is that:
   a. many people wanted the U.S. to take over Canada.
   b. many people thought it was all right for the U.S. to take whatever land it wanted on the continent.
   c. many people wanted another war with England.
   d. Mexico did not want the U.S. to take Texas.

My answer is _____ . (30)

174

5. **Map Skills:** Look at the map on pg. 171 and then answer the following questions:

   a. Austin's settlement was on the _____ River.

   b. The boundary between Texas and Mexico is the _____ River.

   c. The city of ____ _____ is on the Mississippi River.

6. **Map Skills:** Look at the map on pg. 172 and then answer the following questions:

   a. What was the largest piece of land the U.S. bought from another country? _____

   b. The U.S. owned all the land it now owns along the Pacific Ocean by the year _____ .

   c. The last piece of land on the east coast to become part of the U.S. was received by the

   _____ Treaty.

   d. The final piece of land added to the U.S. was _____ .

   e. The original thirteen colonies declared their independence in 1776. The United States

   received its last piece of land in _____ . How many years later was that? _____

Chapter 32
Events of 1848

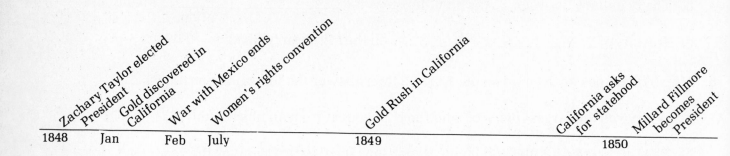

Zachary Taylor elected President
Gold discovered in California
War with Mexico ends
Women's rights convention
Gold Rush in California
California asks for statehood
Millard Fillmore becomes President

| 1848 | Jan | Feb | July | | 1849 | | 1850 |

1. Many important things happened in the year 1848. The war with Mexico ended. The United States got the rights to Oregon, and the land that was to become California, New Mexico, Arizona, Utah and Nevada.

2. In California, a man named John Marshall found gold at Sutter's Mill.

3. In Seneca Falls, New York, many American women held a meeting and demanded their independence.

4. The gold rush was certainly one of the most important events in American history. In the long run, however, what happened at Seneca Falls may have more lasting meaning for many Americans.

5. Women were not treated much better in 1848 than they had been treated in the colonies before the Revolutionary War. Women could not vote. They were not allowed to hold jobs. Most colleges would not allow women to enter. They were supposed to stay at home, taking care of the house and children.

6. Not all women were happy with that lot in life. Two women, **Elizabeth Cady Stanton** and **Lucretia Coffin Mott,** decided that it was time for a women's rights movement.

7. They called for a convention to be held at Seneca Falls, New York. Women came from all over the east to take part.

8. At the convention the women talked about what they wanted from life. They talked about the problems they had.

9. Discussion was often heated. It was plain that the women were angry at the way American women were being treated by men.

10. Before leaving, the women at the convention wrote and published a **Declaration of Independence for Women**. It said, in part:

11. *We hold this truth to be understood by all, that all men and women are created equal.*

12. *The history of mankind is a history of repeated wrongs against women. Here is the evidence that what we say is true:*

   *Man has never allowed woman to vote.

   *He has not allowed her to work at good jobs.

   *He has not allowed her to get a college education.

   *He has not allowed her an equal position in either government or the church.

13. *Therefore, it is the right of all women to fight for those rights which we have not been granted.*

14. The Seneca Falls Declaration of Independence was not taken seriously by many people. However, it was the beginning of the movement that led to women getting the right to vote. The same movement is even stronger today, working for completely equal rights. (For more on the Seneca Falls Convention, see the Spotlight for this chapter.)

18. People gave up everything they were doing to rush to the area where gold had been found. They hoped to find gold and become rich themselves.

19. All over the nation, stores closed down. Families broke up. Schools closed, as both teachers and their students left for the gold fields.

20. The people who rushed to California to seek their fortunes in the gold fields were called **forty-niners** because of the year, 1849.

21. People had, of course, gone west before the forty-niners. They had gone to find new land and a new way of life. Now the search for gold made thousands of people head west.

22. Getting to California was not easy. Most people traveled the shortest, most direct way—overland. They went in wagons, usually grouped with others in **wagon trains**. The

Thousands of people headed west in wagon trains.

Gold Rush

15. In 1848 what was happening in California seemed much more important than the women's convention in Seneca Falls.

16. In January of that year some men were building a new sawmill near what is now Sacramento, California. John Marshall was in charge of the building work. He was walking along the stream leading to the mill when he came across some yellow stones in the stream. He had them tested. They were gold.

17. California was thousands of miles from the rest of the United States. It took almost a year for the news about finding the gold to get to the east. When the news did arrive, the "gold fever" hit hard. Soon, people from all parts of the United States were heading for California.

Some ships went around South America to California carrying passengers to the west during the Gold Rush.

wagons were pulled by horses, mules or oxen. By traveling together, the forty-niners had support, company and protection.

23. Most of the wagon trains left from St. Louis, Missouri, about half-way between the Atlantic Ocean and the Pacific. (Look back at the map on pg. 161 in Chapter 29.)

24. Unlike today, when a trip from St. Louis to California would take only a few hours by air or a few days by car or train, the trip in 1849 could take months. There were many problems and dangers in using this overland route.

25. Weather was one problem. Travelers leaving St. Louis too early in the spring might be bogged down in muddy roads as the snow thawed and melted.

26. Those who left too late in the year would reach the passes through the mountains after the first snow had fallen. When snow was on the ground, the mountain passes could not be used. Many people died from exposure or starvation when their wagons became stuck in snow in the high mountains.

27. Indians who were hostile to white settlers often attacked the wagon trains heading west. Many also died trying to cross the wide, hot, waterless desert. Yet thousands braved the dangers of this route for a chance at easy riches.

28. Others took the longer but safer route by ship from the east coast to California. Some ships went all the way around South America to California. Others would drop their

Gold diggers lived in crowded mining camps.

passengers on the east coast of Panama. The forty-niners would then go overland to the west coast of Panama, where they would be picked up by another ship. This second ship would take them to California.

29. All of the people who joined the travels of the forty-niners to California expected to come home rich. Most did not find any gold. Many went home poorer but wiser. Others stayed in California, opening up shops or starting farms.

30. The life of the gold miners was unlike any the easterners had ever seen. Here's a description of what it was like by a man who went to the gold fields of California in 1849:

31. "Most of what were called houses were made of paper or whatever else the miners could find to shelter them from the rain and wind. They gave such names to their 'towns' as Poker Flat, Hangtown, Skunk Gulch, Red Dog and Dry Diggings.

32. "Rooms in the regular boarding houses rented for $1,000 a month. Eggs were $10 a dozen. The only people getting rich on the gold fields were the people who sold goods to the miners.

33. "Mixed together in these camps were Missouri farmers, New York teachers, Georgia crackers, English shopkeepers, and Mexican peons. There were also **heathens** (people who do not believe in God) and assorted murderers and other criminals."

34. Thousands of these people from very different walks of life stayed on in California. Before the Gold Rush, there had been only a few settlers in California.

35. By 1850, there were enough people living in the territory to apply for statehood. Their application for statehood touched off one of the angriest arguments ever in Congress. You will read about it in the next chapter.

Women met in Seneca Falls, New York for the first women's rights convention.

Spotlight On The Seneca Falls Convention

36. The first women's rights convention did not get off to a very promising start.

37. The convention was to be held on July 19 and 20, 1848. The women were promised the use of the Wesleyan Chapel in Seneca Falls, New York. A large number of women from New England and the east coast had come.

38. When the women got to the chapel, they found it locked. Nobody, the minister included, seemed to be able to find the key.

39. Many of the women angrily yelled at the minister. They were sure he had "lost" the key because of the large number of women who had come to the meeting.

40. A small boy took care of the problem. He crawled into the chapel and opened the door

for the angry women. So began the first meeting in U.S. history called to discuss equal rights for women.

41. Once inside, the women were not sure how to get started. James Mott, the husband of one of the women who had called for the convention, took over. His wife, Lucretia Mott, gave the opening address.

42. The women voted to issue a Declaration of Independence for Women. (See pg. 176.) The Declaration was a ringing reminder of all the wrongs done to women, but few took it seriously.

43. "It was a hens' convention," one newspaper reporter wrote. "Women were trying to crow like roosters."

44. "They are trying to put men into petticoats and set them to do the dishes," wrote another.

45. Women's rights leaders like Elizabeth Cady Stanton did not give up the fight. She was not used to giving up anything. Born to a family of five daughters and one son, she saw her brother get all the schooling and attention. He then died at an early age.

46. Elizabeth decided to get an education. She went to a minister and begged him to teach her Greek. She did so well that the minister praised her to her father.

47. "She should have been a boy," was all her father would say.

Later Conventions

48. Elizabeth Stanton, Lucretia Mott and others continued the fight. Each year after Seneca Falls the women held a convention in a different city. Often large crowds would come to hear them.

49. Most often the women were laughed at by many men and the press. This didn't matter to them. They kept going, and soon many respected men joined their fight.

50. While women were not allowed to vote for another 72 years (in 1920), the Seneca Falls Convention was the first step in a long journey that is still going on today.

Understanding What You Read

1. Which of the following things did **not** happen in the year 1848?
   a. the Women's Declaration of Independence
   b. the end of the war with Mexico
   c. Texas becoming a state
   d. discovery of gold in California

   My answer is _____ . (1-3)

2. The women meeting in Seneca Falls said that:
   a. women are better than men.
   b. men should do all the housework.
   c. women and men are created equal and should be treated equally.
   d. only men should be allowed to travel to the gold fields.

   My answer is _____ . (11)

3. The real importance of the Gold Rush was that:
   a. many people got rich.
   b. new overland routes from New York to California were found.
   c. enough people went to California to allow it to apply for statehood.
   d. women got their rights.

   My answer is _____ . (35)

4. The first gold strike in California was made at _____ . (2)

5. Two leaders of the first women's rights convention held in Seneca Falls were _____

   _____ and _____ _____ . (6)

6. List some of the things the women at Seneca Falls were angry about. (12)

   _____

   _____

7. Some of the problems the forty-niners faced in traveling overland to California were

   _____ (25) and _____ . (27)

8. Two routes to the gold fields of California were _____ (22) from

   St. Louis to California, and by _____ around the tip of
   South America. (28)

9. Many people did not get rich trying to find gold in California. Some went home poor. Others stayed and opened _____ or started _____ . (29)

10. **Word Skills:** Solve the puzzle below using the clues provided.

Puzzle Clues

Across

1. _ _ _ _ would close the passes across the Rockies.
3. a baby cow
6. _ _ what!
7. The Seneca Falls Declaration asked for _ _ _ _ _ _ _   _ _ _ _ _ _ .
8. Some people in the gold rush towns lived in a _ _ _ _ _ made of paper.

Down

2. Many people traveled by _ _ _ _ _ train.
3. the territory the forty-niners went to
4. a person who searched for gold was called a _ _ _ _ _ _   _ _ _ _ _ _ .
5. one event of 1848
6. The women's convention was held at _ _ _ _ _ _ Falls.

182

Chapter 33
The Compromise Of 1850

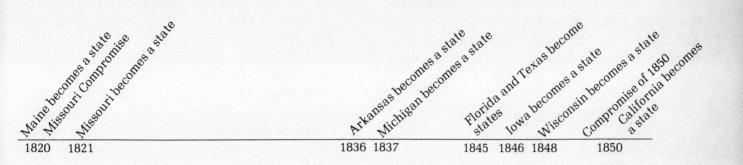

Maine becomes a state
Missouri Compromise
Missouri becomes a state
Arkansas becomes a state
Michigan becomes a state
Florida and Texas become states
Iowa becomes a state
Wisconsin becomes a state
Compromise of 1850
California becomes a state

1820 1821   1836 1837   1845 1846 1848   1850

1. The Gold Rush had brought many new people to California. Enough people were there for the territory to apply for statehood in 1850.

2. Some men in Congress were not sure that they wanted California to become a state. Others thought that California should become a state as soon as possible.

3. The question, whether California should become a state, started such an argument that it would one day lead to war.

4. The argument was about whether California should be a slave or a free state. A slave state was one that allowed slavery within its borders. A free state did not allow slavery within its borders.

5. This was not the first time the question had come up in Congress. The argument over slave and free states had begun in 1819. To understand that argument, let's look at what happened from 1819 to 1850.

6. In 1819 Missouri asked to become a state. Most of the settlers in Missouri had come from the slave states of the south. They wanted Missouri to become a slave state as well, so that they could use slaves to do their farm work.

7. Congressmen from the north did not want another slave state admitted to the Union. They refused to admit Missouri unless it came into the Union as a free state.

8. The same year Maine also asked to be admitted to the Union. An agreement, called the **Missouri Compromise**, was reached. (A compromise is a way to settle an argument when both sides give in a little to get a part of what they want.)

9. In this compromise Missouri was allowed to come into the Union as a slave state. Maine was allowed to come as a free state.

10. Congress also drew an imaginary line across the middle of the United States, running from the east coast to the Pacific. (See the map on pg. 184.) The line separated slave states from free states.

11. Any new state entering the Union that was south of that line could have slavery if it wished. Any state north of that line would have to come into the Union as a free state.

12. Maine became a state in 1820, Missouri in 1821. For the next fifteen years, no states entered the Union.

13. From 1836 to 1850 six states were admitted to the Union: Arkansas (1836); Michigan (1837); Florida and Texas (1845); Iowa (1846) and Wisconsin (1848). All of these states came under the rules of the Missouri Compromise. Arkansas, Florida and Texas were slave states. Michigan, Iowa and Wisconsin were free states.

Testing The Compromise

14. California asked to be admitted to the Union in 1850 while Millard Fillmore was President. The Missouri Compromise would be tested. The California territory was split almost in half by the Missouri Compromise line. Half of the territory was south of the line, half was north. Should California come into the Union as a free state or a slave state?
15. A bill was introduced in Congress that said any land received from Mexico could not become part of a slave state. That would have made California a free state.

16. Many southern Congressmen said that their states would leave the Union if such a bill was passed by Congress. The argument got so bad that some Congressmen went to Congress armed with Bowie knives or with pistols.
17. Henry Clay, the man who had worked out the Missouri Compromise, came out of **retirement.** That is, he came back to work. He wanted to try to work out another compromise, so California could come into the Union. He worked out the **Compromise of 1850.**
18. The north got its way on California. That territory would enter the Union as a free state. In addition, the selling and buying of slaves was outlawed in Washington, D.C. People who lived in Washington could, however, still own slaves.
19. The south also got a lot from the compromise. Some of the land received from Mexico was broken up into two states—New Mexico and Utah. The people in those states

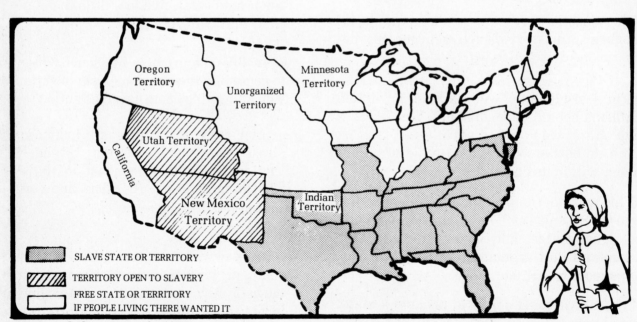

Free and Slave States in 1850

would be allowed to decide for themselves whether they wanted slavery or not.

20. The south got a law it very much wanted. That law was called the **Fugitive Slave Law.** It said that any slaves escaping from the south to freedom in the north should be returned to their masters if caught.

21. The south wanted that law because many slaves were escaping to freedom in northern cities. The new law made it easier for the southern plantation owners to get their runaway slaves back.

22. Any person acting for the slaveowner could take a slave back to the south. Men, called **bounty hunters,** because they received a **bounty** (pay) for each slave returned, went north to look for escaped slaves.

23. Any black person could be picked up on a street in the north, identified by a bounty hunter, and taken to the south. The black person had no right under the law to prove who he or she really was.

24. Many free blacks came close to being sent into slavery by bounty hunters who brought back the wrong man. Some did, in fact, become slaves this way.

25. Any citizen might be told by the bounty hunter to help capture a runaway slave. If the person did not help, then he or she could also be punished under the law.

26. The Compromise of 1850 pleased people from both the north and the south. The compromise kept the nation from splitting apart over the question of slavery for at least the next eleven years.

Spotlight On Slavery

27. By the time California became a state, slavery had been used in the Americas for over 200 years. Slavery had become of major importance to the south. Many slaves were needed to work on the cotton and tobacco plantations. These large plantations could

Slaves were sold in open markets to the highest bidder.

never have been run without the cheap labor of black slaves.

28. The first black slaves had been brought to the Jamestown Colony in Virginia in 1619 by the Dutch. Most of the colonies used slaves from 1619 to the 1750's.

29. The northeastern states, however, made a great deal of money from slavery. Rum was shipped from New England to Africa where it was sold or exchanged for slaves. Most of the slaves were then taken to the islands of the West Indies. They were traded for molasses there. The molasses was sold in New England to make more rum. The New Englanders also brought some slaves to the United States. This was repeated over and over again.

30. Slowly, however, the north rid itself of slaves. The climate and type of work in the north did not fit the African slaves as well as the climate and type of work in the south. The number of slaves in the south increased.

31. In the year 1790 the north had about 40,000 slaves, the south about 650,000. By 1850 the number of slaves in the south had grown to more than 3,000,000.

Slaves worked long, hard hours
on cotton and tobacco plantations.

32. At that time in the north there were only about 250 slaves. They had mostly come to the north with their masters. The rest of the blacks living in the north were free. Many had run away from southern plantations.

33. Slaveowners in the south claimed that blacks were not as good as whites. They said that the slaves were happy living on the plantations. They were given food and clothing. That was all they needed to be happy, so the slaveowners thought.

34. Slaves were treated very differently from one plantation to the next. Some were treated better than others, but some were treated very cruelly.

35. Some slaves worked inside the houses. They cooked, cleaned and cared for the children of the white family who owned the plantation.

36. These slaves were generally better cared for than those who worked in the fields, picking cotton and tobacco.

37. The blacks who worked in the fields often worked from before sunrise to after sunset. They lived in dirt-floored huts.

38. Their pay for long hours of work was almost nothing. Ex-slave Frederick Douglass described it as "eight pounds of pork or fish each month for food, one pint of salt and a bushel of corn."

39. Some slaves worked in factories in big cities, such as Atlanta and New Orleans. They were paid no money for this and worked long, hard hours inside hot buildings.

40. By the 1830's some people began to speak out against the hard life slaves had to lead. By the time of the Compromise of 1850 people in all the free states were speaking out against slavery. Because slavery was so important to the south, people there would not listen.

Understanding What You Read

1. A compromise is_____

   _____ . (8)

2. The Missouri Compromise of 1820 allowed _____ to enter the Union

   as a free state and _____ to enter as a slave state. (9)

3. The six states admitted to the Union between 1836 and 1850 were:

   _____ , _____ , _____ ,

   _____ , _____ , and _____

   _____ . (13)

4. When California asked to be admitted to the Union, the Missouri Compromise was tested

   because half of California was in _____ territory and half was in_____

   territory. (14)

5. Under the Compromise of 1850, the state of_____

   came into the Union as a free state. (18)

6. Under the Compromise of 1850, the south got a promise that two new states, _____

   and _____ , could decide for themselves

   whether they wanted slavery or not (19) and a new _____

   law. (20)

7. The Fugitive Slave Law said that runaway slaves _____

   _____ . (20)

8. Any citizen who did not help a bounty hunter could be _____

   _____ . (25)

9. The first slaves were brought to the _____ Colony by the Dutch in

   _____ . (28)

10. Most slaves who worked in the fields of the south worked from _____

_____ . (37)

11. **Map Study:** Look at the map on pg. 184 and then answer the following questions:

a. Most of the slave states were in the _____ .

b. The free states were in the _____ .

c. The territories that were to be free were _____ ,

_____ , and _____ .

d. The territory that was to be slave was _____ .

e. On the map there are _____ slave states.

f. The territories that were neither slave nor free, but were open to slavery if the people who

lived there wanted it, were _____ , and

_____ .

Chapter 34
Abolition And Rebellion

Nat Turner's rebellion
The Liberator is published
National Antislavery Society formed

Uncle Tom's Cabin written

1831   1833   1852

1. Many people in the United States, mostly in the southern states, wanted to believe that slaves were happy on the plantations. This was not true. A number of events in the early and middle 1800's showed people how unhappy the slaves were.

2. Slaves sometimes ran away from their plantations. Others decided to stay where they were and fight against their masters.

3. Two of the most famous slaves who decided to fight were **Denmark Vesey** and **Nat Turner.**

4. Vesey planned a major slave **rebellion** (fight against owners) near Charleston, South Carolina in 1822. The plan was soon found out by the slaveowners. They quickly put a stop to both the rebellion and Vesey.

5. Nat Turner's rebellion turned out differently from Vesey's. In 1831 Turner led the largest slave uprising in U.S. history. By the time it ended, more than 60 whites and 100 slaves, including Turner, were dead. (For more on the Nat Turner Rebellion, see the Spotlight at the end of the chapter.)

6. The slave rebellions worried the plantation owners. Slaves were valuable property. In 1790 a good field hand had been worth about $300. By 1860 the price rose to nearly $2,000.

7. After the rebellions, armed guards rode the roads of the south each night. Large attack dogs ran at their sides. Any slave found on the road at night was punished unless he had a signed pass from his master.

8. Southerners **defended** slavery (said it was a good thing) in the newspapers and in books as well. They defended it even from the pulpits of southern churches.

9. Many religious southerners believed that the Bible approved of slavery. They pointed to the Old Testament where the use of slaves was often mentioned.

10. They argued that slaves were better off on the plantations than workers in northern factories. Slaves were given free food, clothing, shelter, and medical care, the slaveowners said.

11. They argued that slaves were just not as good as the white man, and that they were as "happy as human beings could be" working on the plantations.

The Abolitionists

12. Other voices were raised in the land. Those voices belonged to people called **abolitionists.** The word **abolish** means to do away with. The abolitionists wanted to do away with slavery.

13. There were many people who had been against slavery for many years. However, it wasn't until the early 1830's that some Americans began to speak out in public against slavery.

14. In 1831 a Boston (Massachusetts) newspaper called *The Liberator* was published. The editor of the paper was an abolitionist by the name of William Lloyd Garrison.

15. Garrison used the newspaper to tell Congress and the world that slavery must be abolished. He called on Congress to free all the slaves and make slavery against the law.

16. Others joined Garrison in his battle against slavery. They believed that no person should ever be allowed to own another person.

17. In 1833 Garrison and others formed the National Antislavery Society.

18. The society published books and papers about slavery. Many of the members traveled around the nation, speaking out against slavery.

19. The abolitionists helped rescue thousands of slaves from the south through the **Underground Railroad** system.

20. The Underground Railroad was not really a railroad nor underground. It was a chain of homes and farms where escaped slaves could go for help. The escaped slaves were secretly taken from one "depot" on the railroad to another until they reached freedom in the north.

21. The abolitionists refused to obey the

Abolitionists helped thousands of slaves from the south through the Underground Railroad system.

190

Fugitive Slave Law that was passed by Congress as part of the Compromise of 1850. That law forced the Underground Railroad to send the escaped slaves further north, to Canada. Once in Canada, the slaves could finally be free.

22. One slave came north a more interesting way. His name was "Box" Brown. Brown mailed himself to the home of an abolitionist in the north. Later he became free, after the abolitionists got him to Canada.

23. Many free ex-slaves took part in the Underground Railroad and in the abolitionist movement. Perhaps the most well-known of these was Frederick Douglass.

24. Douglass was born a slave. He taught himself how to read and write. He ran away to the north.

Harriet Tubman led hundreds of slaves to freedom on the underground railroad.

25. He wrote and told of his life as a slave. He gave **lectures** (speeches) to groups of abolitionists all around the country. He told the truth about slavery.

26. Douglass' voice and the voices of other ex-slaves, such as Sojourner Truth, made people in the north realize just how bad slavery was. They helped to show people that a slave's life on the plantation was not as the slaveowners had said.

27. Another black woman who helped the abolitionists was Harriet Tubman. She personally guided more than 300 slaves to freedom along the Underground Railroad, often at great risk to herself. She would have been killed if she had been caught.

Uncle Tom's Cabin

28. The real push against slavery began with a book, *Uncle Tom's Cabin*. It was written by Harriet Beecher Stowe.

29. Harriet Beecher Stowe lived in Hartford, Connecticut. Her father was a leading abolitionist. She had visited a plantation in Kentucky when she was younger. After seeing this, she decided to write a book about the cruelty of slavery.

30. *Uncle Tom's Cabin* was published in 1852. It was an immediate best-seller in the north. It was made into a play and drew large audiences wherever it played in the north. Many northerners got their ideas about slavery from reading the book or seeing the play.

31. The book was about a cruel slaveowner named Simon Legree. He mistreated all the slaves on his plantation. But, most of all, he mistreated a young black slave, and Uncle Tom, an older slave.

32. Tom tried to be as nice as he could to Legree. The nicer he was, the more he was punished. Legree whipped and killed poor old Uncle Tom.

Northerners got their ideas about slavery from seeing the play based on the book *Uncle Tom's Cabin*.

33. People who saw the play booed Legree and cheered noble Uncle Tom. They believed that slavery must be bad if it could kill a nice old man like him. The book was **banned** (not allowed) in the southern states. Nobody was allowed to read it or see the play.

34. In the north it was given away by members of the new Republican Party who were running for office. They were against slavery spreading into new states.

35. *Uncle Tom's Cabin* heated up the nation as no other work had since Thomas Paine's *Common Sense* before the Revolutionary War.

36. Not all northerners agreed with the abolitionists. Garrison and Frederick Douglass were beaten by mobs who did not like their speeches about the equality of blacks. Many northerners turned in runaway slaves for the reward.

37. Many northern workers were afraid that blacks would take their jobs. Others believed that if the slaves in the south were freed they would all come to the north and start riots.

38. Slavery was an issue people felt they had to take sides on. Many were for it. Many were against it. No one could forget it.

Spotlight On Nat Turner

39. Nat Turner led what was perhaps the best known of the slave uprisings in the south. It certainly was the largest.

Nat Turner led a large slave uprising against southern plantation owners.

40. In 1831 Turner brought together some other slaves. He convinced them that he had been sent by God to lead them out of slavery.

41. After the uprising Turner hid for six weeks. He was finally tracked down by dogs. When he was caught he gave a confession to his lawyer. Here, in modern language, is some of what he had to say:

42. "We gathered at the home of my master, Mr. Travis. We decided that we would spare nobody, not children nor women. Everyone white was to be killed.

43. "We broke into the Travis house and stole the guns. I decided that, as the leader, I had to spill the first blood. Armed with a hatchet, I entered my master's bedroom. It was dark and I missed with my first blow. My master yelled to his wife. One of the other slaves finished him with a blow from an ax, while I killed his wife where she lay.

44. "We killed all five members of the family in no more than a minute's time. We forgot the infant in its crib, but Will went back and finished the job."

45. Slaveowners fought back. Many of Turner's men were killed. Many slaves who did not even know of Turner or his uprising were also killed.

46. Nat Turner was tried, found guilty and hanged. Turner's bold uprising struck fear into the south. Never again could they be sure that the black people living on their plantations were going to obey them, or even let them live.

Understanding What You Read

1. **True Or False:** Decide if the following statements are true or false. If the statement is true, place a **T** in the correct answer space. If the statement is false, change the underlined word to make it true.

_____ a. Two slaves who started slave uprisings were <u>Nat Turner</u> and Denmark Vesey. (3)

_____ b. Slaveowners defended slavery by saying that the <u>Bible</u> stated it was all right to have slaves. (9)

_____ c. People called <u>abolitionists</u> were against slavery. (12)

_____ d. The Underground Railroad helped take slaves to the <u>south</u>. (20)

_____ e. <u>Frederick Douglass</u> wrote *Uncle Tom's Cabin*. (28)

_____ f. *Uncle Tom's Cabin* was banned in the <u>north</u>. (33)

_____ g. <u>Nat Turner's</u> slave uprising left many whites dead. (43-49)

2. In the year _____ Nat Turner led the largest slave uprising in history. In it more than

   _____ whites and _____ slaves died. (5)

3. Southerners tried to defend slavery in _____ , _____ and

   in _____ . (8) They argued that slaves were better off than workers in

   _____ factories. (10) They were given free _____ , _____ ,

   _____ , and _____ _____ . (10)

4. The abolitionists wanted to do away with _____ . (12) They formed the

   _____ _____ Society in 1833. (17)

5. The Underground Railroad was a chain of _____ and _____ where escaped slaves were taken. (20)

6. Because of the Fugitive Slave Law, the abolitionists had to send slaves further north to

   _____ . (21)

7. One black woman, _____ _____ , helped more than 300 slaves to escape. (27)

8. The Republican Party was against_____
_____. (34)

9. In the space below, match the numbers in Column **B** with the names in Column **A**.

Column A

_____ a. William Lloyd Garrison (14)

_____ b. Box Brown (22)

_____ c. Frederick Douglass (23-25)

_____ d. Harriet Tubman (27)

_____ e. Harriet Beecher Stowe (28-30)

_____ f. Simon Legree (31-32)

_____ g. Nat Turner (39-46)

_____ h. Sojourner Truth (26)

Column B

1. wrote *Uncle Tom's Cabin*

2. killed Uncle Tom

3. edited *The Liberator*

4. guided more than 300 people on the Underground Railroad

5. ex-slave writer and speaker

6. mailed himself to freedom

7. ex-slave woman abolitionist

8. led famous slave rebellion

Chapter 35
Update To History

The questions on this page are written so you will think about the meaning of this history for today's Americans.

1. The idea of Manifest Destiny — that the United States had a right to all the land in America— was popular with some people and unpopular with others. How might America be different today if the British, French and Mexicans still owned sections of the country? We also took land from the Native American population. Was this fair to them? How do you think we should have treated the Native Americans?

_____

_____

_____

_____

_____

_____

2. The women's movement began in Seneca Falls, New York, in 1848. Read again (pg. 176) what women wanted at that convention. Which things that women wanted in 1848 do women now have? Which things do they not have? Do you agree with the aims of the women's movement today? Why? Why not?

_____

_____

_____

_____

_____

_____

3. What effect did the Missouri Compromise and the Compromise of 1850 have on today's America? How might things have been different in today's America if those two compromises had not been made?

_____

_____

_____

_____

_____

_____

_____

4. The fact that most black Americans first came to this nation as slaves had had a deep effect on the history of America. How does this still affect America today? How does it affect you as an individual person?

_____

_____

_____

_____

_____

_____

_____

Time Line Update: In the space below make a time line for the entire period this unit covers. Start with 1820 and end with the Compromise of 1850.

1820 _____ 1850

Unit 7
A Nation Divides

Chapter 36
The Break Widens

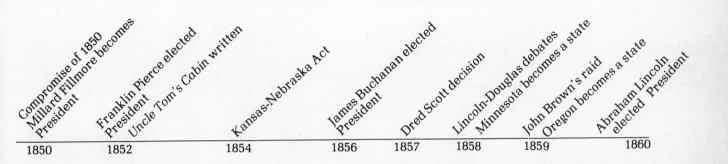

| 1850 | 1852 | 1854 | 1856 | 1857 | 1858 | 1859 | 1860 |

Compromise of 1850 / Millard Fillmore becomes President — 1850

Franklin Pierce elected President / *Uncle Tom's Cabin* written — 1852

Kansas-Nebraska Act — 1854

James Buchanan elected President — 1856

Dred Scott decision — 1857

Lincoln-Douglas debates / Minnesota becomes a state — 1858

John Brown's raid / Oregon becomes a state — 1859

Abraham Lincoln elected President — 1860

1. The Compromise of 1850 helped to bring California into the Union. On the other hand, it did little to quiet the argument over slavery.

2. Abolitionists in the north continued to ask Congress to do away with slavery and free all the slaves. Southerners continued to defend slavery. They pointed out that slaves were needed to work the plantations, which supplied cotton to the northern factories.

3. People in northern states were angry that the Fugitive Slave Law forced citizens to help bounty hunters. (See Chapter 33, pg. 185.) Many of the northern states passed laws of their own saying that state officers could not help capture runaway slaves. These state laws were in direct conflict with the federal law.

4. Captured slaves were often held in local jails waiting to be taken south. In many cases, mobs of abolitionists helped free those slaves.

The Kansas-Nebraska Act

5. In 1854 the argument over slavery became part of the American political scene again. At this time Franklin Pierce was President.

6. Congress wanted to open up the area west of Missouri and Iowa so that a railroad could be built across America. The railroad would start either at St. Louis, Missouri or at Chicago, Illinois. In either case, the railroad would go west to California.

7. Before the railroad could be built, the land over which the railroad was to run had to be settled. That meant Congress had to decide whether the territory it would pass through would be free or slave.

8. Senator Stephen Douglas from Illinois was one of the men pushing for the new railroad. He introduced a bill called the **Kansas-Nebraska Act.** The act, which was passed by Congress, created two new states out of the land the railroad would travel over. The two new states were Kansas and Nebraska.

9. The Kansas-Nebraska Act also **repealed** (did away with) the Compromise of 1850. That compromise had said that there could be no slave states north of an imaginary line which divided the nation roughly in half.

10. The Kansas-Nebraska Act gave the people of those two states the right to choose whether they wanted slavery or not. It did not matter that they were both north of that line.

11. Many northerners were angry about the law. They were afraid that there would be two more slave states in the Union.

12. Most southerners were happy about the act. They saw it as a victory for the idea that Congress could not forbid slavery anywhere in the Union.

13. The north wanted to make sure the two states became free states. The south wanted to make sure the two states became slave states. Both sides took steps to help the states go their way.

14. Northern abolitionists formed the **Emigrant Aid Society.** The society found people who believed that Kansas should be a free state. They gave those people money, wagons, guns, and supplies. Then they sent those settlers into Kansas.

15. The southerners who wanted Kansas to become a slave state formed a group called the **Blue Lodge.** This group paid armed settlers to move from Missouri into Kansas.

Bleeding Kansas

16. The fight between the pro-slavery and anti-slavery forces in Kansas became an open war in 1855. It was called **Bleeding Kansas** because there were bloody battles all over the state.

17. Both sides formed governments. Each demanded that Congress declare it the real government of the state of Kansas.

18. Congress did not want to act too quickly. There would be a Presidential election in 1856. Congress wanted to see what the new President would do to quiet down the war.

19. Slavery became the big issue in the election of 1856. The Whig party had been one of the strongest political parties in the country. At this time it split in two because of the argument over slavery.

20. The Whigs could not agree on how the party should stand on slavery. The Whigs who were in favor of slavery became the American Party. The Whigs who were against slavery became the Republican Party. The major

The fight between pro-slavery and anti-slavery forces led to a bloody war in Kansas.

party against both the American and Republican Parties was the Democratic Party.

21. The Presidential election of 1856 was won by a Democrat, James Buchanan. The Democrats were able to win by taking all the southern states.

22. In March, 1857, the new President gave a speech. He said that the question of slavery had to be left to the Supreme Court.

The Dred Scott Case

23. The court did not take long in answering the President's wish. Their answer came in a court decision in the case of **Dred Scott against Sanford.**

24. Dred Scott was a slave. He had been brought by his master from Missouri, a slave

Abolitionists saw the Dred Scott case as a good test of slavery.

Justice Roger Taney said. He had no such right because he was property, not a person.

28. The founders of the United States did not intend for blacks to become citizens, the court said. Therefore, because they were not citizens, they did not have the right to sue.

29. Then the court went even further. It said that any act of Congress or of any state which did anything against slavery was **unconstitutional** (against the Constitution and therefore not allowed). The court said that such a law would take away a slaveowner's right to own property.

30. Many northern Republicans decided not to obey the court's decision. "It holds no more weight than a decision made in any barroom," said one Republican.

31. The south, on the other hand, was happy that the Supreme Court had ruled in favor of slavery. The leaders of southern states told northern leaders that the ruling must be obeyed or the south would think about leaving the Union.

Lincoln-Douglas Debates

32. In 1858 another important election was held. This election was not for President of the United States, but to elect a Senator from Illinois. The election was important to the nation because of the two men who were running for that office.

33. One of the candidates was Stephen Douglas, the man who introduced the Kansas-Nebraska Act. He was in favor of letting states decide for themselves whether they wanted to have slaves or not.

34. The other candidate was Abraham Lincoln, a young lawyer. Lincoln wanted all new states to be free. He did not, however, want to stop slavery in the states where it was already present.

35. Douglas was a Democrat. Lincoln was a Republican. The two men held a series of

state, to Illinois, a free state. Scott lived as a slave on free soil for four years.

25. Then his master took him back to Missouri. The abolitionists saw the Dred Scott case as a good one to test slavery. They gave Scott money for a lawyer to sue his master for freedom. Scott's lawyer argued that two facts made Scott a free man. He had lived on free soil, and his master had kept him as a slave on free soil.

26. The case went to the Supreme Court. The court was made up of nine men. Five of them were southern Democrats who believed in slavery.

27. On March 6, 1857, just days after Buchanan's speech, the Chief Justice of the Supreme Court read the court's decision. Dred Scott had no right to freedom, Chief

debates (public arguments).

36. The debates between Lincoln and Douglas drew large crowds. Newspapers all around the country printed stories about them. What Lincoln and Douglas had to say helped many Americans decide how they really felt about slavery.

37. Lincoln lost the election for Senator to Douglas by only a few votes. Many people thought he would soon run again for some other office.

38. Abolitionists were unhappy about the way things were going. The Dred Scott case had gone against them. Douglas winning in Illinois was seen as a victory for slavery. They were sure that slavery would continue to grow in the U.S.

39. One abolitionist was angrier than the others. He did not want to wait for political change. **John Brown** wanted to free the slaves by force. Brown thought he had been sent from heaven to free all the slaves and punish all the slaveowners.

40. In October of 1859 Brown and 18 of his followers took over the federal **arsenal** (a place where weapons are kept) at Harpers Ferry, Virginia. Brown hoped that slaves in the countryside around Harpers Ferry would come to help him. He thought the slaves would take guns from the arsenal and go out to punish their masters.

41. No slaves came, but a group of U.S. Marines, led by Colonel Robert E. Lee, did come. They attacked the arsenal, killed ten of Brown's men and captured Brown.

42. Brown was tried on charges of treason and murder. He was found guilty and hanged.

43. Many people in the north thought Brown was a great man who had given his life to free the slaves. Most southerners thought of him as a crazy troublemaker who deserved to die.

44. Each group, north and south, became more and more convinced that they were right. The north thought that slavery must be stopped once and for all throughout the nation. The south felt that slavery must be allowed wherever people wanted it.

45. America drew closer to a civil war.

Spotlight On The Lincoln-Douglas Debates

46. In June of 1858 the Republicans chose Abraham Lincoln to run for the Senate from Illinois.

47. Two nights after he was chosen, Lincoln gave a speech which has become very famous in American history.

48. "A house divided against itself cannot stand," Lincoln said. "I believe that this government cannot last as long as America is half slave and half free.

49. "I do not expect the Union to fall apart — the house to fall. I do expect that it will become either all one thing or all the other — either all slave or all free. Either the people against slavery will stop it forever, or it will become lawful in all the states, old and new, north and south alike."

50. Douglas quickly answered Lincoln's speech with one of his own.

51. "Abraham Lincoln is talking about a war," Douglas said. "He is wrong. The American government was made by the white man to be for the white man and ruled by the white man."

52. For most of the summer and into the fall, Lincoln and Douglas traveled around Illinois together. They held debates wherever people would gather to listen to them.

53. They stopped in large cities and in places where only small farms stood. They traveled by steamboat, rail, and horseback.

54. Many of the debates lasted three hours or more. First one of the candidates would speak, then the other. Then both would speak again, arguing against what the other had said.

55. People came hundreds of miles to hear the

The Lincoln-Douglas debates helped many Americans decide how they felt about slavery.

debates. They became important not only to Illinois, but to the nation as a whole, because the major topic of the debates was slavery.

56. Douglas said that the only way America could have peace was by following the rule of the Dred Scott case.

57. Lincoln argued that blacks also had the right to life, liberty, and the pursuit of happiness called for in the Constitution. Even though he called for these rights, he did not look for "political and social equality between the races". He did not intend for blacks and whites to be together.

58. Lincoln also said that he did not want to do away with slavery if the people in any state wanted it. He hoped it would die out one day.

59. On a rainy and cold election day Douglas beat Lincoln for the Senate seat from Illinois. Only a few years later Lincoln and Douglas would be facing each other in a much bigger election.

Understanding What You Read

1. The main idea of this chapter is that:
   a. a slave named Dred Scott was freed by the Supreme Court.
   b. runaway slaves had to be returned to the south.
   c. the question of slavery was splitting up the Union.
   d. Abraham Lincoln lost an election to Stephen Douglas.

   My answer is _____ . (1-4)

2. Under the Fugitive Slave Law, people in the north had to:
   a. help slaves get to Canada.
   b. run the Underground Railroad.
   c. own slaves themselves.
   d. help bounty hunters catch slaves in the north.

   My answer is _____ . (3)

3. Warfare broke out in "Bleeding Kansas" over:
   a. whether people from the north or the south should be allowed to come there.
   b. whether Lincoln or Douglas should win the election in Illinois.
   c. whether *Uncle Tom's Cabin* was a good book or not.
   d. whether the state should be slave or free.

   My answer is _____ . (16)

4. The Dred Scott case was decided by the Supreme Court. The court said that:
   a. Scott was a free man.
   b. a slave was property and could not sue anyone.
   c. slavery was to be outlawed in the state Scott came from.
   d. Scott should never have been made a slave.

   My answer is _____ . (27)

5. The _____ Act created two new states
   and repealed the Compromise of 1850. (8,9)

6. The big issue in the Presidential election of 1856 was _____ . (19)

   The election was won by _____ . (21)

7. John Brown thought he had been sent from _____ to free the slaves. (39)

   He thought slaves would _____ . (40)

8. a. What did Stephen Douglas think about slavery? _____

   _____ (51)

204

b. What did Abraham Lincoln think about slavery? _____

_____

_____ (57,58)

9. **Word Search:** Find the hidden words in the puzzle below:

RUNAWAY		S U P R E M E C O U R T
SLAVE		J S T C N E B R A S K A
COMPROMISE		O A B O L I T I O N E R
KANSAS		H B F M G D R E D A O E
NEBRASKA		N L K P V W X S K Z A P
ABOLITION		B E T R U N A W A Y T U
BLEEDING		R E O O U K A N S A S B
DRED		O D X M A S D L C M L L
SCOTT		W I Q I N L T E O S O I
SUPREME COURT		N N R S S A O V T X B C
REPUBLICAN		Z G T E A V C F T N A A
JOHN BROWN		G B A R S E N A L Q R N
ARSENAL		

Chapter 37
Lincoln Is Elected President

1. Abraham Lincoln and Stephen Douglas appeared again before the American voters in 1860. It was only two years after Douglas had beaten Lincoln in the election for Senator from Illinois.

2. Now they were running for President. Lincoln was the candidate for the new Republican Party. Douglas was the Democratic candidate.

3. Slavery was once again the main issue in the **campaign** (time before an election when candidates try to get people to vote for them). The question of slavery was threatening to tear the 75-year-old Union apart.

4. The question of slavery went deeper than money, even though southerners felt slavery was needed to keep the cotton plantations going. Many southerners really believed that the black slaves would not be able to care for themselves if they were set free.

5. Most southerners also believed that each state should have the right to makes its own laws concerning things such as slavery. That belief is called **States' Rights.**

6. Most northerners, on the other hand, believed that slavery was **morally** wrong (not the right way to live). They believed that ownership of slaves had to be stopped so that the blacks could have the freedom promised them by the Constitution.

7. Violence over the question of slavery was seen in every big city in the nation. Abolitionists speaking in **border states** (those near the south) were often badly beaten by pro-slavery mobs.

8. People who came to the north to find runaway slaves were often beaten by mobs of abolitionists.

9. The nation was like a bomb waiting to be set off. Many people feared that if a war came, the United States would be destroyed. They were afraid that if would never again be one strong nation.

10. Because of the slavery problem, the

Lincoln became President during a difficult period in U. S. history.

Library of Congress

election of 1860 became a very important one. Four candidates were running for President.

11. Abraham Lincoln was the candidate of the Republican Party. The Republicans wanted no slavery in the new states, but did not want to do away with slavery in those states that already had it.

12. Stephen Douglas was the candidate of the Democrats in the north. The Northern Democrats wanted each state to decide for itself to be slave or free. Douglas, however, made no secret of his pro-slavery feelings.

13. John C. Breckenridge was the candidate of the Southern Democrats. The Southern Democrats wanted slavery in the new states.

14. John Bell was the candidate of the new Constitutional Union Party. That party called for the support of the Constitution. They did not say what they meant by that. They said nothing at all about slavery.

15. The election was held in November of 1860. Lincoln won the popular vote by more than 500,000 votes. He also won most of the votes of the Electoral College. (For more about the Electoral College, see Part 1 of this book, pgs. 111-112.)

16. Lincoln got 180 electoral votes, Breckenridge 72, Bell 39, and Douglas 12.

17. Lincoln won most of the electoral votes in the north, in California and Oregon. Breckenridge won most of the votes in the south. Bell won in Virginia, Kentucky and Tennessee. Douglas won electoral votes in only two states, Missouri and part of the votes from New Jersey.

18. Abraham Lincoln was now President of the United States.

19. Many people in the south were angry over the election. Some southerners called Lincoln a "baboon, a wildman from nowhere," and "the reckless leader of the abolitionists".

20. Many southerners demanded that the southern states leave the Union. They wanted to form a new nation with its own government and flag. It would be a confederacy of southern states.

21. The Civil War drew closer.

Spotlight On Abraham Lincoln

22. It has often been said of Thomas Lincoln, Abraham's father, that he worked his way down in the world. He started out with some money and wound up living in a log cabin in the wilderness.

23. This was not to be the story of his son. Lincoln was born in a log cabin in Kentucky. When he was seven, he went with his family to Indiana. There he spent the first winter living in an open shelter. The family ate whatever game the father could hunt with his rifle.

24. Lincoln attended a real school for only about one year. He taught himself to read and write by the light from an open fireplace in a cabin.

25. By the time he was 17, Lincoln was working for local farmers. He also worked splitting logs and clearing land. He was tall and strong, and could put in a good day's work for a day's wages.

26. Around 1830 Lincoln and his family moved again. This time they went to Illinois.

27. The young Lincoln was always a good speaker. In 1834 he decided to get into politics. He ran for a seat on the Illinois state legislature and won.

28. Lincoln worked hard getting ready to be a lawmaker. He read lawbooks and talked with lawyers. He became a lawyer while he was in the state legislature.

29. Lincoln spent several years in the legislature. Then he decided to leave and open his own law office. He was called back by the public to run against Stephen Douglas for Senator from Illinois.

30. He lost that race but came back two years later to win the election as President of the

United States.

31. Lincoln became President at a very difficult time. The Union was about to split up over the slavery issue. Many southerners hated him. Many northerners thought of him as a "country bumpkin" without the brains necessary to do the job as President.

32. Lincoln, however, had faced tough situations for most of his life. He was used to hard work and difficult problems.

33. Lincoln's first speech told the nation that he did not want the Union to split apart.

34. "We cannot remove one section of the nation from any other section," Lincoln said. "We are not enemies, but friends. We must be friends.

35. "A husband and a wife may be divorced from each other and move away from each other. The different parts of this country cannot do that. They will always physically be together. They must get together in friendship."

36. The war that Lincoln did not want to happen was only a short time away.

Understanding What You Read

1. The main issue of the election for President in 1860 was:
   a. how many new states should be made.
   b. whether to make a railroad from St. Louis to California.
   c. slavery.
   d. whether to print more U.S. dollars.

   My answer is _____ . (3)

2. During the election campaign, Lincoln was in favor of:
   a. freeing all the slaves.
   b. allowing slavery everywhere in the United States.
   c. no slavery in the territories and new states, but keeping it in the states where it already was.
   d. passing a new Kansas-Nebraska Act.

   My answer is _____ . (11)

3. Lincoln was afraid that the slavery issue would:
   a. lead to a break-up of the Union, with the southern states forming a new nation.
   b. kill thousands of white people.
   c. spread to Canada and Europe.
   d. cause England to go to war with the United States.

   My answer is _____ . (33-34)

4. People who believe in States' Rights believe that _____

   _____ . (5)

5. Finish the chart below by putting in the number of electoral votes for each of the candidates in the 1860 election and the areas or states in which they won: (16,17)

Candidate	Electoral Votes	Area or States
Lincoln		
Breckenridge		
Bell		
Douglas		

6. After Lincoln's election, many southerners wanted to _____

_____ . (20)

7. **Word Skills:** Solve the puzzle below using the clues provided.

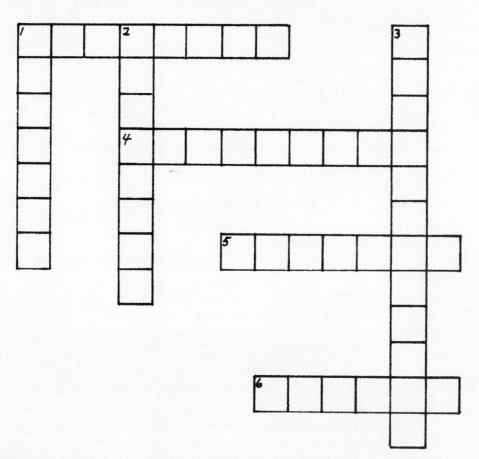

Puzzle Clues

Across

1. Abraham Lincoln lived in
   a _ _ _ _ _ _ _ _ _ _ .
4. In 1860 Lincoln became

   _ _ _ _ _ _ _ _ _ _ .

5. The Republican Party was
   against _ _ _ _ _ _ _ _ in
   the new states.
6. Lincoln met Douglas in a
   public _ _ _ _ _ _ _ .

Down

1. Abraham _ _ _ _ _ _ _ _
2. what people do when they
   run for office
3. Many people in the south
   believed in _ _ _ _ _ _ _

   _ _ _ _ _ _ _ .

Chapter 38
The War Begins

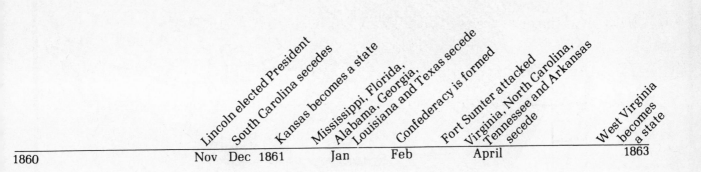

Lincoln elected President — South Carolina secedes — Kansas becomes a state — Mississippi, Florida, Alabama, Georgia, Louisiana and Texas secede — Confederacy is formed — Fort Sumter attacked — Virginia, North Carolina, Tennessee and Arkansas secede — West Virginia becomes a state

1860 — Nov — Dec — 1861 — Jan — Feb — April — 1863

1. With Lincoln's election in 1860, the Civil War became almost a certainty. Spokesmen for the south made that clear soon after the election returns were final.

2. One southern Congressman told the people of the southern states:

3. "The argument is over. All hope of settling the slavery question peacefully is gone. The Republicans are not going to give anything to the south but trouble.

4. "We are sure that the only way the southern people can now live in peace is to form a separate nation—a Confederacy. The aim of each slaveholding state should now be to get out of the Union as soon as possible."

5. A spokesman for one of the slave states, South Carolina, said:

6. "Written constitutions are worthless if they are not also written in the heart. They must be founded on the interests of the people. There is no longer a common bond between the north and the south. All efforts to keep the Union together will now do no good."

7. South Carolina was the first to **secede** (withdraw, leave) from the Union. (See map on pg. 212.) The legislature of that state voted to secede on December 20, 1860.

8. The legislature of South Carolina asked the other slave states to join in forming a new nation. By February of 1861, six other states from the lower south followed South Carolina's lead. Those states were Mississippi, Florida, Alabama, Georgia, Louisiana and Texas.

The Confederacy Is Formed

9. Those seven states formed a new union they called the **Confederate States of America** in February of 1861. They said they could no longer be a part of the United States.

10. The United States, they said, had broken the contract set up in the Constitution between the states and the federal government. That contract gave states certain rights. These rights were now being taken away, according to the southern states.

11. The Confederacy argued that the United States had failed to enforce the Fugitive Slave Law. The government also would not allow slavery in the new territories.

12. Because of those reasons, they said, the slave states had the right to "become free and equal", and form their own union.

13. Many people in the upper (northern part) of the south wanted to remain with the Union. Virginia was one of those states which remained with the Union for the time being.

14. One Virginia newspaper said, "So important do we regard the Union that pulling it down would be like tearing down our own homes. We know that we shall never find any

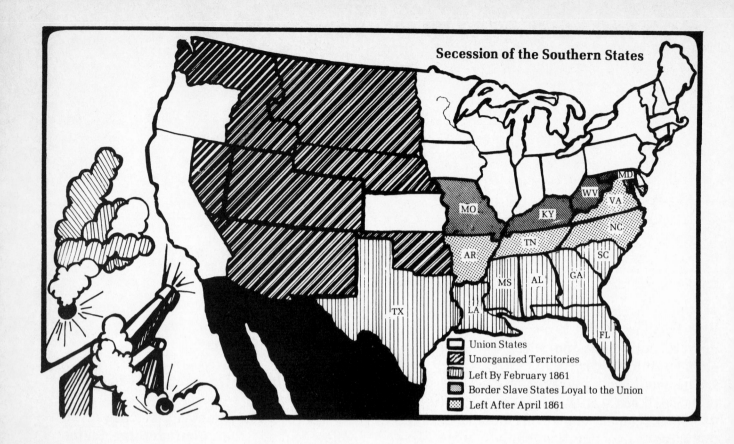

Secession of the Southern States

Legend:
- Union States
- Unorganized Territories
- Left By February 1861
- Border Slave States Loyal to the Union
- Left After April 1861

other such country.

15. "However, it does not matter what we feel about the Union. If the north decides to fight those states which left it with the sword, every southerner will fight to the death against them."

16. Lincoln reached Washington to become President at the end of February 1861. By then seven slave states had left the Union. Eight slave states remained in the Union.

17. Lincoln told of his feelings in his first speech as President. He said that it was wrong for the states to leave the Union. Lincoln told the southern states that they should accept the will of the majority of the people. They did not want the territories to have slavery.

18. He said that he would not use force to get the states back into the Union. He only wished that they would do so on their own.

19. He said that he would be in favor of an **amendment** (change) to the Constitution saying that slavery could be used in the south. "The north and south are not enemies, but friends," he said. "We should stay together."

20. The Confederacy did not listen to Lincoln. The north and south were not to be together much longer.

Fort Sumter

21. Those states which had left the Union began taking over forts on their land from the federal soldiers. There was no fighting.

22. Soon, the only federal forts left to the Union in the deep south were Fort Pickens in

Florida and Fort Sumter at Charleston, South Carolina.

23. Both forts were surrounded by Confederate troops.

24. In April, 1861, Lincoln sent word to Jefferson Davis, the President of the Confederacy. He was sending needed supplies to the troops at Fort Sumter, South Carolina.

25. Jefferson Davis knew that he had two choices. He could let the supplies in and seem to be weak, or he could order his troops to fire on the fort and begin a war.

26. Jefferson Davis ordered his troops to fire on Fort Sumter. The fort returned the fire. The Civil War had begun.

27. When word of the attack on Fort Sumter reached the north, mobs of people crowded the streets. They called for war against the south. Many people in the south also called for war.

28. Within a few days Virginia voted to leave the Union and join the Confederacy of southern states. North Carolina, Tennessee, and Arkansas followed shortly after Virginia.

29. The slave states of Missouri, Kentucky, Maryland and Delaware remained loyal to the Union. During the war people in western Virginia who were loyal to the Union formed a new free state, West Virginia.

30. The Confederacy had its own flag. The flag was blue and had a single star. Many southern soldiers sang a song about that flag as they marched into battle during the Civil War. It was the *Bonnie Blue Flag.*

31. *We are a band of brothers and native to the soil.*
Fighting for the property we gained by honest toil.
And when our rights were threatened, the cry rose near and far
Hurrah for the bonnie blue flag that bears the single star.

Hurrah, hurrah, for southern rights, hurrah.
Hurrah for the bonnie blue flag that bears the single star.

32. The North had a song of its own. The Union soldiers sang *The Battle Cry of Freedom.*

33. *Oh, we'll rally round the flag, boys.*
We'll rally once again, shouting the battle-cry of freedom.
We will rally from the hillside, we'll gather from the plains, shouting the battle cry of freedom.
The Union forever, hurrah, boys, hurrah,
Down with the traitor and up with the star.

34. The songs were brave. The men were brave. Thousands of young American men died with the two songs on their lips.

Spotlight On The North And South

35. There were brave men on both sides, men who thought that their side would easily win the war. Both sides greatly **underestimated** (thought less than they should have of) each other.

36. The first Confederate Secretary of War said, "I'll be able to wipe up with my pocket handkerchief all the blood that will be spilled."

37. Lincoln called for volunteers for the Union army. At first, he asked men to volunteer for only three months. He was sure the war would be over in three months' time.

38. Both were wrong. It would be a long, hard war for both sides. At the beginning, however, both sides were very sure of themselves.

39. The southerners thought that they had better soldiers. Their soldiers were fighting for a cause they believed in. "Southerners are fighting for a way of life," people said.

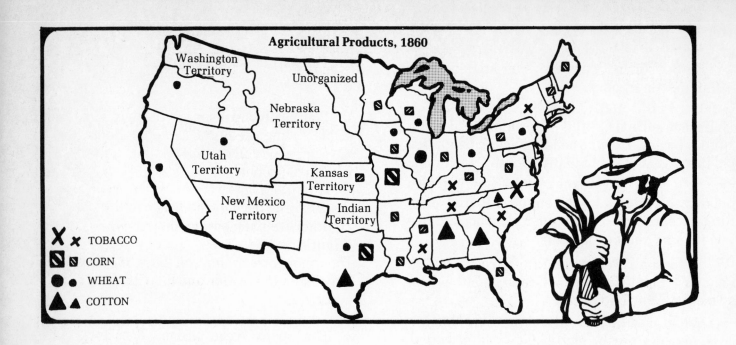

Agricultural Products, 1860

Washington Territory

Unorganized

Nebraska Territory

Utah Territory

Kansas Territory

New Mexico Territory

Indian Territory

✗ ✗ TOBACCO

◧ ◩ CORN

● ● WHEAT

▲ ▲ COTTON

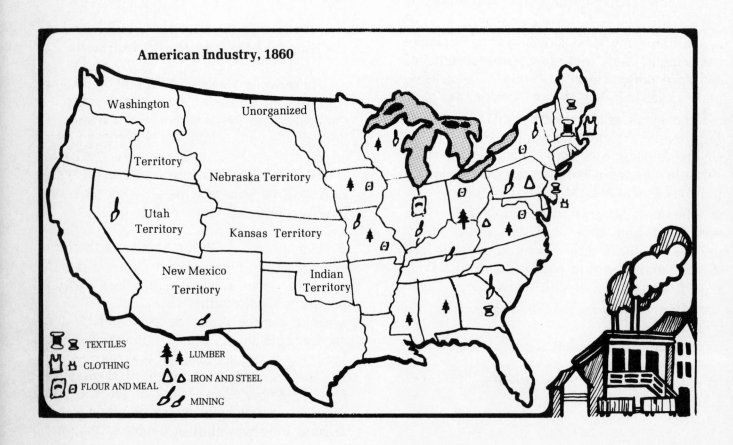

American Industry, 1860

Washington

Territory

Unorganized

Nebraska Territory

Utah Territory

Kansas Territory

New Mexico Territory

Indian Territory

▤ ▨ TEXTILES   🌲 🌲 LUMBER

▥ ♯ CLOTHING   △ △ IRON AND STEEL

⬭ ⬭ FLOUR AND MEAL   MINING

214

The south lost cotton trade with England during the Civil War.

	North	South
Population	*22 million	9 million (3½ were slaves)
Military Leaders	Few good trained leaders	*Many trained military leaders
National Leaders	*Lincoln was a good leader	Jefferson Davis had little experience
Economy	*Many factories to make war material; few farms	Few factories to make war material; many farms with cotton to sell
Ships	*Many war ships	Few war ships
Land	Fighting on "foreign soil"	*Fighting for own homes
Money	*Most banks and money were in the north	Few banks, little money

40. The southerners also believed that cotton would be a big help for their side. They thought that England, a nation that used much cotton, would help the south in its war against the north.

41. The north also expected an easy victory. They had more men, more factories, and more weapons.

42. Both sides were right about some things. However, both were wrong about the length of the war and the number of people who would be killed.

43. The following chart shows the strengths and weaknesses for each side in 1860, at the start of the Civil War. A star (*) shows which side is stronger.

44. Even though the north was stronger in most ways, the south had some strengths in the beginning, as well.

45. As the war went on, the north grew stronger. They had more factories to make weapons, uniforms and all the other things necessary to fight a war. The southern army often found itself short on supplies for their fighting men. Many southerners **deserted** (left the army) because they didn't have the things they needed for fighting.

46. After many early mistakes, northern

215

Many textile mills and factories grew in the north.

military leaders became as good as those in the south.

47. Cotton was not as important to other countries as the south had expected it to be. The English found other places, such as Egypt and India, where they could get the cotton needed for their mills.

48. England did not help the south in the war. In fact, England sold many war goods to the north, because the north had cash with which to pay for the goods.

49. As more and more southerners fell in battle, the number of men available to fight for the south grew even smaller. There were still many able-bodied slaves on the plantations, but most of them stayed to help the families of the men who went to war. The north also lost many, but had more men from which to draw an army.

50. The little strength the south had soon slipped away. Most experts now agree that the southerners were fighting a lost cause from the first shot at Fort Sumter.

Understanding What You Read

1. The first state to leave the Union was _____ . That

    state left the Union on _____ . (7)

2. Six states were next to leave the Union. They were _____ ,

    _____ , _____ , _____ ,

    _____ , and _____ . (8)

3. Three of the reasons the south gave for leaving the Union were _____

    _____

    _____

    _____ (10, 11)

4. President Lincoln tried to get the southern states to stay in the Union by promising to try to get

    an amendment to the Constitution that would have _____

    _____ . (19)

5. The Civil War began with the southern troops firing on _____

    which was in the state of _____ (24, 26)

6. Each side in the Civil War had a marching song. The southern song was called _____

    _____ . (30)   The northern song was called

    _____ . (32)

7. Many people thought the war would be a short one. What did Lincoln do that shows he thought

    this? _____ (37)

8. Look at the chart on pg. 215. Find two ways in which the south was stronger than the north at
    the beginning of the war.

    _____

    _____

List two ways the north was stronger than the south at the beginning of the war.

_____

_____

9. **Map Skills:** Look at the map on pg. 212 and then answer the following questions:

   a. The border slave states that never left the Union were _____ ,

   _____ , _____ , and _____ .

   b. The seven states that left the Union by February, 1861 were _____ ,

   _____ , _____ , _____ ,

   _____ , _____ , _____ .

   c. The four states that left the Union after April, 1861 were _____ ,

   _____ , _____ , and _____ .

10. **Map Skills:** Look at the farming and industry maps on pg. 214 and then answer the following questions:

   a. The major crop of the south was _____ . Other important

   crops were _____ and _____ .

   b. Was manufacturing more important to the north or the south? Explain your answer.

   _____

   _____

   _____

   c. What do you know about climate and geography that would help you to understand the

   differences in business and farming between the north and the south? _____

   _____

   _____

Chapter 39
The War Rages

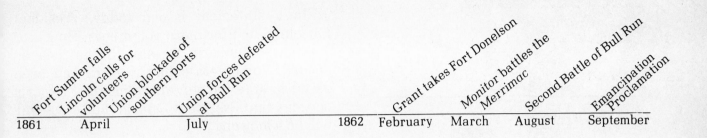

Fort Sumter falls	Lincoln calls for volunteers	Union blockade of southern ports	Union forces defeated at Bull Run		Grant takes Fort Donelson	Monitor battles the Merrimac	Second Battle of Bull Run	Emancipation Proclamation
1861	April		July	1862	February	March	August	September

1. The war that began with the shelling of Fort Sumter soon spread.

2. Northern generals had three aims in mind when the war began:
A. They wanted to split the south in half by sending soldiers and **cavalry** (soldiers on horseback) from Ohio down to the Gulf of Mexico.
B. They wanted to take the Confederate capital, Richmond, Virginia.
C. They wanted to use the U.S. Navy to **blockade** and capture southern ports. A blockade means that no ships are allowed to go in or out of a port.

3. The Union generals wanted the blockade because they did not want cotton to be shipped to England. They also did not want ships bringing supplies to the south. They believed that they could starve the south into **surrendering** (giving up) if they could keep supplies from reaching southern ports.

4. President Lincoln called for a blockade of the southern ports only five days after the fall of Fort Sumter.

5. Civil War battles were fought from Washington, D.C. to Florida and from Pennsylvania to New Mexico. There were hundreds of battles fought by thousands of men. Many of these battles were small, but many were major, with thousands on both sides killed or wounded.

6. In the next pages you will read about some of these battles as newspapers from that day might have reported them.

Fort Sumter Falls To South

7. **April 14, 1861.** After 40 hours of continuous shelling, Fort Sumter fell to southern forces today.

8. The South Carolina fort, far out in Charleston harbor, took many shells. One soldier in the fort, Captain Abner Doubleday, told us that "one-fifth of the fort was on fire. Many of us would have choked to death had we not left the fort."

9. The southern commander gave permission for all the Union troops to leave safely, which they did.

10. The southern troops took over the fort early this morning.

President Lincoln Calls For Army Volunteers

11. **April 15, 1861.** President Abraham Lincoln today called for army volunteers from all states remaining in the Union.

12. President Lincoln wants to raise an army to fight against the Confederacy. Stating that he thinks the war will be a short one, the

The Civil War began when Confederate troops fired on Fort Sumter.

15. After the defeat, what was left of the Union army retreated to the capital. The southern army regrouped and picked up their wounded from the field.

16. In a statement issued today, President Lincoln called for more volunteers. He asked the new volunteers to stay for as long as needed. Volunteers called in April had been asked to stay for only three months. Experts now say that President Lincoln thinks the war will be a long one.

President asked for only three months' service from each volunteer.

Northern Army Retreats From Bull Run

13. **July 21, 1861.** The southern army completed a big victory today by turning back a larger Union army in Virginia.
14. The battle was fought at Manassas Junction near Bull Run Creek, only thirty miles south of Washington, D.C. Because it is so close to the capital, many Congressmen and their wives watched from behind the battle lines.

Fighting Hot Along The Mississippi

17. **February 16, 1862:** In a move to end the war more quickly, the Union army gained control of the Mississippi River. A force of 15,000 men led by General Ulysses S. Grant attacked Fort Donelson, a **rebel** (Confederate) fort on the Mississippi River.

18. Joining Grant in the attack were six Union gunboats which had sailed down the river from St. Louis.

19. The fighting raged for three days. In an unexpected move, the rebel army charged the Union positions outside the fort. They were forced back into the fort.

20. The southern general, S. B. Buckner, sent the following note to Grant:

Sir: Because of the position we find ourselves in, I ask the commanding officer of the federal troops to agree upon the terms of our surrender.

Your servant,
S.B. Buckner
Brigadier General, C.S.A.

21. General Grant sent the following note back to Buckner:

Sir: No terms except **unconditional** *(complete) surrender can be accepted. I will move on your fort and take it if you do not accept my terms.*

Your servant,
U. S. Grant
Brigadier General, U.S.A.

22. Buckner sent Grant his answer quickly.

Sir: I have no choice but to accept your demands, as ungentlemanly as they are. We have fought well and should be given good treatment when we surrender. However, we do accept your demand for unconditional surrender.

Your servant,
S. B. Buckner
Brigadier General, C.S.A.

23. Grant took 12,000 Confederate prisoners and 40 cannons from Fort Donelson. According to Union sources, this cuts off the Confederate supply line from the western territories to the forces fighting in the east.

Ironclad Ships Battle
For First Time

24. **March 9, 1862:** For the first time in the history of mankind, two ironclad ships battled today. The battle lasted for hours, with both ships pouring shells at the other. After the battle both ships sailed back to their home ports. Neither side won the battle.

25. The Confederate ironclad is an old wooden ship called the *Merrimac.* The *Merrimac* has been rebuilt with iron all around the boat and a heavy iron ram on the front. The Confederate ironclad has sunk several Union ships in the past months.

26. For that reason, the Union built an ironclad ship of its own. Named the *Monitor,* it has hunted the Confederate ship until they met today.

27. Our reporter was able to speak with one of the sailors on the *Monitor.* Here is his view of the battle.

28. "As the *Merrimac* came closer, the captain passed the word to start firing. I ran to the port side and to the gun. I fired the first shot.

29. "Throughout the battle, we loaded and fired as fast as we could. After every shot, I would ask the captain how we did. Most of our shots hit the mark.

30. "Five times during the battle the two ships came so close that they touched each other. Each time we touched I fired a shell. If the *Merrimac* were made of wood she would have been sunk by any of those shots.

31. "Once she tried to run us down with the ram on her bow, but she did not damage our iron hull. We fired for hours. Then the *Merrimac* broke off the battle and headed away. We were under orders not to follow.

32. "The only damage to our ship were dents in the turret. The only men injured were hurt when a shell struck the iron turret with them inside. They lost their hearing for a few hours."

33. Confederate sources tell this paper that the *Merrimac* will probably never sail again as a result of the battle. Other ironclads will soon join the *Monitor* in the Union fleet.

Confederate Army Calls For Men

34. **April 16, 1862:** There is a shortage of fighting men in the ranks of the Confederate army. It was announced today that all white men between the ages of 18 and 35 must serve in the army.

35. The Confederate generals hope that this order will bring in enough men to replace those killed or wounded on the field of battle.

36. Men involved in necessary work at home

can stay out of the army. It is also reported that those who can afford to pay can send others to take their places in the army.

Both the northern and southern armies lost many men in the Civil War.

Union Forces Lose Major Battle

37. **June 25, 1862:** Confederate troops claimed a major victory today when they surprised a Union force ready to attack Richmond. The Union troops were forced to retreat to Washington.

Union Troops Beaten At Bull Run For Second Time

38. **August 29, 1862:** For the second time in the course of the war, the Union army was defeated at Bull Run Creek.

39. The large Union army was marching on Richmond, the Confederate capital, when they met the southern troops. After a fierce battle, the Union troops were forced to retreat once more to Washington.

Robert E. Lee Takes Command Of Confederate Forces, Takes Forces Into North For First Time

40. **September 17, 1862:** General Robert E. Lee of Virginia today took command of all Confederate forces. In a speech to his generals, Lee promised to carry the fight to the enemy.

41. Lee did not take long to carry out his promise. In a swift raid, Lee and his forces crossed over the Potomac River into northern territory. Lee was blocked from Washington, D.C. by a large Union force.

42. In one of the bloodiest battles of the war Lee and his troops fought the Union army to a standoff.

43. Lee realized that he and his army were in bad position to receive supplies. He then withdrew his troops over the Potomac to Virginia and southern territory.

Lincoln Frees All Slaves

44. **September 22, 1862:** President Lincoln today issued a **proclamation** (law) freeing all the slaves in the south. Lincoln's document is called the **Emancipation Proclamation,** because it **emancipated** (made free) the slaves.

45. Many people think that Lincoln did this to please the abolitionists who are his supporters. They had urged Lincoln to free the slaves. President Lincoln has nothing to lose. Those who would be angered by his freeing the slaves have already left the Union.

46. Our reporters in the south say that the Emancipation Proclamation will have little effect on southern slavery. The states which seceded think of themselves as a separate nation. Most slaves continue to work in the plantations alongside the families of their masters.

47. In the north, however, many people are calling Lincoln's move "one of the most important things to happen in the history of man". Northerners now see the war as a war not only to save the Union, but to keep the slaves free as well.

Spotlight On Lee And Grant

48. When most people think of the generals in the Civil War, they think of two people. They think of General Ulysses S. Grant of the Union army and General Robert E. Lee of the Confederate army.

49. The two men had a lot in common. Both officers were graduates of the military academy at **West Point.** Both fought in the Mexican War of 1846. And, when the Civil War came, both served the side they thought was the right side.

50. Grant was born in Ohio in 1822. He entered West Point at the age of 17. As a young lieutenant he served in the Mexican War.

51. After that war Grant left the army and went into business. He tried to be a lumberman, a farmer and a storekeeper, but failed at everything he tried.

52. When war broke out, Grant wanted to get into the Union army. Even though he was almost forty years old, he helped to form the Illinois militia.

53. In May of 1861, Grant applied for a job in the Union army. He was given command of a **regiment** (a large number of troops) from Illinois because the north had few experienced leaders.

54. "I served for fifteen years in the regular army, including four years at West Point," he wrote. "I believe it is my duty to support the government in this war."

55. Grant proved himself in the fights along the Mississippi River. He soon became a general and was given command of all the Union armies in March, 1864. He attacked and attacked until the north finally won a victory over the Confederate forces of Robert E. Lee.

56. Robert E. Lee was born in Virginia in 1807. His family was wealthy and had many slaves. Lee was one of the top students in his class in West Point and became a good military leader.

57. Lee led the raid that captured John Brown, the abolitionist who wanted to start a slave uprising. Lee really did not believe in slavery. He wanted to see it end peacefully.

58. When the Civil War broke out, Lee was asked to command the Union forces. He refused. When Virginia seceded from the Union, Lee resigned from the Union army. He could not fight against his home state.

59. Lee later took over command of the Confederate armies. He led many victories over larger Union forces until his men ran out of energy and ammunition. Then he surrendered to Grant and the Union army.

Understanding What You Read

1. Which of the following was *not* an aim of the northern generals at the beginning of the war:
   a. to capture California.
   b. to capture Richmond, Virginia.
   c. to cut the southern forces in half by capturing the Mississippi River.
   d. to blockade southern ports.

   My answer is _____ . (1-4)

2. On July 21, 1861, the south won a big victory by defeating the Union army at _____

   _____ near _____ Creek. (14)

3. During the battle for Fort Donelson, on the _____ (17)

   River, General _____ , the Union general, told the Confederate

   commander that he would accept only an _____
   surrender. (21)

4. The first battle of ironclad ships was when the _____ fought

   against the _____ . (25, 26)

5. Southern men between the ages of 18 and 35 could stay out of the Confederate army if they

   _____ or if they

   _____ . (36)

6. The Emancipation Proclamation freed _____

   _____ . (44)

7. Lee and Grant had some things in common. Both were graduates of _____

   _____ and both fought in the _____ . (49)

224

8. Refer to the newspaper stories and match the event in **Column A** with the date in **Column B:**

Column A

_____1. Fort Sumter falls (7-10)

_____2. Lincoln calls for volunteers (11)

_____3. North loses at Bull Run (13)

_____4. Grant takes Fort Donelson (17)

_____5. The *Monitor* fights the *Merrimac* (24)

_____6. The south calls for men (34)

_____7. Lee takes command (40)

_____8. Lincoln frees the slaves (44)

Column B

a. March 9, 1862

b. April 16, 1862

c. April 14, 1861

d. July 21, 1861 and August 29, 1862

e. April 15, 1861

f. February 16, 1862

g. September 17, 1862

h. September 22, 1862

Chapter 40
Two Brothers

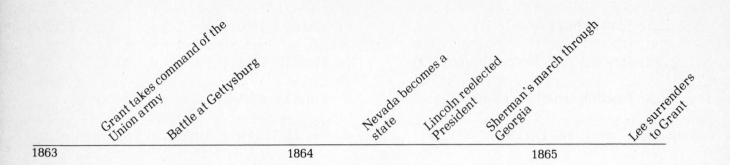

Grant takes command of the Union army

Battle at Gettysburg

Nevada becomes a state

Lincoln reelected President

Sherman's march through Georgia

Lee surrenders to Grant

1863   1864   1865

1. The Civil War has been called a war between brothers, because in many families, fathers, sons and brothers fought on opposite sides.

2. One Civil War song tells of the terrible sadness of a family breaking up. The song is called *Two Brothers*.

3. *Two brothers on their way,*
Two brothers on their way,
  One wore blue and one wore gray.
One wore blue and one wore gray as they
  marched along the way.
The fife and drum began to play,
  All on a beautiful morning.

One was gentle,
  One was kind.
One came home,
  One stayed behind,
  All on a beautiful morning.

Two girls waiting by the railroad track,
  One wore blue,
  One wore black.
One wore blue and one wore black, waiting
  by the railroad track,
Waiting for their loved ones to come back,
  All on a beautiful morning.

4. The sadness of the two girls, one whose husband wore a blue uniform (Union), and one who wore a gray uniform (Confederate), touched many families.

5. Only one of the husbands came back alive. His wife wore blue to honor her Union husband. The other wore the black clothing of a widow as she waited by the railroad tracks for the body of her dead husband.

6. The following letters are like many that crossed the battle lines. They passed between family members serving in opposing armies, often facing each other in battle.

July 10, 1863

Dear Caleb,

7. Here it is, 87 years after our nation was born, and we are fighting each other like enemies.

8. It's been only about seven months since I joined the Union army, but I've seen a lot of action. I was with the Union forces that attacked Lee's camp in Virginia. We won such a big victory that you must have heard about it by now.

9. Caleb, I just can't understand why you joined the rebels. We never had slaves, or anything like that. Why did you do it?

10. I don't know where you are fighting, but Mother tells me she can get this letter to you. I only hope you are not fighting around northern Virginia. If so, we might be forced to kill each other one of these days. That would be terrible.

11. Yesterday we finished fighting the largest battle I have ever been in. Maybe you were there, too. I've no way of knowing. Our army met an army of rebels led by General Lee at a place called Gettysburg, in Pennsylvania. I've heard that more than 140,000 men took part in the battle, and we fought for three days.

12. Thousands died. Some of my best friends were killed by southern shots. It was all so mixed-up and confusing. We charged the rebel lines. They charged us. There was smoke and dying all around.

13. I heard from our officers that Lee lost about one-third of his army in the battle. I hope you were not one of them.

Your brother,
Frank

June 10, 1864

Dear Frank:

14. Your letter finally reached me about two weeks ago, but I couldn't write back until now. I've been too busy shooting at Union soldiers. I hope that you weren't among the ones I shot.

15. I find it hard to tell you why I joined the Confederate army. I think the reason is that I believe each state has the right to decide for itself how it wants to act. The Union wouldn't allow the south to do that, so the southern states peacefully formed their own nation. It was Lincoln and his abolitionist crew that forced us into a war.

16. I did fight at Gettysburg, but luckily, I am still alive. Your people did all they could to kill me though, and I was slightly wounded. It

Union soldiers relax in a field awaiting their new orders.

doesn't matter. The south needs men, and I'll keep on fighting for what is right until we win or I can no longer fight.

17. We have been having trouble ever since Grant became your commander in March. He seems to be a better general than the last three you had. The fighting is constant and we have been forced to give up ground each day.

18. We have been taking heavy losses. Your army has also lost many soldiers, but you have more men and ammunition, and will probably win in the end.

19. We are fighting with our backs to Richmond now, and the capital will probably fall soon.

20. I hope to see you at home by planting time next spring. Maybe peace will come to all of us by then.

Your brother,
Caleb

21. By this time the war was going very badly for the south. General Lee felt that it was only a matter of time before the Confederate army had to surrender.

22. There was little food to eat in the south. Confederate money was almost worthless. The army had almost no supplies. In November President Lincoln was reelected for a second term. The Union army prepared to finish the war.

Christmas, 1864

Dear Caleb,

23. I sit here rereading your letter. It is sad that something as terrible as this war must keep us apart on this holiday.

24. I am serving with General Sherman, and we took Atlanta, Georgia. We set the city on fire. I'm not sure that I agree with Sherman. He says that we must destroy everything so that the rebels cannot use it against us again.

25. Shortly after taking Atlanta we marched across Georgia to the sea. We destroyed

General Sherman marched across Georgia to the sea destroying everything in his path.

everything in our path—plantations, crops, even women and children.

26. I can't say that I liked my job, but I'm a soldier and this is a war. It's a war that the rebels started and we are finishing. I tried to do as little as possible, but I had to do some things I'm not too proud of. I hope to talk to you about these things when the war ends and we can be together again.

Your brother,
Frank

April 10, 1865

Dear Frank,

27. The war ended yesterday, and today I got a letter from you. I hope you are still alive now that the war is over.

28. About a week ago, Lee realized that he had no hope of holding Richmond. The city was in ruins. There was fire and death everywhere. I have lost a hand to a Union shell. Wouldn't it be strange if you had fired that shell?

29. Lee's army left Virginia and headed for Pennsylvania. We hoped to meet up with other Confederate forces there, but Grant's army surrounded us. We were finished. Lee surrendered to Grant at a place called **Appomattox Courthouse.** The war is over. If you are still alive, I will see you soon.

Your loving brother,
Caleb.

The End Of The War

30. The Civil War ended on April 9, 1865, almost four years to the day after Fort Sumter fell. The north had lost almost 365,000 men. The south had lost almost 260,000 men. Most had died in battle, but many others had died of sickness or in prison camps on both sides.

31. The economy of the south was in ruins. Thousands of acres of good farmland had been destroyed. Whole plantations had disappeared from the face of the earth.

32. Southern soldiers going home found their families gone, their homes and crops destroyed. Families were split up, fortunes lost. The south had changed forever.

33. The north was not affected as much as the south. The economy of the north was stronger because it had fed on war industries. Little fighting had been done in the north. The land and its people had not been touched the same way as they were in the south. Few women or children had been killed. The Union soldiers going home found things much as they had left them.

34. Some things had changed. Before the war most women had stayed at home. During the war women had served as nurses or as workers in the factories of the north. When the war was over, many women did not want to go back to their old role of wife and mother.

35. One woman, **Clara Barton,** had even served on the lines with the Union army. She went on to begin the **Red Cross** after the war. (See the Spotlight at the end of this chapter.)

36. Also, many black soldiers had served in the Union army. Those soldiers showed that the black man could fight as well as anyone. Many all-black units won medals for bravery on the battlefield.

37. Most northerners wanted to forget about the war after its end. They wanted to get on with other things.

38. Many southerners remained angry about the outcome of the war. They thought that Lee had quit too early in the fight. They did not want to give up.

39. That made it hard to bring the divided Union back together again.

Spotlight On Clara Barton

40. Clara Barton was said to be the first woman ever to "stand between bullets and beds". She did this when caring for the wounded on the battlefields of the Civil War.

41. "My job," she often said, "is stopping blood and feeding the men who do the fighting."

42. She had not always been so brave, however. When she was younger, Clara was so shy that her mother took her to a **phrenologist** (a man who claimed to be able to tell about a person by the bumps on his or her head).

43. The phrenologist felt the bumps on Clara's head and proclaimed that she would have a great future some day. She did.

44. The youngest of five brothers and sisters,

Clara Barton cared for the wounded on the battlefields and later founded the Red Cross.

Clara learned to do "men's work" as well as women's. She could cook and sew, and she could also do carpentry work and ride horses.

45. The only work open to a woman in those days, though, was teaching. So Clara became a teacher. At one time she had seventy pupils in her small school.

46. Clara later went to work in the Office of Patents in Washington, D.C. She was so good at her job that she earned a **promotion** (a higher job). It was stopped by a man higher up who said that, "There is something wrong in mixing the sexes within the walls of a business office."

47. After the start of the Civil War, Clara saw the bloody, ragged soldiers coming into Washington from the battlefields. She wrote to newspapers and got people to give food and supplies.

48. As the supplies came in, Clara wanted to take them right to the battlefield. It was unheard of for a woman to go to a battlefield at that time. She kept arguing, however, and soon received a pass to the battle areas.

49. She went there with supplies and helped to care for the wounded.

50. In one case, she was on the battlefield when a Union soldier was hit nearby. She stripped off her petticoat and wrapped it around the wounded man's arm until medical help came.

51. After the war Clara Barton helped to identify the dead Union soldiers.

52. Clara continued her nursing work after the war. She later **founded** (started) the Red Cross to help people in times of war, floods, fires, and other disasters.

Understanding What You Read

1. The song *Two Brothers* is about _____

    _____

    _____. (2-4)

2. One of the biggest battles of the war took place at _____,
   Pennsylvania. (11)

3. General Sherman and his army marched across _____. (25)

    Many people thought his actions were wrong because he _____

    _____. (25)

4. The Confederate army under General _____ surrendered to the Union

    army under General _____ at a place called _____

    _____ . (29)

5. List some of the things that southern soldiers found when they returned home. (31, 32)

    _____

    _____

    _____

6. Who was Clara Barton? Why was she important? (35) _____

    _____

    _____

7. **Word Search:** Find the hidden words in the puzzle below and circle them.

BLUE	A C C C D E L E E I J A
GRAY	K L O N L I N C O L N B
CONFEDERACY	S E N O G R A Y A G I O
LEE	H O F U B V W X W R N L
GRANT	E S E Z L A B N R A E I
REBELS	R T D D U N I O N N O T
UNION	M R E Y E R G T O T P I
LINCOLN	A Q R L O Q S R U V M O
ABOLITIONIST	N E A M C B A R T O N N
RICHMOND	G J C L A R A B W C D I
SHERMAN	H K Y N R E B E L S P S
CLARA	I R I C H M O N D X R T
BARTON	

Chapter 41
Update To History

The questions on this page are written so you will think about the meaning of this history for today's Americans.

1. What did Lincoln do in his childhood and early manhood that showed what kind of President and statesman he could become? Which modern Presidents have had the same kind of childhood? Did that kind of childhood help them to become good Presidents?

    _____

    _____

    _____

    _____

    _____

    _____

2. When Lincoln said, "A house divided cannot stand", he meant that America could not remain a nation as long as it was divided over slavery. Does this saying have any meaning for today's Americans? Is America divided now over any one issue as it was over slavery? If so, what is that issue? Explain your answer.

    _____

    _____

    _____

    _____

    _____

    _____

3. The ending of the Civil War brought the southern states back into the Union. What would the United States be like today if the southern states had remained a separate nation?

_____

_____

_____

_____

_____

_____

Time Line Update: Complete the following time line for the entire unit. Begin with Nat Turner's uprising in 1831 and end with 1865, the end of the Civil War.

1831 _____ 1865

the Spotlight on page 239.) They wanted to control black people by force. They began to frighten, beat and kill many black people.

Black Codes

18. After the 13th Amendment had been passed, the feelings of the southern white people towards blacks did not change. Black people were still mistreated by many southerners.

19. Many of the former slave states passed laws called **Black Codes**. These codes kept black people from voting, serving on juries, getting a job, owning land and going to school.

20. "Ours is and ever shall be a government of white men," the governor of Mississippi told a cheering white crowd.

21. Some southern states forced black people back into slavery with a legal trick. Blacks who did not have jobs were arrested for **vagrancy** (having no work and no home). As vagrants, they were fined. If they could not pay the fine, their labor was sold to the highest bidder until the fine could be paid off.

22. Most blacks could not find work in the ruined south. Many found themselves again working for their old masters.

23. To work against the Black Codes, the federal government set up **Freedmen's Bureaus** in the south. The bureaus gave food, clothing, and medical care to ex-slaves who needed help.

24. The bureaus also tried to help ex-slaves get their rights under the law. The government also set up schools throughout the south to teach the ex-slaves how to read and write.

25. In 1866 all of the states that were to come back into the Union held elections for state government and for representatives to Congress. Almost all of the men elected had held office in the state or Confederate government during the Civil War.

26. This made Congress angry. The Radical Republicans in Congress passed stricter rules for allowing the southern states to come back into the Union.

14th Amendment

27. Each of the states would have to ratify the 14th Amendment. That amendment said that all blacks were now citizens of the United States and were to have all the rights of other citizens. Any laws against black people were no longer constitutional.

28. The amendment also said that nobody could hold state or federal office if they had helped the Confederacy in any way.

29. Ten southern states refused to ratify the amendment. That meant they could not come back into the Union.

30. The Radical Republicans now had full control of the Congress. They wanted to force the southern states to come back into the Union.

Federal Troops Go To The South

31. Congress divided the south into five military districts, each governed by a general. Union troops were sent to the south to see that black people were given their rights. They were also there to force the south to accept the 14th Amendment.

32. The troops also made sure that the new southern governments did not allow ex-Confederate soldiers to vote or hold office. Ex-slaves could vote and hold office and many were elected to state positions.

33. While many blacks were elected in the years following the Civil War, they did not truly run the governments of their states. They had little or no education, and did not know what to do. Running the government was left to northerners who came to the south to find power and money. These men were called

Richmond, Virginia was left in ruins after the Civil War.

carpetbaggers because they often came to the south with all they owned in an old suitcase made of a piece of carpet.

34. Most of the carpetbagger governments were **corrupt.** That means, they ran the government not for the people's good, but for the money they could make for themselves. The carpetbaggers would take money for getting laws passed, giving railroad rights, and helping certain people.

The Radical Republicans Gain In Congress

35. While the Radical Republicans were working in Congress to punish the south, they were also working to change the federal government. They tried to make Congress the most powerful of the three branches of government.

36. They passed a law that the President could not appoint new members to the Supreme Court when an old member **resigned** (quit). They passed another law that a President could not remove one of his advisors without the permission of Congress.

37. President Johnson decided to test the law. He dismissed the Secretary of War, Edwin M. Stanton. Johnson was immediately **impeached** by the House of Representatives.

38. He was brought to trial in the Senate under the rules of the Constitution (See Part 1, pg. 110 for impeachment rules.) The trial in the Senate lasted for two months. At the end of that time the Senate voted 35-19 in favor of

238

removing Johnson from office.

39. A two-thirds majority was required to remove the President. The Radical Republicans needed 36 votes and only had 35. They failed by one vote. President Johnson completed his term in office, thanks to one vote in his impeachment trial.

40. He was followed in office by U.S. Grant, who was elected President in 1868. Grant had defeated the Confederate army and ended the Civil War.

All States Back In The Union

41. With the help of northern troops, the southern states all accepted the 14th Amendment and were back in the Union by 1870.

42. In that year the 15th Amendment to the Constitution was passed and ratified by the states. That amendment gave the right to vote to all black males over the age of 21.

43. At one time, there were 700,000 blacks in the south with the right to vote, and only 625,000 whites. This frightened many southerners.

44. Many people in the south were angry at the way the Radical Republicans were treating them. Reconstruction under the Radical Republicans was very hard on them. They did not like the way the carpetbaggers were running the state governments for their own gain.

45. They did not like having Union troops on southern soil. Many of the Union troops had fought in the south during the war and had seen friends die there. They did not always treat southern ex-soldiers kindly.

46. More than anything else, the southerners did not like the fact that blacks could vote and hold office. Many southerners still believed that blacks were not as good or as smart as whites.

47. The federal troops finally left the south in 1877. The fighting had ended at Appomatox in 1865, but the Civil War really ended when the troops left the south.

48. Though the war was over, many of the problems that brought on the war in the first place remained. Some of them would cause more trouble for America in years to come.

Spotlight On The Ku Klux Klan

49. The time was late December, 1865. The place was Pulaski, Tennessee. Six young men were sitting around, looking for something to do. All of them had been Confederate soldiers. They had come home from the war to find that everything they had owned had been wiped out.

The Ku Klux Klan terrorized blacks in the south.

50. "Let's form some sort of club," one of them said. The others agreed.

51. "What should we call it?" another asked.

52. "How about Kuklos?" Richard Reed suggested. He explained that was the Greek word for circle.

53. The others liked the idea and the Kuklos Klan was born. The men decided to go out and bother those people they didn't like — mainly blacks.

54. Here is the way one person described the birth of the Klan:

55. "They were so excited about their new club that they wanted to go out in public. But they didn't want their friends to know who they were, so they made simple Halloween costumes out of sheets. They got on horses and rode through the streets.

56. "Many of the blacks in the town were frightened by the white-sheeted riders. They believed them to be ghosts risen from the graves. Many of the town's blacks left the streets and ran for the safety of their homes."

57. Others in the town joined the Klan. They wanted to scare blacks, also. They didn't worry if sometimes a black person was roughed up a bit, if that's what it took to scare him.

58. The idea spread to nearby towns, then to other parts of the state, then to the entire south. Within three years the Ku Klux Klan became a terror group that burned, whipped, and murdered blacks and carpetbaggers alike.

59. In 1867 a convention of all the local Klan groups was held in Nashville, Tennessee. The convention made up rules for all the Klan groups in the south.

60. The Klan became a police force in the south, making sure that blacks and carpetbaggers didn't "step out of line".

61. In 1871 a Congressional committee studied the Klan and listed 260 Klan crimes against people. These included 7 murders and the whipping of 72 whites and 141 blacks. The following is their report of what the Klan was doing at that time:

62. "The Klan, in carrying out the purpose for which it was formed, took action against the colored citizens of the south. They broke into the houses of colored people in the dead of the night, dragged them from their beds, and, in many cases, murdered them."

63. In April of 1871 Congress passed a law known as the Ku Klux Klan Act. This law made it unlawful to take away the rights of any citizen of the United States. The government was able to use that law against the Klan, because they were taking away black people's rights.

64. Many members of the Klan were punished under the act. Some parts of South Carolina were put under federal rule for a short time because the Klan operated so openly there.

65. In 1879 the Ku Klux Klan officially disbanded. Years later the Klan would appear again. For the time being, however, it became just another group that had tried to change the face of America.

Understanding What You Read

1. **Cartoon Reading Skills:** Look at the cartoon below and then answer the following questions:

   a. This is like a cartoon that appeared in a newspaper. Do you think the paper was printed in the north or in the south? Why? _____

   _____

   b. What do you think the cartoonist is trying to say? _____

   _____

   c. Would the Ku Klux Klan agree with what the cartoonist is trying to say? Why? Why not? _____

   _____

   d. Would the Radical Republicans in the north agree with what the cartoonist is trying to say? Why? Why not? _____

   _____

2. Write the letters from **Column B** in the correct spaces in **Column A**.

Column A

_____ 1. Andrew Johnson (11-13)

_____ 2. Black Codes (18-21)

_____ 3. Freedmen's Bureaus (23-24)

_____ 4. 13th Amendment (15)

_____ 5. 14th Amendment (27-30)

_____ 6. 15th Amendment (42)

_____ 7. Ku Klux Klan (49-65)

_____ 8. Carpetbaggers (33)

_____ 9. Radical Republicans (14)

Column B

a. passed tough laws for the south to come back into the Union

b. northerners who ran southern governments

c. became President when Lincoln was killed

d. frightened away black voters and beat them

e. gave food, clothing and medical care to ex-slaves

f. kept blacks from getting their rights

g. gave the right to vote to all black males over the age of 21

h. made slavery unconstitutional

i. Black Americans were made citizens of the United States

3. Lincoln asked the southern states to do four things before they could come back into the Union.

They were _____ ,

_____ , _____

_____ , and_____

_____ . (8)

4. When ten of the southern states would not accept the 14th Amendment, Congress sent in

_____ . (31)

5. President _____ was impeached by the House of Representatives,

but was not found guilty by the _____ . (37-38)

242

6. President Johnson had a hard time enforcing Lincoln's rules for the reconstruction of the Union

   because _____

   _____

   _____ . (13)

7. The Black Codes kept the blacks in the south from _____

   _____

   _____ . (19)

8. The Freedmen's Bureaus were set up to _____

   _____

   _____ . (23-24)

9. The _____ was an organization that took action against the
   black citizens of the south. (62)

10. President Lincoln was killed by _____ . (10)

Chapter 43
Changes In The United States After The War

1. The Civil War and Reconstruction brought many changes to both north and south.

2. In the years following the war the north became, more than ever, a strong manufacturing region. Many factories had grown by making war goods. They now turned to making the goods needed in everyday life.

3. There were social changes in the north as well. Many women had worked in factories while their husbands were on the battlefields. Many of these women did not want to go back to being just cooks and housekeepers for their husbands. They wanted to work outside the home and have more freedom.

4. Another group was also demanding social change. They were the **immigrants** (people who go from one country to live in another country.) These people wanted better jobs and better places to live.

5. Up until 1800, only about 5,000 immigrants per year came to the United States. Then the number of people coming to the United States began to grow. By 1860 an average of over 200,000 immigrants a year came to the United States.

6. Most of the immigrants came in search of a better life than the one they had had in Europe. Many came because of **political beliefs** (how they felt their countries should be governed). They had been punished in their home countries for their beliefs, so they came to the United States to find freedom.

7. Others came for economic reasons. They had not been able to make a living in their home countries. Some had not had enough to eat in their home countries.

8. The main food for Irish peasants was the potato. In 1845 there had been a **blight** (disease) that killed all the potatoes on the vine. One million people died in Ireland because of the potato blight. Another million came to the United States. More came during and after the Civil War.

9. Most of the immigrants moved into the already overcrowded cities of the north. The people there did not like having so many new people coming in.

10. The immigrants had a hard time finding jobs. Some factories posted signs saying, "No Irish need apply here."

11. The cities of the north were alive with the sounds of foreign languages and the smell of foreign food.

Conditions In The South

12. The changes in the south after the Civil War were much greater than in the north. Gone were the large plantations that had grown most of the cotton before the Civil War. Gone was the free slave labor to work the cotton fields. Gone were most of the able-bodied men.

Farmers called sharecroppers paid for their land with a share of the crop that they grew.

13. For the last years of the war the few remaining plantations were run by women and loyal slaves. After the war, some owners tried to keep their plantations by hiring ex-slaves to work the land. Many of the black people no longer wanted to work on the plantations. It was too much like being a slave again.

14. It cost a great deal of money to hire people to work the land. The plantation owners did not have the money to hire people to help them. Many of them broke their land up into small pieces. They sold those pieces of land to both black and white farmers who wanted their own farms.

15. Some plantation owners rented their land to the farmers, instead. These farmers were called **sharecroppers** because they would pay for the land with a share of the crop that they grew. Most sharecroppers were ex-slaves or poor white farmers.

16. Southern farms continued to grow cotton and tobacco. By 1870 cotton production was back up to what it had been before the Civil War. By 1890 cotton production doubled what it had been before the Civil War.

17. The south had not changed in one very important way. Blacks were still treated as second-class citizens. As soon as white people got control of the southern states again from the federal government, they began to make laws to keep the blacks in a low position.

18. One of these laws was the **Grandfather Clause**. It said that no person could vote unless his grandfather had voted before the Civil War. Since no blacks could vote before the Civil War, this law kept southern blacks from voting.

19. Another law said that people had to pay a tax to vote. Many blacks and poor whites could not afford to pay the tax and were not allowed to vote. Many other laws were passed that kept blacks from using the same facilities as whites.

20. It is true that black people were no longer slaves. However, it would be many years before they could become first-class citizens of the United States.

Mexico And Alaska

21. In the 1860's, most people in the United States were thinking about what was happening at home. However, important things were happening in other parts of the world.

22. In 1861 French troops, under the command of Napoleon III, had taken Mexico. Napoleon wanted to make a new French empire in Mexico.

23. Because of the Civil War, there was little the federal government could do about the French going into Mexico. All of the American troops were tied up fighting the Confederacy.

Southerners tried to keep blacks from voting.

245

24. When the war ended, the government sent 50,000 troops to the Rio Grande River, the Mexican border. William Seward was Secretary of State for President Johnson at this time. He helped persuade Napoleon to leave Mexico without a fight. The French withdrew in 1867.

25. That same year the Russian minister to the United States came to Seward with an idea. Russia owned Alaska. That frozen land was too far away for the Russians to control it or use it. Would America like to buy Alaska, Seward was asked.

26. In a few hours the Secretary of State had arranged a treaty. The United States agreed to buy Alaska from the Russians for $7,200,000. That was about 2 cents an acre.

27. Many called Alaska **Seward's Folly** or **Seward's Icebox**. The treaty was passed, however, by both the House and the Senate. Alaska became a part of the United States of America.

Spotlight On The Stereotype Of Black People

28. In printing, a **stereotype** is a kind of printing plate which makes the same picture over and over again.

29. The word stereotype also has another meaning. A stereotype can be an idea that people have. This idea is that everyone who belongs to a certain group is just alike, does the same things and thinks the same way. This can't possibly be true, but people who believe in stereotypes think this way. They think that certain groups all act the same way and they treat all of the group in the same way.

30. There are many stereotypes which some Americans believe. Some of these are: all blonds are dumb, everyone who wears glasses is smart, all Jews are rich, all Italians eat spaghetti. There are many others. Some are harmless, but others are cruel.

31. The black stereotype was one of the first. It began on the plantations of the south.

Blacks were always pictured as lazy, slow-moving people who loved to eat watermelon and dance.

32. In 1828 a white man by the name of Thomas "Daddy" Rice published a song called *Jump, Jim Crow*. The song didn't make any sense at all, but it was very popular. Many white people thought all blacks, like Jim Crow in the song, were lazy, shiftless people who only wanted to sing and dance.

33. The name Jim Crow became another name for **segregation** (keeping blacks and whites apart). The laws against black people are still called **Jim Crow laws.**

34. In the late 1800's and early 1900's, a very popular kind of entertainment was the minstrel show. In minstrel shows white men would color their faces and hands black. They would sing and dance and tell "corny" jokes.

35. As time went by, the movies picked up the stereotype. All the black actors and actresses played stereotyped parts. They would play the maid or the shuffling hired hand who was scared of his own face in the mirror.

36. Television carried on the stereotype of the black person. In the early days of TV, all blacks were maids or cabdrivers. The women were full of wisdom and loved only the people they served. The men were dumb and always getting into trouble because of some get-rich-quick idea they had thought up. They were also so scared that they ran at the first sign of trouble.

37. Today the stereotype can no longer be seen on TV. Black superheroes fight bad guys with all the skill and daring of any other man. TV shows now try to show what black life in America is really like.

38. Most of the old stereotypes of the black person are no longer seen. Many people in America have tried to stamp out the old stereotypes. However, those stereotypes have deeply affected the way blacks have been treated in the United States.

Understanding What You Read

1. The main idea of this chapter is:
   a. America was the same after the Civil War as it was before.
   b. Blacks were much better off in the south after the Civil War.
   c. Many things changed after the Civil War.
   d. Black stereotypes changed after the Civil War.

   My answer is _____ .

2. Many immigrants came to the U.S. Some came to find a _____

   _____ , others for _____

   _____ . (6)

3. Many of the large plantations were broken up after the Civil War. The land went to small

   farmers who paid for the land with _____ ,

   so they were called _____ . (15)

4. The U.S. bought Alaska from _____ for about

   _____ per acre. (26)

5. The stereotype of black people was that all blacks were _____

   _____ . (31)

6. Fill in the following chart. Compare the way things were before and after the Civil War. You will find this information in paragraphs 1-20.

	Before The Civil War	After The Civil War
Life in the cities of the north		
Factories in the north		
Plantations in the south		
Life in the south		
Black Americans		

Chapter 44
Update To History

The questions on this page are written so you will think about the meaning of this history for today's Americans.

1. Do you think that other organizations like the Ku Klux Klan could get started and grow today? Why? Why not?

_____

_____

_____

_____

_____

_____

2. Can you think of any stereotypes about a group of people which are still around today? Do you think they are fair or unfair to the group they are supposed to be about? Why?

_____

_____

_____

_____

_____

_____

3. The Jim Crow laws were unfair and cruel to black people. They are no longer laws today. Do you think that black people are treated as if there were still Jim Crow laws? Why or why not?

_____

_____

_____

_____

_____

_____

Time Line Update: Complete the following time line for the entire unit. Begin with Lincoln's assassination in 1865 and end with 1877, when the last federal troops left the south.

_____

1865

1877

INDEX

This index lists all the important people, places, events and subjects in this book. They are listed in **alphabetical** order. After each subject or **heading**, the page numbers are given where you can find information on the subject. For example, if you wanted to look up the pages containing information on George Washington you would turn to page 258 and see this **entry:**

Washington, President George,
89, 130, 151
as first president, 93, 95
French and Indian War and,
95
Revolutionary War and, 71,
73, 75, 95

As you can see, the index provides sections under the name. These sections, called **sub-entries,** give you the exact type of information found on the pages.

In some cases the index will send you to other entries. If you looked for information under "American Indians," you would find the message *see* Indians.

If you have any trouble finding information in the index ask your teacher to help you.

Women (continued)
	Civil War and, 229-230
	Equal Rights Amendment
		(ERA) and, 121
	in the French colonies, 36
	Reconstruction period
		and, 244, 245
	Seneca Falls Convention,
		176, 179-180
	in the Spanish colonies, 36
	voting rights for, 180
Woodland Indians, 15

Y

York, Duke of, 40, 41
Yorktown, Virginia, 73-74